In 1940, age six, Roddy Mackay ⸎ ⸎e Scheme," whereby more than ¹ ⸎ ⸎ere taken from their parents an⸎ ⸎ens of thousands more were sent to A⸎ ⸎land, and South Africa. This is Roddy's story ⸎ ⸎t Fairbridge Farm, serving in the Canadian Army, ⸎g a new life in the United States, and eventually, reuniting with his family.

Feb 3, 1934
Jan 31, 2021

Abandoned children of Britain 1850 - 1950

A forgotten Child at Fairbridge Farm School

Roddy Mackay

Mackay Enterprises
California

Abandoned Children of Britain 1850-1950
A Forgotten Child at Fairbridge Farm School
Roddy Mackay

Second Edition 2020
First Edition 2018
Originally published as *The Memoirs of a Guttersnipe*

ISBN 9781652021094
Mackay Enterprises

COMMONWEALTH OF AUSTRALIA
MIGRATION & SETTLEMENT OFFICE.

MEDICAL EXAMINATION.
Instructions to Medical Examiner.

In cases where the Medical Examiner is unable to describe the applicant as being in good health, he should state under "REMARKS" the exact nature of the defect which he finds and whether it is of a temporary or permanent nature. Any disablement received on Active Service or otherwise should also be noted and commented on, and if a Pension is received the amount of it should be stated.

The presence of Pediculi or Nits should be noted. In the case of married women, if pregnant, please note the fact in "Remarks" column, and state number of months.

CERTIFICATE.
Replies by Applicant to Questions.

NAME MACKAY Roderick
(Full Name in Block Capitals)

ADDRESS 2 Kilburn, East Newport, Ffestine

1. Have you ever had any serious illness or surgical operation? NO
2. Have you or has any member of your family ever been in a Sanatorium or other institution or attended thereat for the treatment of Tuberculosis? NO
3. Have you ever had Enuresis or any sign of disease of the Genito Urinary Organs? NO
4. Have you or has any member of your family ever suffered from mental disease or epilepsy or been treated in an institution of any kind for these Diseases? NO
5. Have you required medical attention during the last twelve months? NO

Results of Medical Examination.

A. Heart Normal

B. Lungs Normal.
   (Particularly Tuberculosis)

C. Nervous System and Mental Condition Normal

D. Intelligence Bright

E. Digestive Organs Healthy

F. Genito Urinary Organs Normal

G. Sight { without glasses RE 6/6 RE 6/6 LE 6/6
          { with glasses (if worn) BE RE LE
          (Snellen's Type)

H. Hearing Good

I. Physique Good

J. Skin Healthy.

K. Number of vaccination scars and date of operation No marks

L. Teeth Good

REMARKS (include particulars of any departure from normal conditions not fully set out in answer to above questions) Tonsils slightly enlarged. has not been vaccinated Good type of boy

AGE 6 years   HEIGHT, in Boots 3 ft 9 ins   WEIGHT, Clothed 48 lbs.

Having read and made myself conversant with the instructions contained in Form KA, supplied me, I certify that I have this day examined the above-named and am of opinion that he
is in good health and of sound constitution, and not suffering from any mental or bodily defect which would unfit him for earning his own living as a labourer

Date 24th July 1940   Signature and Qualifications W. H. Dickinson M.D

Address 6 PORTLAND TERRACE 24 JUL 1940 NEWCASTLE-ON-TYNE

I hereby certify that the information supplied by me to the Medical Examiner is correct in every particular:—
Signature of applicant which must be made }
in the presence of the Medical Referee. } Williamina Mackay for
TO:— Roderick Mac
         THE DIRECTOR,
MIGRATION & SETTLEMENT OFFICE, AUSTRALIA HOUSE, STRAND, LONDON, W.C.2.
(FORM K.)   PLEASE TURN OVER.

*See page 23

CONTENTS

PART II

PART III

PART IV
1960-2010

ABANDONED CHILDREN
OF BRITAIN

PROLOGUE

I'd been waiting for this moment for nearly 70 years. At long last, someone in power, prestige and authority was acknowledging and apologizing for the terrible wrong done to thousands upon thousands of innocent children over the decades. On a late February morning in 2010, I joined dozens of other former victims of misguided government programs in a reception at the British House of Commons.

When Prime Minister Gordon Brown came forward to shake my hand and the cameras flashed, all I could think of was the appropriate caption for the photograph: "The Guttersnipe Meets the Prime Minister," and I could not help but marvel at the long, bumpy journey that had taken me out of the depths and up to the heights, and to reflect back on how it all began.

— RODDY MACKAY

Author's Notes

Before I delve into my story, it's important to relay some back-story. I was institutionalized for 12 years, and no one ever explained why or how I was tossed into a system that was aptly referred to as "The Scheme." As I got older, I yearned to learn more about what happened to me, and the other kids who I grew up with.

I began by reading books and archival papers written on the topic of Britain's Child Migration. However, information was hard to come by. Official records were not accessible. The little I did find did not give me a complete picture; none of it answered my biggest questions. I knew I was one of 329 girls and boys sent to Fairbridge Canada, but I still didn't understand how or why we had been collected in the U.K. and then sent to Canada.

When I told others my story, many would say, "Oh! You must have been one of those child evacuees of WWII."

For a long time, I simply responded with, "Yes."

Back then, I assumed my schoolmates and I had, in fact, been taken away because of the war. Before leaving, most of us had experienced the nightly bombings of Britain's industrial cities. Many of us thought our parents or relatives had sent us out of harm's way.

However, this rationale began to break down when considering that children had been coming to Fairbridge before the war began, and they kept coming after it ended.

Other people would say, "Oh, I see you were an orphan," to answer them it was easier to agree that I was. It saved me the embarrassment of explaining how my parents had abandoned five children.

A real revelation came when I picked up a book on the subject, *The Little Immigrants* by Kenneth Bagnell. That title led me to discover that my schoolmates, and I were part of a much larger program: The Scheme.

The Scheme included well over 120,000 British children shipped to Canada alone. Tens of thousands more were sent to Australia, New Zealand and South Africa. There were three other Fairbridge Farm Schools located in Australia alone. All the receiving nations were one-time colonies of the old British Empire.

This removal, or mass migration, of children from the shores of Britain began as early as 1830.[1] Like many countries in the early 19th century, Britain had a problem with overcrowding and poverty in its industrialized cities. Millions of families suffered in extreme poverty and thousands of abandoned children were living on city streets, begging for scraps.

Workhouses were built, and the poor and homeless were thrown in. The conditions in these buildings were terrible and disease was endemic. Children as young as three were forced to labor in mines, working naked in the overbearing

1   As stated earlier, many professional authors and scholars have written extensively on this subject. For an in-depth perspective on the Scheme, I would recommend books listed in the bibliography. There are also Fairbridge Farm School Associations sites listed on the internet.

heat in the dark, filthy shafts.

The Canadian newspaper *The Globe and Mail* wrote, "Any drearier or more forlorn prospect than what lies before a pauper child or guttersnipe in England is not easily imagined."

That was the problem. The Scheme was proposed as the so-called "solution."

The basic premise was simple: remove poor children from the overcrowded cities and send them to the colonies.

Now, I have no doubt that there were compassionate and socially conscious individuals, government officials and groups that sympathized with the plight of poor families—especially the children—and wanted to give them more promising futures. The humane concern was there. However, not all the child welfare agencies supported by the government were driven by it.

Several well-intentioned upper-class British citizens took an interest in the plight of impoverished children. I will only briefly touch on one of the most prominent, Thomas Barnardo.

Barnardo was born in Ireland to a Jewish family who later converted to radical Protestantism. As a young man, Barnardo moved to London, intending to become a doctor and a missionary in China. He failed in both those endeavors, so instead he became a missionary for homeless children. He opened infirmaries, homes for the deaf and mute, and homes for the abandoned. These Barnardo Homes were emblazoned with the sign "No Destitute Child Ever Refused Admission."

He came into conflict with several fellow missionaries and

other child welfare agencies. One rival missionary, Frederick Charrington, made public accusations, stating, "His homes were outposts of sodomy, drunkenness, blackmail and other vices of the most depraved sort."

Many of the accusations leveled against Barnardo were true. For one thing, he used forged credentials to pose as a doctor. Oddly enough, the judge exonerated him of all the serious charges. Life at his homes would continue uninterrupted.

It was a bad life, no better than what the infamously terrible workhouses offered. Children were pulled from their beds at 5:30 a.m. and forced to work until 6:30 p.m. Those caught trying to escape their prison faced solitary confinement.

Barnardo not only lured children with promises of a better life, but his organization snatched children right off the street—homeless or not—to fill his homes. Once they were in, they had little hope of seeing their families again.

Though nothing has been proven, I strongly suspect an agreement was brokered between operators like Barnardo and the British government to take poor children and send them away so they could be unceremoniously dumped in the colonies and taken in by foster parents or institutions there. The first party of Barnardo's children arrived on Canada's shores in 1882. And thus The *Scheme* was created.

Politicians would've easily seen the strategy as a great way to cut current and future welfare costs. If the youngest welfare recipients were removed, they wouldn't grow up needing support for years to come. However, the benefits didn't stop with money. This same design to relieve overcrowding in cities would also build up the white population in places like Canada and Australia.

Unlike Barnardo, other early social workers were far more humane and rightly deserved to be called philanthropists. Among them was Kingsley Fairbridge, the founder of our Fairbridge Farm Schools. By all accounts, Fairbridge was a good man with an optimistic mission to improve children's lives and give them a future.

His vision, which he called the *"Vision Splendid,"* was to bring children out of poverty and destitution to wide-open farmlands in Canada and Australia and teach them skills. Boys would learn the practical skills of farming and animal husbandry, so they could be farmers or farm hands, and girls would learn domestic skills to become farmer's wives.

It sounded like a good idea, but the goals were so limited that I find it hard to think of the vision as especially "splendid."

Fairbridge established the first school in Western Australia in 1912, with the first party of boys arriving in 1913. More schools bearing his name were founded after his death, including ours in Canada in 1935.

Fairbridge had two administrations. The first was the London-based Board of Governors, which oversaw our Canadian school and the three sister schools in Australia, which controlled all the finances. Board members included a laundry list of Britain's who's who—titled aristocrats, a Lord and Lady, an Earl, a Duke, a Viscount and high-ranking retired military leaders. This was quite an illustrious panel of board members for an institution full of lowly guttersnipes.

The second was the local residential staff that operated the Fairbridge schools. The Principal (or as I refer to him, Headmaster) was in charge. During my 10-year stay at the school, three different men would hold the position. I suppose back then women were never considered for that lofty station. The vice principal frequently served as the duties master, a man much-feared by Fairbridge kids because he was in charge of discipline.

Our school had 12 cottages where the kids lived, and a cottage mother supervised each one of them. The cottage mothers lived and slept in the cottages in a separate suite. Because they were so close to us, the cottage mothers left indelible, lifelong impressions. Our days became dramatically more or less bearable depending on how kind or cruel she was. Her temperament could shape one's entire perception of the Fairbridge years.

Kingsley Fairbridge as an idealistic young man who envisioned home, that offered comfort and happiness for children. It was meant to be a home. However, far too many children experienced the exact opposite of that. If he had lived to see the schools' functioning, he would've been disappointed and ashamed by the conduct of many staff members.

Canadian child welfare officers Laura Holland and Ruby McKay wrote, "In their view, Fairbridge (schools) was reminiscent of an orphanage of the last century. The English ambience that seemed so quaint and charming was stifling and regressive! We observed children eating off metal plates in front of staff members eating off china dinnerware. An early report by a Government health inspector indicated terrible sanitation with food stored in the main kitchen, also most of the children wearing dirty clothing."

I do not recall the dirty clothing, but the food was definitely questionable. It was often tasteless and we frequently found maggots in our porridge.

The school continued receiving new parties of child migrants until 1948. Financial problems and critical reports by Canadian health and child welfare representatives finally led to the school's closing in 1951.

The Fairbridge boys toiled as farm laborers. We milked cows, shoveled manure, fed the pigs, shoveled more manure, fed the chickens and then shoveled even more shit. We worked in the fields, pulling weeds, stacking hay, and loading it onto horse-drawn wagons. The list of chores was nearly endless. At age 15, most of us became full-time farm trainees and received no more academic schooling. With our future destiny already decided, finishing high school was not a necessity. We were destined to become no more than farm hands, after all, regardless of what occupations we may have been interested in.

Farm owners employed most of the boys leaving Fairbridge at minimal wages. I seriously doubt that government standards for minimum wages existed back in the 40s. My first part-time job was working an eight-hour day for a local farmer for $2 per day.

On the bright side, several boys taken in by local families did manage to complete high school and get accepted to universities. However, they make up only a small fraction of the 200 or so boys sent to Fairbridge.

The girls were instructed in domestic chores: laundry, sewing, ironing clothes and so on. I feel they actually had it worse than the boys did after leaving Fairbridge. They had fewer prospects open to them. For many, the only choice was to become a maid for the wealthier families in Victoria.

Not surprisingly, The Scheme is a piece of British history that is swept under the rug today. The full details of the overseas evacuation programme are kept buried, even from those who were once part of it. I'm still angry with both Fairbridge and the British government for not sharing the existence of our own personal files. Ethics aside, some may argue that they did not conceal these files from us so they did nothing illegal, which technically may be true. They simply forgot to tell us that our personal files existed, which is just as bad in my mind. It wasn't until I was 66 that I finally learnt my personal files and Minnie's were stored in the archives' section in the Birmingham Library. I had to write for special permission just to view mine. Then, on at my own expense I flew to Birmingham, England, to read all of my files and make copies for my records.

The media of the day published many articles about the Fairbridge Farm Schools, most of them positive reviews explaining how the organization functioned and how children were educated and trained for future employment. However, I have yet to see a single comprehensive report published about what kinds of jobs they were actually able to find.

I would not wish my early life upon any child—thrown into an unsympathetic system at the age of 5, without explanation, and kept in that system's vice-like grip for a dozen years, shielded from any sense of what a loving and nurturing childhood looked like.

One thing I can say about Fairbridge is that it did toughen me up for the world that awaited me. The most valuable lesson I took away was not how to care for livestock or harvest alfalfa; it was the value of true friendship. When I went through some extremely difficult times in life, often it was a friend who reached out and gave me a hand. For the past 30 years, that friend has been my dear wife Betty, and I am eternally grateful for her.

Today, in my 80s, I have clear and detailed recollections of around a dozen of my Fairbridge schoolmates. The names of many more come back to me, but other details about them elude me. The ones I remember best are the shipmates from my trans-Atlantic journey, including Brian, Roy, the brothers Leon and Louis—who died too young—Mitch, Clifford and Hughie. We stuck close together in the early years. Most of us lived in the same cottages. We stayed friends after leaving Fairbridge. There were other friends and characters I remember well, who came on with other parties on other ships: John, Jock, Eric and Leon and Louis' brothers, Phil and Eugene. The list goes on and will go on long after I'm gone. The names of many staff members have been changed for obvious reasons, and of schoolmates out of respect for their privacy. The full names of staff members I did include are given because I feel they deserve recognition as decent people and good caregivers.

PART I

1934-1951
Toddler to Teen

EDINBURGH, SCOTLAND

People have a saying: "It could have been worse."

When I think about my childhood, I'm much more likely to say, "It could have been better."

Perhaps my life began badly because I was born under the unlucky number 13. Our family lived in tenement flat #13. The family flat was in a substandard tenement building in the urban heart of Edinburgh, Scotland. Obviously, two adults with five children living in a two-room flat in the tenements would indicate they would be struggling financially, many close to the poverty level. However, poverty didn't have to mean complete misery. Thousands of low-income families in the U.K. lived in these low rents 'Tenement's, buildings and managed to keep their families together and reasonably happy... The fateful splitting of our family began in 1939. I was only five years old at the time. My brother Rob was ten, and my sister Minnie was eight.

It was also, coincidentally; the same year Britain entered World War II. On September 3, 1939, Prime Minister Neville Chamberlain declared war on Germany after Chancellor Adolf Hitler's armies attacked Poland, which would have drastic and tragic consequences for Britain, Europe, and the world.

However, it was not the war but my parent's divorce that was the pivotal moment in my life, even if I was too young to remember it. To this day, I still do not know why they ended their marriage, and so I have no reason to judge them for it.

Even though none of us remember her being a bad mother, the divorce judge ruled that, for whatever reason, she was unfit to take care of us. My father got custody instead, which was highly unusual for the time.

Father was a member of the Territorial Reserve Army. With the declaration of war, he was reassigned to the active forces in the Royal Medical Corps, and our care fell to his sister Kate. She took us in for a while but could not to keep us as she had four children of her own. I cannot imagine how her flat could've possibly accommodated two adults and nine children.

Soon after we were taken from Aunt Kate's, the powers that be placed Rob, Minnie, and me in a child hostel in Fifeshire, Scotland. At the time, Rob was old enough to realise what was happening, and as the eldest, he felt it was his responsibility to keep us together. That was a hopeless responsibility for a ten-year-old child up against a huge, callous system.

The three of us were shuffled from home to home. Rob became rebellious. He made many escape attempts to get us out of those terrible homes. He would pull me along behind him through the streets. Several times he carried me on his back when I couldn't keep up or carry on. He refused to leave me behind. However, every time the police eventually found us and carted us back to whichever home we had escaped from, where a thorough beating awaited us.

Rob's defiant behavior eventually landed him in various

juvenile detentions centers, commonly known as Borstal Homes, and basically disappeared from my life.

In 1940, Minnie and I were placed in the Middlemore Homes, where earliest childhood memories begin.

John Middlemore, a wealthy Birmingham citizen who was a pioneer in rescuing homeless boys and girls from the crowded city slums, founded Middlemore, located in Birmingham, in 1872. He took the children off the streets, housed them, and provided them decent food and clothing in preparation for a one-way journey to Canada.

Middlemore, along with Dr. T.J. Bernardo and others, pioneered these Child Emigration Homes, often caustically referred to as "Gutter Children Homes." The children themselves were called "guttersnipes," a terribly degrading insult.

Life at Middlemore was quite grim and Minnie was a source of much-needed comfort in those times. Our days were dictated by stiff routines and filled with chores. Discipline was strict.

To begin each morning, the staff members had us line up. There were around a hundred kids at the home altogether. The matron doled out a tablespoon of cod-liver oil to each of us. Our faces contorted into grimaces as we forced ourselves to swallow the awful-tasting stuff. Afterward, we got rewarded—or perhaps bribed—with a spoonful of sweet treacle.

These little rituals stayed constant through the chaos of the WWII Blitz. The matrons and staff probably tried to keep life as normal and orderly as possible for us. But those days could hardly be described as "normal." War was a reality that colored our daily lives and left a vivid impression.

When we looked out our windows at night, the bright beams of searchlights scanning for German bomber planes pierced the dark skies. Now and then, the golden beams landed on an enormous white barrage balloon, anchored in the ground by heavy steel cables. If an unsuspecting bomber plane flew close enough to clip the cables, their wings snapped off, and they fell from the sky. We visualized the German planes flying into the cables while we shot them down with our imaginary machine guns from the windowsills.

Sometimes the wailing of the air-raid sirens woke us up in the middle of the night. We threw off our bedclothes, our hearts hammering, and huddled close together. Some of the younger children screamed. The staff members came rushing in and shouted, "Children stay calm." They got us to settle down and line up, and then they lead us single-file at a brisk pace to the cellar, which served as our air-raid shelter. Once they closed the doors, the noise from outside was muffled to near silence.

It was terrifying back then, but today those nights are only distant memory. For several years as if by instinct, low-pitched sirens often made me jump, bringing images flooding back. I can practically hear the staff yelling, "Keep calm!" over the din.

My mate Hughie T., who was seven at the time, has clearer memories and fills in the missing details. Here is his description:

"Middlemore Home was not a very pleasant place. It seems that new groups arrived weekly, and fistfights between the children were a constant. The advent of the war in 1939 brought a bit of relief as the usual routine changed—we were missing days of school. We spent a portion of our day searching the fields and collecting shrapnel. It was exciting fun seeing barrage balloons released by the Home Guard in a nearby park.

"During the bombing raids, we would sleep in a ground floor room on thin mattresses lined up in rows with strategically placed 'pee buckets for answering nature's call. I well remember the night, heeding the call; I struggled my way down the narrow passageway to the assigned bucket. On my return to my pallet, I found that some enterprising chap had used my mattress as his port of call.

Glaring at my pee soaked mattress "I immediately began to holler at the indignity done by some fool kid who could not distinguish between a mattress and a bucket. Suddenly, one of the nurses screamed at me to shut up lest the German pilots hear; they will drop bombs, and we would all be killed!

"'Yeah, right,' I thought."

During the days, the staff insisted that we carry our gas masks everywhere and wear them when we went outside. In spite of their dire warnings, we took them off as soon as they walked away. Most of the adults around us did the same.

The masks were large and clunky things that hung in a box around our necks. They gave us long snouts when we wore them. We called them Mickey Mouse masks because kids with big, protruding ears looked like the familiar cartoon character while wearing them. Of course, they got hassled: "There goes Mickey Mouse!" someone would shout.

However, gas was not the only potential danger of war we faced.

One morning, a lad ran into the dining hall with his eyes wide, insisting we come outside quick—there was a huge hole in the ground near the building. We rushed out to find the sizeable crater. The kids in the back jostled to get a better view. It was the result of an incendiary bomb, which was meant to set buildings on fire. A few feet farther and it would have hit the building, igniting it in flames. Similar bombs were responsible for starting the massive fires of the London Blitz.

Another time, my friend Roy M. stepped outside during a day air raid. Looking up at the sky he could see a lone plane circling and he was certain he was about to get shot. He ran back inside as fast as his legs could carry him, shaking from fear. He still remembers the incident vividly 75 years later.

Small groups of us used to go out into the surrounding fields in our spare time eagerly looking for spent bombshells. At that age, we had no idea how dangerous playing in those fields might have been. Like so many children in war-torn countries, we were oblivious to some of the dangers, even when we were so sensitive to the sight of a bomber plane overhead.

Even today, kids can be seen throwing stones or bottles at tanks on the TV evening news. It seems like an act of sheer childish recklessness, but I understand why they do it. It's a game to them. Nothing more. The fact that they could be killed or seriously injured doesn't even cross their minds, just like it didn't for us in those fields.

I spent approximately a year at Middlemore Homes. Though I didn't know it at the time; I had been signed over to the Fairbridge school system, which had institutions in South Africa, Canada, and Australia. Middlemore was only an intermediary stop that funneled most of its young residents to one of these schools. There was no choice about where I wanted to go, or if I did, I don't remember it. Quite honestly, at that age I had no idea where any of those countries were or what they would be like. A few of the older kids remember getting a say.

At some point, I was in the process of being sent to Australia. I underwent a medical examination for the trip. My brother Rob and sister Minnie signed the form in childish block-letter scrawls.

The fact that an eight- and ten-year-old was verifying medical information for their younger brother shows how absurd and callus the child welfare bureaucracy was. They would take just about any signature to get a child sent away. To top off the cold, clinical cynicism of these proceedings, the paper was little more than a standardized form used for a child of any age. The medical examiner only filled in a few blanks.

I was deemed "In good health and of sound constitution and not suffering from any mental or bodily defect, which would unfit [him] for earning [his] own living as a [LABOURER]."

Yes, at six years old, I was pronounced suitable for a life of hard labour. And most likely my parents were not even required to sign their consent. If they were, I will never know.

I did not end up going to Australia, however. Whoever was making decisions about my future selected Canada as my destination instead. Friends from Middlemore, like Hughie, Roy, and Brian, sailed with me on the SS *Bayano* to Canada.

Minnie did not. She failed to meet the very strict health standards for children with no parents or adult relatives because she had an eye defect.

So when I left Middlemore, I lost the comfort of having my big sister by my side. She was effectively the last remaining family member I had in my life. As if losing her wasn't bad enough, the older boys teased me about her. "Hey, Mackay, your sister is boss-eyed!" they would yell after me.

Now it was time for me to go upon a journey across the Atlantic.

Goodbye Britain,
Hello Canada

My destination was chosen: the Fairbridge Farm School in Canada.

Officially, its title was The Prince of Wales Fairbridge Farm School, renamed after the Prince of Wales donated €1,000 to the school. It certainly gave the school a more refined air. I admit I did drop the "Farm School" crap and called it "The Prince of Wales Fairbridge" on résumés and applications, figuring an employer would think my upbringing was far more dignified. But who in pursuit of some form of advancement in life isn't guilty of a little embellishment at times?

In reality, Fairbridge could not be mistaken by a long shot for the posh institution that its full name suggested.

I did not know it at the time, but the course of my life was about to take a major turn when I left Middlemore. I barely understood what was happening. How could I? My life had been uprooted at such a young age, and I had to rely upon the guidance of my siblings up until then. All I knew was trying to get through the day without getting on the matron's bad side at Middlemore. Now I was going to be shuffled to a new home again—this one overseas—along with fourteen of my Middlemore peers.

In preparation for the journey, we received a series of immunizations over several weeks. Then we were sent by train to the port city of Liverpool where we stayed overnight in one of the Bernardo homes. There they issued us new clothes with our names sewn on each garment. Each of the children who had made the journey before us had received a small inventory of items to take across the Atlantic:

1. A small Bible
2. A gray flannel suit
3. Two pairs of short trousers
4. Two shirts
5. One Fairbridge school tie (gold and brown horizont al stripes)
6. Two pairs of pyjamas
7. Two under vests
8. One Mackintosh (raincoat)
9. One pair of boots
10. One pair of sandals
11. Two handkerchiefs
12. Two pairs of stockings
13. One jumper
14. A face cloth
15. One towel
16. A wash kit
17. One comb
18. One toothbrush and a bar of tooth cleanser in a small round can.

Out of all the things we received, I was most fascinated by the tin of tooth cleanser. I had never seen anything like it, and at first I had no idea what it could be for. It seemed strange that I should use this chalky, bitter-tasting white paste to clean my teeth. At the time, toothpaste in a tube did not exist.

All of our things had to be packed in a brown suitcase much smaller than the carry-on bags that airline passengers carry today. Oddly enough, we seemed to be the only party not issued a school uniform like we were supposed to. In all the photos taken of us, we were never wearing the grey blazer, matching short pants, and school tie. I suspect the government was saving cloth to use for soldiers' uniforms.

From the Bernardo home, we were bussed to the Liverpool docks where we boarded the ship *SS Bayano*, a pre-war banana freighter. We sailed in a convoy of merchant ships carrying some military personnel and several civilian passengers. A few British warships escorted the convoy to protect it from Nazi submarine wolf packs.

Once we were aboard the ship, our four adult escorts assigned us to cabins. I argued with my cabin-mate for the top bunk. It was very possible that a lad might pee in his bed during the night, and it was not a good idea to be the one sleeping below when it happened.

Otherwise, though, being on a ship sailing away from England to a faraway land seemed like a grand adventure after being cooped up in Middlemore. We felt like explorers, eagerly gazing over the decks and watching the English coastline recede, in the distance, and we imagined our lacklustre old lives were disappearing with it. Any destination would be an improvement, but we were especially excited about going to Canada. Some of the older boys had told us it was the land of cowboys and Indians, the land where frontier legends were made. That got our imaginations stirring over all the adventures we would have. In our minds' eyes, the former cargo vessel felt like the finest of luxury liners. What did we know of true luxury ships at the time, like the Duchess ships of the Cunard Lines, anyway? Interestingly enough, most of the prewar and postwar kids did sail with the Duchess ships.

While on board, I became quite close with some of my shipmates who were around my age. Roy M. became one of my closest friends over time. He could be a bit quieter and introverted than the others, but when he talked, he always had something clever or witty to say. There was also Eric F., better known as Mitch, Brian T., and Hughie T., who were a fellow Scot.

The November 10, 1941, issue of the *Victoria Daily Times* printed a photo of our party disembarking, subtitled "Orphans of Blitz," and described our arrival:

"Tired out after a perilous journey from Great Britain but excited about the prospects of the new life in Canada before them, sixteen small children of the average age of eight were welcome to the happy colony at Fairbridge Farm School, Cowichan, Saturday afternoon. These little orphans of the 'blitz' come from some of the worst bombed areas in Britain. The terrors of modern warfare are very real to them, and most of them have spent much of their young life in air raid shelters. Even on their way to Canada, they came very near to death, as their ship was the leading ship in the convoy, which was being escorted by the ill-fated American destroyer when it was torpedoed. A U.S. oil tanker in the same convoy was sunk. Depth charges were dropped all the way across, but despite the excitement occasioned by the submarines attack upon the convoy, the boys' only regret was that they did not have to get into the lifeboats according to Reverend W. Buckingham, the senior conductor of the party."

I certainly do not remember that particular episode. What I do remember is getting seasick, because, after all, this was winter on the North Atlantic, and the seas could get rough. The submarine attack may well have happened while I was bent over the loo throwing up.

When I was not attached to the loo, I ran around on deck with the others, shooting imaginary German planes out of the sky. Being on a ship in submarine-infested waters apparently did not faze us. More than likely, they did not tell us about the dangers that may be lurking underwater.

Two of my old friends recently shared their personal experience of the sub attack with me. Roy recalls seeing a sailor being transferred between ships on a bucket seat attached to a steel cable. Clem G., who was about ten years of age at the time, told me how we had slept on the stern deck of the ship during the attack. He said he'd seen the torpedoed ship go down. Our caretakers herded us out of sight of the action, but he'd managed to slip away and see everything unfold from the rails and watch the ship disappear under the water.

Other crews of kids crossing the Atlantic were not as lucky as we were. The ship *SS City of Benares*, carrying 90 children from Britain to Canada, was torpedoed in September of 1940, only a year before we embarked. The ship was part of a convoy similar to ours. When the *Benares* was attacked, 258 of the 406 passengers and crew died. Of the child evacuees, 77 perished and only 13 survived.

Tom Nagorski's book *Miracles on the Water* chronicles the incident, and the extraordinary courage displayed by some of those children. One naval officer later called it "courage beyond praise." One youngster, Colin Richardson, was in a lifeboat watching other boats capsizing and people dying around him as the temperatures plunged into the night. An elderly nurse in his boat perished. He had the good sense to keep himself and his remaining companions awake through the night so they didn't succumb to hypothermia. Two girls survived alone on a life raft for eight days without food, battered by vicious storms. They were near death on rescue, but they did recover.

When reading the grim account, I found myself thinking that this could easily have been our fate. I wondered how we would have survived the same terrible ordeal; how I would have coped if the decks suddenly buckled beneath me. Would I have had the presence of mind to get to the lifeboats, much less find my panicking friends and pull them out of harm's way like the children of the *Benares* did?

The book also describes how Winston Churchill was opposed to the scheme of evacuating children by ship to North America. The author writes:

"First he argued that ships carrying the children would be vulnerable to attacks by German submarines. Churchill also argued that this mass evacuation of children sent the wrong message to the enemy. He felt this would damage Britain's world image. It would appear that possibly his attitude centered more on national pride than safety of the children. On October 2, 1940, the British Government suspended the child evacuation program, having determined that it could no longer assure the children's safety in the North Atlantic."

In the book *Blitz*, Margaret Gaskin also states that

Churchill was strongly opposed to the child evacuation program: "The symbolism of Churchill's people fleeing danger was too powerful as a propaganda tool for the enemy."

I would agree with Churchill's opinions. German submarines were sinking Allied ships on the North Atlantic with great regularity from 1940 through 1944. It was no place for children to be yet there we were.

Even in spite of the danger and Churchill's disapproval, the programme resumed and ran again as it had for many decades. The British government did, however, place new restrictions on it. One of new policies stipulated that each party must have one adult caretaker for every four children. I still do not understand how the additional adult escorts would have helped us if our ship had been torpedoed.

Though our convoy lost one ship, with a second seriously damaged, the old banana freighter docked safely in Montreal. We were booked into a hotel for the night.

Roy still remembers us seeing a revolving door for the first time. This amazing contraption stunned us all—a door that just kept turning. Roy and I ducked in between two panels and pushed the door around and around. We were in the lobby, and then back outside again. In and out, around and around we spun inside the door. We wanted to see how fast we could make it spin.

The chaperone soon noticed our little game and demanded we get out immediately. We were sent to our room to reflect on our misbehaviour. Of course, the only thing we reflected on was why on earth did he have to spoil our innocent fun?

For the next leg of our journey, we boarded a Canadian

Pacific Railway train, destination Vancouver, British Columbia. We hoped to see dashing cowboys on beautiful horses galloping over the sagebrush, chasing wild Canadian Indians across the countryside, but we were gravely disappointed. I guess they were all in Hollywood making movies.

We gazed out at vast, wide-open, snow-covered prairies that seemed to stretch onward forever. They could not have been more different from the crowded cityscapes we were used to. Something about all that sheer emptiness unsettled me deeply. I made up my mind on that train that I would never live in a prairie or desert; it would be far too lonely and terribly boring.

The snow, however, excited us greatly. Every time we stopped in a station we made the most of it, throwing snowballs, sliding down hills on our behinds, catching snowflakes on our tongues. Many of us would have experienced snow in the U.K., but most likely never so much at one time. We still were fascinated and marveled at the massive snowdrifts blanketing the Canadian prairies.

Each stop brought us closer to Canada's West Coast, until we finally pulled in to the Vancouver station.

The air was crackling with anticipation as we departed from the train. After such a long journey, we would finally see our wonderful new home, the Prince of Wales Fairbridge Farm School. How could it be anything but wonderful? We exchanged theories, each more elaborate than the last, as we boarded the ferries for the shortest and next to final leg of our journey.

Arriving at Fairbridge

"We are Fairbridge folk, all as good as e'er,
English, Welsh, Scottish and Irish we have come
  from everywhere,
Boys to be Farmers and Girls for Farmer's wives,
We Follow our Fairbridge Founder."
                    — AUTHOR. some Fairbridge kid

An edge of anxiety crept into my excitement as the bus brought us closer. My stomach churned and I could not help wondering, if this would be one more miserable home like Middlemore. I silently prayed it wouldn't be.

The bus pulled through the main gates of Fairbridge. I was about to find out.

The gates were large, ornate, and painted stark white. Appropriately, a friend later dubbed them "the pearly gates to hell."

Gravel crunched under the tires as we drove up the dirt road past an apple orchard. We pulled up next to a cluster of buildings, where a large crowd of staff members and our new schoolmates were gathered to meet us.

As I stepped off the bus, a woman with a thick Scottish accent asked me if my name was Roddy Mackay. She was Mrs. Sinclair, a cottage mother.

I puffed up and answered her proudly, "Yes, and I'm from Edinburgh, Scotland!"

The staff members and the crowd of kids who greeted us all seemed friendly, yet I still had some sense of foreboding about this new home. After all, I had experienced a lot of changes in very short time. So even though my first impression was wonderful, I was still edgy.

Leading the welcoming party was a white-haired gentleman with a very scholarly appearance and an impeccable suit. He was Professor H.T. Logan, the school's headmaster, more commonly referred to as the principal of Fairbridge. To avoid confusion between Professor Logan (head of Fairbridge I refer to him as *Headmaster* and Mr. Grant head of the day school, *the Principal.*

Professor Logan led the staff and children in a rousing British "Hip, Hip, Hurrah" cheer in welcome. I was a bit star-struck; I thought this sort of reception was reserved only for very important adults. How could someone so sophisticated greet us so reverently? At Middlemore, we'd always been treated like nobodies.

After the welcoming party, we were all shepherded to the school hospital for a medical examination. The doctor inspected us for nits, ringworms, and lice. When he found some, we all had to get our heads shaved. It didn't bother us boys so much, but the girls were humiliated. Still, the clippers seemed far better than the alternative: dousing our scalps with a harsh, stinging solution, as they used to do in Middlemore.

When we were in the hospital, we slept in the biggest and softest beds I had ever lain on. The bedspreads were pure white, and the pillows were so fluffy it felt like resting on a cloud. I began to think we had arrived in heaven, and the nurse attending us must be an angel. She was very kind and had a gentle smile, and brought us fresh fruits and desserts along with our meals. These were delicacies we had never enjoyed before.

While we stayed, there were boxes full of games and toys for us to play with, and plenty of books to read. We could amuse ourselves most of the day. It all felt very luxurious.

They discharged us from the hospital in small groups. The hospital's daily record book shows that I was the last to leave:

Nov. 8: New party of 16 children admitted—
    Routine baths, shampoos, etc. Sixteen
    children examined by Dr. McHaffie.

Nov. 10: Twelve children held for vermin in hair.

Nov. 13: Eight new children remained.

Nov. 14: Four children discharged, four
    remain.

Nov. 15: One new child (R. Mackay) remained
    in the hospital for general care.

Nov. 26: New child R. Mackay discharged to
    cottage F.

No diagnosis was listed in the book other than "general care," so I have no idea why they kept me for 18 days, but I certainly didn't object.

During those short days in the hospital with everyone being so nice to us, I began to let go of my initial worries. I thought maybe I could be happy here. The hospital was so bright and cheerful. The green playing fields and the distant forests surrounding the grounds that we saw through the windows looked wonderful, especially after the gloom of Middlemore. We couldn't wait to explore them and climb the trees. The cottages were situated nearby. We knew we would soon be living there; they looked neat and well kept, cozy even.

Yes, I looked forward to finding my niche here.

ORIENTATION TO FAIRBRIDGE

I would soon learn my way around the Fairbridge Farm School. The whole place was pretty huge. At 1,100 acres, it was about the size of a modern-day university campus. It was bigger than any of the previous homes I had lived in. The whole school has often been compared to a village. It certainly was pretty insular, situated a few miles away from the nearest town, Duncan.

The main hub of the school was the residential area, where the cottages, hospital, dining hall, and other buildings sat along a horseshoe-shaped drive. The day school and the chapel were on opposite ends of this drive. Lots of trees grew here. They dotted the landscape and made small groves near the cottages. We also had the thick forests of hardy evergreens on the far reaches of the property.

Most of the school's land was dedicated to the farm, including animal pastures, barns, fields of alfalfa and oats, apple orchards, and gardens of vegetables like tomatoes, corn, turnips, cabbage, and beets. The fields stretched out far.

Most of the buildings were built in the old English style. Each of the seven duplex cottages could house 15 boys or girls divided between two suites. The girls' cottages were strategically located away from ours at the far end of the residential. Honestly, they looked more like large military barracks than cottages—all of them uniform and practical.

Each cottage also was named after a royal family member or prominent noble. A few bore the names of wealthy Canadian businessmen who filled the Fairbridge coffers.

So Queen Mary mingled with Mr. Blodell of the lumber company Macmillan & Blodell. However, for the kids, each cottage was simplified to a single letter, like R or S Cottage. I wonder if they thought we were too stupid to memorise the names.

In addition, four single houses could accommodate 12 children each. Other staff members lived in smaller buildings.

I would soon move from the hospital into my first cottage and discover what it was like to live in a cottage with a group of boys under the care of a cottage mother who lived with us. I would also discover how my cottage mother would have the biggest role in my daily life, and how her attitude would set the tone for my days at Fairbridge..

MRS. GREEN

If I forget every other detail of the cottages, I will never forget the floors. Cream-colored linoleum tiles in the kitchen, dark-brown hardwood with nearly black grain covering most of the second story where we slept in our dorms and the cottage mother had her suite. Every day the tread of 15 pairs of boys' shoes would heavily scuff those floors. The first floor (the basement) was mostly concrete, including the playroom, furnace room, and a large bathroom with toilets, sinks, and showers.

I remember the floors so vividly because I spent countless hours on my knees with a brush and rag in my hand scrubbing and polishing them. For the dorm floors, I used an unwieldy, oddly shaped tool called a bumper. It had a long handle with a heavy-metal square on the end, where I would wrap an old piece of cloth for polishing. The wooden stairs, though, were the worst and took the longest. They had to be perfectly shined until I could almost see my reflection. My knees were already sore, and then I had to perch awkwardly on a narrow stair while scouring the one above it. The chore seemed like an endless task.

Standing over me while I toiled, ready to punish me at the slightest provocation, was the woman who made my life hell.

In later years I was to think of her as "The Witch of Buchenwald" after an infamous female guard of a Nazi concentration camp. Back then, we knew her as Mrs. Green[2] of S Cottage, our cottage mother.

She was a woman in her late forties, her dark brown hair

2   Her name has been changed.

streaked with touches of gray. She carried herself like an army sergeant with a stiff military bearing everywhere she went. But she wasn't ugly or crone-like. Perhaps she may have even been a handsome woman if she had not been so stern.

We had to call her "Mum" when addressing her. It made me sick to my stomach to force that word out as I looked at her. Even though I had no recollection of my real Mum, I found it impossible to think of this woman as a surrogate.

For her part, she had no problem snarling at us. "You are filthy little guttersnipes," she would spat when she was upset with us, which was often. The term was a terribly derogatory slur, something the English upper class used to refer to poor children who spent their days living in the gutters of city streets.

"Mackay, you are a filthy guttersnipe, come here now!" she would yell, her shrill voice broached no disobedience. If I didn't appear at her side immediately, the consequences would be dire; most likely, a belt strapping.

My pal Hughie from the *Bayano* gave her the nickname Mrs. Grief. It was quite appropriate as she definitely brought much grief into our lives. Her husband died in the trenches during WWI. Quite possibly the poor chap had gone "over the top," meaning he'd been ordered to jump out of the trenches and charge the enemy line with a section of men, a move which always ended in a bloodbath. The German machine guns mowed them down like grass. Sure, he sacrificed himself for King and Country, but we all agreed that he'd probably gone out to meet his end gladly rather than return to a life with that nasty, malicious woman.

Kingsley Fairbridge once gave a speech to the Colonial

Club in London describing his vision for the caretakers of his proposed farm schools. He said, "The men and women of the staff must be gentlemen and gentlewomen of culture and refinement in order to bring up the children in a clean and wholesome atmosphere."

Gentlewoman; This woman was the complete antithesis of that mild-mannered lady Kingsley Fairbridge envisioned. If he had seen her caring for the children in his namesake institution, he would be cringing in his grave.

Unlike Mrs. Green, my first cottage mother was a very caring woman. I do not remember her name because I wasn't with her very long, but I do remember her kindness. She doted on me because I was the youngest, speaking softly and whispering reassurances to me and the other younger boys. She also gave hugs generously. They were the last hugs I ever received from a cottage mother.

To add to my misery the older boys in the cottages frequently mocked me for being her pet. They hassled me in mocking, babyish tones or slapped me upside the head when our cottage mother wasn't around.

I thought that was bad enough. Not even the Middlemore boys were that mean to me. Worse days were in store for me when I left that first cottage. I was being transferred to S cottage. The next four years living under the tyranny of Mrs. Green would be the worst years of my childhood.

One of my first mistakes upon arriving at S Cottage was asking one of the older boys what the "S" stood for.

His response was both quick and threatening. "S stands for 'Shite,' and you will get plenty of that, you little shitehead."

I would soon learn to fear this boy.

Mrs. Green was a sadistic disciplinarian. Her preferred form of punishment was flogging us with a belt. Technically, only the duties' master had the authority to use a belt on us, but she did it anyway. These floggings left bruises and welts on our backs and buttocks for weeks afterward.

Fairbridge followed the precedent of British public schools (the equivalent of private schools in America), which had several levels of discipline. The cottage mother was supposed to deal with the smaller infractions. The duties master administered major punishment to the boys for more serious offenses. Discipline was the duties master's main job. Only he was supposed to use the strap on us. In reality, though, we could receive far harsher beatings and punishment, i.e. confinement, from certain cottage mothers like Mrs. Green.

She targeted some of us more than others. She had a mental list of "troublemakers" that she would automatically blame if something went wrong or something ended up missing from the Pantry. Sadly, it was the youngest and most defenseless boys at the cottage who found themselves on the receiving end of her cruelty more often than others.

Her harsh treatment and excessive punishments would have been bad enough on their own, but she also turned a blind eye to the bullying that went on in the cottage.

Two of the older boys terrorized the younger ones relentlessly. These boys were already teenagers; they should never have been housed together with six- and seven-year-olds to begin with. However, during this period of time, that was the way some of the cottages were set up.

The bullies of Cottage S picked on us for their sadistic pleasure. They taunted us in the hallways. They remembered my innocent exchange with Mrs. Sinclair at the welcoming, when I proudly asserted by Scottish roots. They chanted, "Watch out for the little shitehead from Scotland, Mrs. Sinclair's wee pet!" I now deeply regretted that exchange.

One of their favourite pastimes was ordering us to fight each other while they watched and egged us on. Then Mrs. Green would beat us, in turn, for throwing punches. They ordered us to misbehave in front of Mrs. Green, so we would get in trouble. If we refused, they would drag us out of bed later that night and beat us up. Because of their tactics, I soon gained a reputation in Mrs. Green's eyes as a problem child.

One time they hoisted me up and forced me to hang by my fingertips from the second-story balcony. The bullies gathered their cronies to enjoy the show as I struggled to hold on, my face turning red as my grip weakened. Many of the younger kids were reluctant spectators, but they stayed rather than risk being targeted as the next victim.

Even though I was terrified, I wished with all my soul that I would fall and fracture my leg on the ground below, so I could end up back in the hospital with its soft beds and kind nurses. However, one of them would always grab me just as I was about to slip.

The constant torment took its toll psychologically. I woke up each morning thinking, "What fresh terrors are in store for me today?" The nightmares of falling into a bottomless pit followed me for years into my adult life, leaving me waking up in a cold sweat a decade later.

In those early years, I wished so badly that Rob or Minnie had come to Fairbridge with me. They would have provided some comfort. Plus Rob, being a fighter, would have given me some protection from the bullies.

However, then again, even if they had come, Rob and I would have been separated into different cottages anyway. It typically happened to siblings sent to Fairbridge together.

Our misery began first thing in the morning when Mrs. Green conducted daily bed inspections. We slept on uncomfortable metal cots lined up in two rows, barrack-style, in the upstairs dormitory. We had two sheets, one blanket, and no pillows. Our sheets and blanket had to be perfectly tucked in with mitered corners and not a single wrinkle. If a bed did not pass muster, she would tear it apart and order the boy to remake it. She might scream at us to redo it several times over.

At night, once we climbed between the sheets; we were not allowed to leave the room for any reason, not even to use the bathroom. For the younger boys, that was generally from 7:00 p.m. until morning. Many nights we had to tiptoe across the dorm and relieve ourselves out of the window. One night, Roy couldn't open the window, so he used the floor-heating vent. He was not too popular with us when the heat was turned on the next night, and the room filled with the rank scent of urine. We were grateful it had not been a number two.

My pal Hughie, like many of the kids, had a problem of wetting his bed. It was little wonder, considering how much we endured at such a young age—broken homes, war trauma, and air raid sirens waking us in the middle of the night. It's incredible that more of us did not wet our beds nightly.

Mrs. Green and a few other cottage mothers certainly didn't consider these factors. She punished "bed-wetters" with something worse than a physical beating: humiliation. She forced Hughie to strip his bed in front of all the other boys. Then he had to take his sheet, pee stains and all, and hang it on the outside washing line in full view of everyone passing by for the entire day. Then he would have to sleep in the same sheet the next night and every night after that until the scheduled laundry day.

For those kids like Hughie, there was no relief from this daily public embarrassment. It's worth noting, though, that shortly after Mrs. Green left the school, Hughie stopped wetting his bed.

If the school administration was aware of her cruel conduct towards the defenseless children, they simply turned a blind eye..

One incident with my friend Hughie demonstrates the callous attitude some of the staff members took. One morning, Hughie came to day school classes with his hands raw and bloody from a thrashing by Mrs. Green, and our concerned teacher took him to the day school principal. His only response was, "Well, very likely he had it coming."

In all fairness, I have to say that not all the staff members shared his attitude. Many, in fact, felt bad for the way we were treated. The problem, though, was that the higher-ups in the administration just didn't care or were incapable of making the necessary changes. I found out years later that a former cottage mother—one of the sympathetic ones—saw the abuse and reported it, but her complaints fell on deaf ears and very little was ever done to change things.

OUR DAILY SCHEDULE

There is a moldy home far, far, away,
Where we get bread and jam three times a day.
Eggs and bacon we don't see,
We get mothballs in our tea.
Now we are gradually fading away.
                    —A song of Fairbridge, possibly carried over
                              from British institutional homes

A big brass bell of Fairbridge dictated our daily routine.

It was an inanimate control freak, constantly commanding us to do something or go somewhere. It ordered us to get up in the mornings, dictated when we ate and went to school, and ordered us to turn up for work details, church services, and special gatherings with its deep, insistent gongs.

It was not housed in a bell tower. Instead, it hung on a simple wooden platform near the dining hall, next to the flagpole on the central green.

We never liked hearing it. In the morning, it made us groan and stick our fingers in our ears. The bell was much like an army bugle call for us, and one WWII army song put the feeling of our frustration into words: "Someday I'm going to murder the bugler."

Nobody actually murdered the bell-ringer, but years later somebody did steal the damned bell. Who did it is still a mystery? However, if someone proposed the idea to me, I would've volunteered gladly.

To be appointed the bell-ringer, though, was a different

story. The job was good fun. When I was on bell duty, I swung it with great gusto while laughing merrily as the sound reverberated throughout the school grounds. Knowing that it was making my friends, and foes moan and grumble made it that much more delightful.

The first gong sounded at 6:00 a.m.

In S Cottage, I woke up knowing another miserable day was beginning. Mrs. Green would be coming through the door soon to conduct daily bed checks. I stole a few more precious minutes under the covers before I got up. I never dared to take more than a few. Then I joined the other boys in the ritual of tucking in our sheets and blankets. The corners had to be perfectly mitered, and the blanket couldn't have a single wrinkle.

After that, we stood beside our beds as Mrs. Green slowly and deliberately inspected our work. We were not allowed to leave the dormitory until our beds were cleared. We held our breaths, hoping that she wasn't in a foul mood that day and started tearing beds apart and screaming to humiliate us.

After we were cleared, we proceeded to the downstairs washrooms to wash up and brush our teeth. By the time we were clean, we had another hour and a half to go until breakfast. In that time frame, we all had our various assigned cottage duties to complete. We might be washing sinks and toilets, scrubbing and polishing the floors and stairs, chopping and bringing in wood for the furnace and kitchen stove, or doing various other chores.

Mrs. Green took especial delight in having us scrub and polish the stairs until they gleamed. She scrutinized all of our work, paying special attention to the easy-to-miss little corners. One spot of dirt and she would be furious.

"They are filthy; you will redo the entire stairway now!" she would scream.

If we missed several spots, she smacked our ears hard enough to leave them ringing.

She could make a hardened sergeant major inspecting barracks look like a choirboy. In a few war movies, I've seen, the officer pulls on his white gloves and runs a finger along surfaces to check for dust. Mrs. Green never needed gloves— she had the eyes like a hawk capable of spotting the smallest gray speck of dust. If she saw anything, we were in trouble.

Finally, the 8:00 a.m. bell released us from our duties to go to the main dining hall for breakfast, if we had finished. Our stomachs would by rumbling by then.

The dining hall, located centrally among the cottages and near the chapel, was like a large soldiers' mess with many long tables. It had to accommodate all of Fairbridge's staff and kids. It had space for over 300 people, although we never had more than 200 kids at any one time. The dining hall also served as the venue for special gatherings like Halloween parties, Christmas dinners, or the occasional dances.

Inside, each cottage shared one long table with benches on either side. All the tables for the boys' cottages were at one end, and the girls were at the other. The staff gathered at the head table in the centre of the hall. Their table always looked much nicer than ours with white linen tablecloths, real napkins, china, glasses, and silverware.

We had no tablecloths. Our knives were always dull and

all our dinnerware was made of metal, including the plates, cups, and bowls. Each week, one boy was assigned to carry all our dinnerware and utensils in from the cottage and set the table.

We waited until Mrs. Green gave us permission to be seated. When all the children were settled, the school minister rose, and we stood up with him to say the very simple grace:

"For what we are about to receive,

May the Lord make us truly thankful.

For Christ's sake,

Amen."

That faithfully followed routine stuck with me. To this day, I still use this simple, old, country grace. I like it best. Too many people, I feel, over-extend the grace by praying for much more than just the meal in front of them.

Our breakfast menu was unchanging. Every morning we had a bowl of porridge (which we called mush), a mug of milk, and bread with jam. We had no butter. The mush was either Cream of Wheat or Sunny Boy Oats. The cereals were shipped in large vats, and sometimes the lids were not sealed tight, so we often found small, white, wriggly maggots in our bowls. Mrs. Green sat at the head of the table where she had a good view of each of us. The youngest children sat closest to her, but not by choice. She arranged the seating order so the youngest boys sat close to her on one end and the senior boys took the far end of the table. The arrangement put us in the striking range of her long-handled serving spoon. She liked to whip it out and smack knuckles and arms for any minor breach of good table manners. Elbow on the table—smack!

Talking at the table was not allowed either. If we let out even a peep, we risked getting whacked.

Meanwhile, the big boys at the far end of the table could get away with practically anything while Mrs. Green's attention was focused on us. Sometimes to amuse themselves, they used a spoon or fork to flick food or a maggot someone had found in the mush at the young "turds," as they liked to call us.

One prank that really cracked everyone up was the farting game. One of the seniors at the far end farted and all the boys on that bench one by one would lift their buttocks to let the, "Honorable Fart," go by like a wave. It had us giggling so hard that Mrs. Green became furious and sentenced the entire cottage to a gating; a punishment much like grounding that confined us to the cottage and its yard.

The girls covered most of the food preparation for the main meals. They may have enjoyed this assignment, but they sure didn't enjoy Cookie L.'s habit of pinching their bottoms when they were bending down.

Even if that could be grounds for firing or arrest today, back then his behavior was simply considered one of those things that horny adult men did. I am ashamed to admit that his habit at times had the boys laughing at the girls' expense. It certainly was not the example that any staff member should have been setting in front of children.

His actual cooking skills were very limited. On the other hand, nothing on our menus ever demanded a chef; pretty much everything from the veggies to the meat was simply boiled and served. Seasoning was unheard of. I think as long as one knew how to boil water, he or she would have been competent enough to be hired as a cook at our school.

Lunch, by the English custom, we called dinner, consisted of various meats except on meatless Fridays when we had fish or macaroni. Suppers were made and eaten in our cottages.

Maggots aside, the food was healthy but tasteless. Most of the food was tolerable, but when I saw either turnips or parsnips getting ladled onto my plate, my stomach recoiled. I could not stand those two vegetables. Even the smell of parsnips made me gag.

Of course, we had to eat absolutely everything on our plates, no exceptions.

I bided my time until Mrs. Green's attention was on another table. I swiftly scooped the parsnips off my plate and into my trousers pocket.

I had started padding my pockets with some toilet paper before mealtimes for this very purpose, just in case. The stain of mashed parsnip on my buttock or trouser legs would have given me away immediately. It was a bit uncomfortable walking around with the wad there, but it spared me the displeasure of eating the repulsive veggie. Better yet, it worked. Mrs. Green never caught me, or else it would've meant a severe tongue-lashing and at least a week of stacking wood.

After we finished breakfast, we might have a few minutes free before the third bell rang at 9:00 a.m. to send us off to the day school. It was a short walk to and from the school building from the cottages and dining hall, but still we were kids, and we would get distracted by our games and arrive late. If we racked up too many "tardies," we got sent to the principal's office for discipline.

After the day school was finished, we returned to the cottages and got ready for the bell to summon us to our daily work details. We had different assignments depending on our age. The older kids went off to do farm chores. Some of them worked on the farm full-time while waiting to be placed for employment. The younger kids like me got assigned to work in the cottages or the residential area around the school.

We did a huge variety of chores such as weeding gardens, mowing lawns, scrubbing and polishing floors, cleaning toilets, washing everyone's clothes and bed linens in the central laundry, sometimes even filling potholes on the main road. There was no end to the list.

In the afternoons, we sometimes got a precious hour—but never more than an hour—of free time to ourselves if we hadn't been gated.

After a full day's work, we went back to the cottages for our evening meal, supper. We prepared and ate supper within our own cottages.

One or two boys were assigned to make the meal and set the tables. Mrs. Green instructed us in the basics of cooking. On the positive side of Fairbridge, those skills came in handy later in life when I was a bachelor.

At the time, though, preparing supper could be an ordeal.

One episode, in particular, involved a friend of mine whose nickname was Coop. I was in the kitchen with him peeling potatoes. He had to prepare the night's dessert: blancmange, a white gelatinous dish made with milk. The adults called it delightful, while the kids called it misery. We mainly rotated between blancmange, rice pudding, and bread pudding for dessert.

Generally, the cottage mothers set out the recipes and the ingredients and supervised the kids to ensure they didn't start a fire or drop an unpeeled spud in the stew. Mrs. Green, however, always watched us with her evil eye, as though waiting for us to make the slightest mistake, so she could pounce.

That day, Coop was extremely nervous, and with good reason. His eyes kept flicking anxiously to Mrs. Green, as though expecting her to jump at him at any moment.

He approached the counter gingerly. Wanting to be extra careful not to make a mistake, he decided to read each ingredient from the recipe sheet aloud as he gathered them on the workspace. He desperately hoped that if he misread something, Mrs. Green would just correct him.

Poor Coop barely reached the third line when he mistakenly read out one cup instead of a half-cup of something or other. *Wham!* Mrs. Green slapped him on the arm and screeched in his ear, "No; that's not the right amount; read your recipe again, you stupid boy!"

Coop got tenser and began making more blunders, only to have Mrs. Green tear into him more each time. I sat in the other corner dutifully peeling my potatoes and listening to that bitch getting more and more worked up. I wanted to throw the paring knife at her, but I knew the consequences would be severe. So I just kept my head down and focused on my task. I felt every bit as scared as Coop did in the kitchen whenever she was there.

THE DAY SCHOOL

Cheerio!
Here we are
Learning hard.

— *The Golden Rule*
At the Fairbridge School

When school was in it dominated much of our day. The day school building stood between the residential area with the cottages and the dining hall, and the farm site with the various barns, fields and orchards. It was the largest building on the site. It had nine classrooms, a full-sized gymnasium with a wood floor, a stage, and a small library. Next to it stood the manual training building where carpentry classes for the boys were held. Unlike today's schools, students did not move between classrooms. We stayed put in the same room throughout the day. Only grades 1 through 10 were taught there. Since the original concept was to take us out of school at age 15 and place the boys in agriculture work and the girls to domestic positions, the administration didn't think we would need more schooling beyond that. The few scholastic lads that reached the higher grades and wanted to continue attended the Cowichan High School in the town of Duncan.

Like some other kids coming to Fairbridge, my unsettled early years meant my previous schooling had been inconsistent at best. Many of us had lost parents, become displaced, and gotten shuffled through the various institutions in Britain before arriving in Canada. I must have missed at least two years of school. As far as I know, there are no records that I even attended school at all in Scotland. I was placed a grade behind most of the kids my age.

I found many classes to be difficult. My evaluations from teachers ranged from "not very bright" to "above average." I felt the odds were stacked against me in certain ways. It seemed that a few kids, like me, got labeled as "slow" for various reasons, and some teachers pushed us even harder because of it and punished us more when we struggled. We very seldom heard words of encouragement in dealing with our learning difficulties.

Though the school building was part of the Fairbridge property, it still came under the jurisdiction of the Canadian Department of Public Education. The school administration and teachers were part of the British Columbian Public School System, not the Fairbridge staff. However, the day school principal and several of the teachers lived on the Fairbridge grounds in the staff houses. Others had homes nearby or in Duncan.

Many of us believe today that because most of the staff lived onsite, several of them felt free to discipline us the same way the Fairbridge staff did, including strapping us. In regular Canadian schools, the punishments such as we received would never have been allowed, not even from the highest authority in the school.

Mr. Grant[3] was the day school principal and was a dedicated teacher covering a wide range of subjects, in

---

3   His name has been changed.

particular math, history, and English. He could be tough and had high standards for behavior and achievement in the classroom. He had less patience for those of us who had learning difficulties or behavior problems. Personally, I think he had a tendency to punish some students more harshly than others.

His disciplinary weapon of choice was an old razor strop—a thick, flexible band of leather used to hone knives and shaving razors. It looked like a short, hefty belt.

When we were sent to his office for discipline, he started with giving us a vicious verbal tongue-lashing. Then we were told to hold our arm out straight with our palm facing up. If we pulled away before the strop came down, we earnt five more strokes. If we cried, grimaced in pain, or showed any emotion, it was considered a sign of weakness. Many a lad struggled to hide his tears and maintain a sense of manliness as he went back to his classroom.

If we had done something to make him really lose his temper, he would seize us by one ear and haul us into the office. This left us with a lot of very sore ears.

Though he may have been a tough disciplinarian, in other ways, he was a good teacher and a great basketball coach. Our senior girls' basketball team won the B.C. Provincial Championship. Many of his students held him in high regard. The bright kids benefited from being challenged to improve in his classes. It helped that they rarely, if ever, had to be disciplined. Ultimately, they thought he was tough but fair. Even I could admit he was a good teacher and knew his subjects well.

Mr. Grant did manage to contribute one particular word to my somewhat limited vocabulary. It was from his one of his report cards, which said, "Roddy is a capable student (not always); however, too often he allows his *pugnacious* attitude to interfere with his daily studies."

Pugnacious. I looked it up: "Having a quarrelsome or combative nature."

I snorted indignantly, but I never forgot it.

Years later at one of the early "Old Fairbridge Reunions," I met him again and thanked him personally for introducing me to the word. When my kids were growing up and really aggravating me with their rebellious attitudes, I called upon that particular word for them. It came in handy. We shared a good laugh about it.

Of course, as with most kids, my favourite part of the school day was recess.

Unfortunately, there was no access to any of the school's sports equipment during our recess periods. There were neither footballs to throw nor basketballs to pass and dribble. So we had to make up games using objects we could find. Even kicking a can around with a friend, games of tag, hide and seek could be fun.

Marbles were some of the most popular toys we had. We called them "miggies" as they do in England. The game of miggies had two players squatting at opposite sides of a circle drawn in the dirt. A small group of kids always gathered around the circle as well to watch and wait for their turn. The players took turns shooting their miggie at the other ones inside the circle by flicking it with their thumb. The one who knocked the most miggies out of the circle was the winner.

At one point, a metal miggie got snuck into the action, and it would smash the glass ones. That added another layer of drama to the game.

Another popular game was called "Conkers." It involved hardened chestnuts drilled through with a nail and threaded with 12 inches strong twine, so they hung like a hard ball at the end of a rope. Chestnuts, or what we called conkers, could be found abundantly on the ground thanks to Fairbridge's many chestnut trees.

We got pretty invested in the process of hardening the conkers, experimenting with different methods to get the hardest, most unbreakable nut. Soaking them in vinegar was a popular method. Others took it a step further by soaking the conkers in their pee. One enterprising lad thought he could speed up the process by soaking the conker in his pee, then sticking it in a hot oven to bake.

However, this would be scientific chap did not realise was that baking pee-soaked conkers made for a very smelly kitchen. Of course, Mrs. Green noticed, and she spent hours opening up drawers and cabinets, sniffing every nook and cranny in the kitchen to try to find the source of the lingering, pungent odour. Fortunately, the culprits were long gone by then.

When we had the conkers hardened appropriately and threaded, they were ready for action. Two players took turns. One of them would dangle his conker out in front of him, and the other would swing his out, trying to break his opponent's conker. We put as much effort into perfecting our swing as we did into the science of hardening them. For each conker we broke, our conker got a point. As they raked up many points from their victories, they could become champion conkers. But then everyone wanted to challenge our champion conker, because if they broke it, they took all the points our conker had.

Eventually, our champion conker became quite vulnerable, much like an aging prizefighter. A tiny, hairline crack would appear on its shell, and then we knew it was only a matter of time. We had to weigh risk and reward: our conker could gain even more notoriety by withstanding another bout, or it could break at last. If we entered the arena again, we found ourselves nervously holding out our prized champion while our smug opponents geared up to destroy it with one mighty swing.

It was very disheartening when our conker lost. But then we just had to go out and find a newer, stronger conker and get back in the ring. It's not a bad analogy for life.

THE SCHOOL CHAPEL AND OUR RELIGIOUS TRAINING

On Sunday mornings, the Fairbridge bell called us to attention at 10:45 a.m. with a series of three gongs repeating over and over. It was as though the bell was commanding us, "Come to church! Come to church!"

At seven years old, I had no recollection of having been inside a church, not even when I'd lived at Middlemore. It was recorded in my file that I had been baptized a Presbyterian, as most Scots were in those days. (My older brother Rob likes to tell me he was baptized in Edinburgh's most noted and historical cathedral, St. Giles. I told him, "Rob, a sinner yes, a Saint you ain't.")

Other than the Catholics, it didn't matter what faith we had come from originally. Whether we had been Presbyterian or Jewish, we were converted promptly to "The Church Of England," at Fairbridge. As most of us had no idea what the differences were between the various religious faiths or what it meant to convert we humbly accepted the new faith. My birth certificate has me baptized, as a Presbyterian so even though I have never attended one of their churches when asked to fill in forms that is what I use.

The chapel was located on the far end of the road running through the residential area, on the opposite side from the day school building. On the outside, the school chapel looked like a fairly simple, humble building, though quite big. It was very long with a rounded apse end, covered in wood shingle siding. It was unadorned on the outside, built in a very similar style to the other buildings at the school. Attached to the front end of the building was a stout and stocky clock tower. The surrounding tall evergreens and maple trees made for a picturesque, pastoral scene.

As soon as I walked inside, I found myself in a wide-open space with an all-wood interior. The stained-glass windows glinted in the sunlight, adding a shot of beautiful vibrancy.

I wasn't sure why, but I felt a felt a sense of peace in there. I felt safe.

I was impressed by the sheer size of the place and the magnificent pipe organ, built by the famous Harrison & Harrison of Durham, England. Its tones reverberated through the whole chapel as students and staff alike came in and found a pew. I perked my ears and listened to those powerful, majestic, and sweet notes. This was music unlike any I'd heard before.

Our chapel building was larger than many churches throughout the area. Its 34 rows of simple wooden pews could comfortably seat a congregation of 300 people or more.

As we settled down and the organ stilled, I began to feel my anxiety creeping up again. I watched everyone around me intently so I would know exactly what to do, so I wouldn't seem out of place. Once all the children and staff were seated, Cannon Hughes commenced the service.

That first day I didn't quite keep up with the motions and the hymns. Soon, though, I became accustomed to the Sunday service. When I came into church, I felt a strong sense of comfort and security in this sanctified space. Here I knew I was safe from receiving beatings and thrashings.

I generally found the sermons rather dull as they were beyond my comprehension at that age. Like many kids my age, I could come up with a whole list of other things that would be more fun than attending church. I did love the music and singing, however. The old hymns filled me with lightness, and I got a lot of enjoyment from singing many of them.

Toward the end of the service, two boys wearing the choir vestments were assigned to walk down the main aisle and pass the offering plate down each row of pews. Every child at Fairbridge was given two cents a week, one for pocket money and one to put in the church plate. The staff members usually gave a few small silver coins from their purses.

The whole cottage sat together in one long pew. I could look down its length and see two or three bullies who almost daily got their kicks out of terrorizing the youngest of us, and the biggest sinner of them all, our dreaded cottage mother who made our lives hell.

Their evil ways did trouble me when I seriously reflected on the sermons. If these people could claim to be good Christians and still do these things to us, it raised serious doubts on my mind for the faith they were instilling in us.

I learnt how to say my prayers in church. When I bowed my head night after night, I raised a plea for some relief from these wicked people.

"Please, God, take these people and send them elsewhere," I prayed silently. After an especially bad day, I added, "Send them all to *hell* where they belong!"

Yet, with each Sunday they would all be there, alive

and well in the house of God. Mrs. Green would be sitting ramrod-straight in the pew focused on the sermon, looking very devout and sanctimonious as usual. The bullies would be huddled together and sniggering among each other, likely plotting new forms of torment to inflict on us.

Everyone, staff members and students, attended morning and evening services conducted by the Church of England, or as we called it, "The C of E." We had a school minister who was charged with our spiritual care. When I came, Reverend Hughes held that office. All of us were issued a copy of *The Book of Common Prayer, according to The Church of England in the Dominion of Canada.*

The only exception was made for the Catholic children, who hopped into the school truck every Sunday morning to be driven to a church of their faith in the town of Duncan. That hardy, multi-purpose truck was also used in all sorts of school duties, including bringing in the milk and taking out the garbage. We used this fact to give the Catholic kids a hard time. One of us would pipe up and say, "What's the truck used for?"

Another would be quick to answer: "Milk, garbage and Catholics."

As mentioned earlier, Mrs. Green took our conduct and presentation at church very seriously. We always had to be perfectly put together and extra respectful of our conduct on Sundays.

One such Sunday, Mrs. Green came down the stairs and began her inspection as usual. She was halfway down the line when she came to an immediate stop, lifting her head up and concentrating as she sniffed the air. The severe, disapproving expression of her face told us that something was wrong, and one or all of us were about to suffer a tongue-lashing or worse.

Then she announced, "There is a foul odour in the air, and one of you boys must have passed gas. I want to know who would do such a vile thing of a Sunday morning."

Of course, nobody was willing to confess. I kept my expression blank as her leering eyes swept over me.

After a minute of glaring at us and getting no response, she ordered us to form a straight line, turn around to face the cottage wall, and bend over. She began at the end of the line and sniffed the rear end of each lad in turn, practically pressing her face against each buttock. I could hardly believe that this was actually happening. I would've been in stitches laughing if I hadn't been one of the suspects.

Halfway down the line she stopped behind Louis.... She'd found her quarry.

She began shrieking at him: "You are the one, you filthy boy! This behavior on a Sunday morning—it's too disgusting!"

Poor Louis, pale was shaking and looked like he was facing a firing squad.

The rest of us breathed a sigh of relief and fought to hold our laughter in.

She continued, "You vile boy! Why didn't you own up when I asked who did it? For that you will be gated for a week, and furthermore there will be no cake at supper for you tonight!"

LIFE IN "S" COTTAGE

A year went by, and I had become accustomed to the daily routine of chores, school, more chores, cooking, Sunday church services, and free time when I could get it.

I had now experienced the full gamut of chores we got assigned each day, from the laundry to the weed pulling. However, the one chore I hated above all others was chopping and stacking wood. Every building at Fairbridge had large stacks of neatly piled wood behind it that would eventually be fed into the furnace. We were the ones who had to maintain the woodpile. Other than the fieldwork in the hot summers, it was one of the most labor-intensive and unpleasant tasks we had to do.

In the summer, it would be hot by the woodpile and in the winter it would be bitterly cold. After a while, the logs would get very heavy. If I had a nickel for every splinter, I got from piling wood; I would have left Fairbridge a wealthy man.

Sometimes we were sent to the homes of staff members to work for the day, including the headmaster's house, which was the largest and nicest residence on the entire Fairbridge property. It was an old English-style building painted white with dark brown, decorative wood panels adorning the front and ivy growing on the sides. It was two stories high, with four bedrooms and a master suite. We all admired that house. I liked being assigned there if only because it meant I got to spend time inside.

When I arrived, I reported to the headmaster's wife and she gave me a list of tasks.

"Here's what you have to do, Roddy," she told me.

I glanced over the list quickly and very politely replied, "Yes, marm."

I wasted no time before getting my bucket and scrubbing brush for the floors and getting right to it. I would also have to mop the basement and pull the weeds in the yard before the day was done. I was used to doing these types of chores in the cottage.

But unlike in the cottage, I heard a welcome call as I neared the end of my chore list.

The headmaster's wife opened the upstairs door and called out, "Roddy, there's a good boy, I have placed a glass of milk and a cookie for you on the steps."

The kindness was there, but she still sounded like she was calling a dog or cat in to be fed. What was more, she put the treat on the steps instead of inviting me into the nice, carpeted parlour upstairs. I guess she was afraid a scruffy urchin would dirty the rug.

Still, I appreciated the gesture. It was more than I ever got from Mrs. Green. The headmaster's wife was a kind and decent person just like her husband, whom I greatly admired.

One of the duties I did not mind was working with the road gang and filling potholes with Mr. Bullcock.

Mr. Bullcock was the school's truck driver. He brought in the deliveries of food and milk, drove the Catholic kids to town for church, drove us back and forth for summer camps and other activities, and handled any other errands that required a drive out to town. Our all-purpose truck was a hardy Dodge with a canvas roof, creating a tent-like canopy over the bed. There were benches fastened to the sides on the bed for us to sit on. It looked much like an army truck used to carry troops.

Mr. Bullcock always tooted the truck's horn when passing the home of his friend on the way to town. But really, it sounded more like a short "tunt." So we gave our driver the nickname "Tunt Bullcock." Of course, we never let him hear us call him that.

The road gang assigned to Mr. Bullcock's work detail got our buckets of gravel and shovels and jumped into the back of the truck.

As we drove around, we sang a little ditty that had been passed down through generations of Fairbridge kids. It had been around for so long that it predated the Dodge and referred to the original Plymmy truck:

There's a Plymmy running back,
Down the old Koksilah track,
On its way to Fairbridge Farm.
There's water in the petrol,
The tires are made of wood,
The spark plugs are a missing,
And the whole damned thing's no good.
There's a Plymmy running back,
Down the old Koksilah track
On the way to Fairbridge Farm.

Mr. Bullcock stopped whenever we reached a pothole. As soon as the truck pulled over and the rowdy, sputtering engine stilled, we jumped out with our equipment at the ready.

Mr. Bullcock gave directions in his thick Yorkshire or Lancashire accent. When he caught me taking a break and leaning on a shovel, he marched over and reproached me: "Ee by gum Roddy Mackay if thee don't get to work, I will kick tharse for thee."

He had a gruff attitude and grizzled appearance, but underneath the roughness was a decent and caring person. He and his wife, a cottage mother, were two of my favorite staff members. Unlike many, they were also parents, with their kids attending Fairbridge, which made them treat us better.

In S Cottage, I earned a permanent place on Mrs. Green's list of problem boys.

That was partly due to the bullies, who took perverse pleasure in making us break rules right under Mrs. Green's nose to provoke her wrath.

With all their terrorizing, I had become so terrified of the bullies whom I would do anything they ordered me to do without hesitation, no matter how humiliating or bizarre. I practically became their slave, washing their stinking socks, cleaning their boots, and performing other menial tasks for them.

One Sunday we were all lined up outside the cottage ready to leave for church and waiting for Mrs. Green to come down the stairs.

One of the bullies stepped out of line and made eye contact with me, his favourite target. I knew from the devilish curl in his smile that this was going to be bad.

I tried to drop my gaze and pretend I didn't notice him, but it was too late. He pointed to the distant hills across the playing fields and ordered me to run. My stomach twisted in fear, knowing Mrs. Green could come down any moment. I knew well that if I refused, I was in for a hard thrashing tonight and probably 'gating' to the cottage for the rest of the week as well.

So, feeling angry yet frightened, I took off running across the playing fields as I'd been ordered. One of the sympathetic older kids ran after me and closed in before I got too far. He caught my shoulder and stopped me, but by then Mrs. Green was already outside.

She was livid.

I broke out in a cold sweat just facing her. The bully, meanwhile, was struggling to hold back laughter.

I didn't dare tell her the truth about why I took off. I knew by now that she probably wouldn't believe me anyway. So I stayed quiet and took my punishment.

Incidents like this solidified my place on Mrs. Green's list. Leon, Louis, Brian, and Roy also joined me on her roster of usual miscreants. We were watched even more closely by her hawk's eye. When something bad happened, Mrs. Green automatically turned her suspicions on us.

For instance, every now and then she found something missing from the cottage pantry. When this happened, she would interrupt our supper to announce that a theft had taken place and demand somebody step forward. When no one did, she dismissed everyone in the room except for three or four of us on her list.

She would confine us in the dining room until one of us confessed.

It was pointless to plead innocence. We were the problem boys and if no one else claimed responsibility, it had to be one of us. That was how her stupid justice system worked. So we took turns coming forward and taking the punishment: a thorough strapping and losing any privileges we may have had.

One time when I was around eight, a small can of sardines had gone missing from the larder. As usual, it came down to the four of us.

The other boys insisted it was my turn to take the rap. So I made my false confession, bracing for the beating that would come. I just wanted to get it over with and go to bed.

But instead of just making me turn around and bend over, she asked me what I did with the empty tin.

Of course, I had never seen the bloody tin. If I were going to steal food, I certainly wouldn't have picked some stinking sardines.

I lied and said that I threw it away on the playing field.

She ordered me to go find that stupid can and bring it to her. I spent several hours on a black and bitterly cold night wandering the fields, shivering and looking for an empty tin that didn't exist. I huddled in my coat and dug my hands into my pockets or armpits—anything to stave off the biting cold attacking my fingers. My hands, feet, and face were completely numb after a while. It seemed like ages before she finally called me back in to receive my thrashing and get sent to bed.

There were times, though, when we stood up to her in subtle ways, or when her viciousness backfired on her entirely.

One time, a cottage-mate was the server of the day after Mrs. Green had given him a severe thrashing for some daft minor incident. The server's job was to go to the kitchen in the dining hall and pick up serving pots or dishes of food and deliver them to Mrs. Green, who doled out portions to each of us. They also brought her food separately on a china plate.

That day, my mate picked up her plate and on his way out through the swinging kitchen door, he spat right in her food. Turning on his heel to face our table, he laid the plate in front of her, saying, "Mum, the food really looks delicious today."

As soon as he sat down, he whispered to the boy next to him what he had done. Word of his revenge spread to every kid at the table. Each of us watched with relish as she dug into her food and finished every last bite.

We were all bursting with pent-up laughter as we sat there. We couldn't wait to be released from the table. Once out of the main doors, we doubled over and laughed ourselves silly. It was one of those rare occasions that had us all united in a common cause.

Another time, several of us were washing our socks in the basement while she monitored us to make sure no one was slacking off. Peter was whispering to the lad next to him, and he called Mrs. Green a bitch.

Peter didn't realize she was close enough to hear his comment, and she was incensed. Her face went purple with rage, and she was about to hit Peter's head as hard as she could.

She flung her arm up so violently that she dislocated her shoulder.

We braced ourselves for the sound of the blow's impact, but it never came. Her face changed from wrath to pain in a split-second, and her chest heaved as she realized what happened. She ran out of the room screaming in pain, cradling her injured arm.

One of the older boys went after her to take her to the school hospital. The rest of us soon put the pieces together, and Peter became an instant hero. We cheered him for instigating the deed.

Of course, when the dust settled, it did cost Peter a trip to the duties master for punishment. He did not regret it; becoming a hero was well worth it in the eyes of your mates.

On another occasion, she caught three of us roughhousing in the basement. She ordered all three to strip off our shirts so she could lay into us with her leather belt.

While she was distracted with the first two, Roy grabbed the strap out of her hand and took off. She stood there looking half-crazed and dumbfounded for a moment, and then strode out of the room.

Roy, of course, became our hero much like Peter, and she never attempted that particular punishment on a group again. Of course, she still had enough ammunition in her bag of disciplinary measures to make our lives miserable.

Even though we endured a lot of misery in S Cottage, we still managed to create good times, as kids often do. We were resilient in the face of all the hard labor and punishments. We didn't let them keep our spirits down for long. We often came up with various games to play. Even something simple like "I Spy" helped make a chore like stacking wood on a hot summer day much more enjoyable. It helped pass the miserable hours when our cottage-mates were running down to the swimming hole but we were stuck inside or pulling time on the woodpile. It even got us laughing.

I still hold on to many happy memories of having fun with my friends, enjoying our games and childhood antics like climbing trees, swimming across the river, and pulling off pranks.

I stayed close with my shipmates from the *Bayano* and met a few more kids at Fairbridge who were my age. My best friends were Roy, Brian, Hughie, Mitch, Coop, and the brothers Leon and Louis. We all struggled with bullies and ruthless cottage mothers. Many of my friends had also been labeled as problem boys. We were the ones being picked on, and that brought us together and united us in solidarity. By sticking together, we knew that we could survive whatever the bullies and adults dished out.

Mitch presented a bit of a contrast to the rest of us. Unlike us, he did very well academically. He was also a star in sports because he had a good physique and was an outstanding athlete. We liked to say Mitch was a Canadian version of Jack Armstrong, the All-American Boy we knew from the eponymous radio adventure series.

We had him pegged as the most likely to succeed in life. I must confess we harbored a little resentment that Mitch had everything going for him while life seemed to be a constant struggle for most of us. But Mitch never used his good standing with the teachers and staff members to lord it over us, as some other kids did. At least, he never used his laurels to take advantage of me.

Brian had an interesting personality. He often liked to be the center of attention. He was quite serious but also funny and loved to do impersonations. In particular, he practiced imitating a variety of British dialects. Between the staff and children at Fairbridge, he had several accents to choose from. There was the Newcastle kids (we called them "the Geordies"), the Scots, the Londoners and many more. Brian loved to take a whack at all of them.

I loved to play along with his games and take a stab at the different dialects with him.

In the school gym, the administration occasionally screened various documentaries produced by the National Film Board of Canada. Quite often, they were news films about the war in Europe. They showed clips of Churchill's speeches interspersed between footage of planes in the sky and tanks rolling across the battlefields. All of us watched in rapt attention, hanging onto Churchill's every word.

I found Brian at the end of the show as we were walking out, and we would have a go at giving our best imitation of our hero Churchill. We did our best to impersonate his deep, gravelly voice, delivering snippets from his famous speech: "We shall never surrender" to our audience of Fairbridge boys.

These times with my friends were the best of times.

Besides my friends, I found one more very special pal—a friend with four legs.

He was a mixed breed mutt with a soft, shaggy fur coat that curled like sheep's wool. That's why we called him Woolie. He looked mostly like an English sheepdog with a bit of wire-haired terrier tossed in.

It was sometime in the mid-40s when this happy mutt adopted all of the children at Fairbridge as his own. The exact day Woolie set paws on Fairbridge is not on record, but it is a day when all our lives became a little brighter.

It is possible that some neighboring Native Americans had abandoned him, and he was wandering around looking for food when he strolled through the school's pearly gates. It didn't take long for some kids to spot him sniffing for scraps and make a beeline straight to his side.

Within an hour, Woolie must've thought he'd found dog heaven. Never had a mutt found so many kids in one place all vying for the privilege of petting him, scratching him behind the ears, rubbing his belly, and throwing sticks for him to fetch. After that, he was a Fairbridge resident for life.

Fairbridge was much like the stereotypical orphanage, devoid of that essential human sentiment of love. It seems very odd when I recall my childhood that love seemed practically non-existent. I remember desperately wanting something to love. So the day I first laid eyes on that brown-eyed, shaggy ball of wool named Woolie, I knew I had found it. I was hooked, like all my other schoolmates.

I adored that mutt. The hard part was trying to get a moment alone with him. Usually it meant fighting through a throng of other kids who all wanted to play with him and squeeze him and feed him.

Many times I wanted to tear him away from all those other selfish kids who were hogging him. I thought how many of them didn't even know how to pet a dog properly. I could certainly do a much better job of it. When he looked at me with those big brown eyes, I imagined I could read the message he was sending me: "Sorry pal, I really want to be with you and just as soon as this little guy gets off my back…"

Woolie accepted all the attention graciously. He even tolerated the youngest kids who pulled his fur. He seemed to know exactly what we needed, and was more than happy to give it. He could lift my spirits even on the worst days.

At Fairbridge, Woolie lived without a care in the world. Even the staff liked him and fed him scraps. His plate was seldom empty, and if it ever was, he simply cocked his head in the air and howled until one of us came to his rescue. He used that same howl whenever he felt lonely and in need of a good scratch. He was never disappointed. A few times, he even howled at the chapel door during Sunday church services, catching the reverend in the middle of his sermon. The minister may not have appreciated it much, but we kids exchanged giddy snickers in the pews.

I didn't have many aspirations about what I wanted to be when I grew up. Others claimed they would become cowboys or ranchers. But because of Woolie, I knew exactly what I wanted out of life. I simply wanted to have my own dog.

When I did grow up, I learned I would never really own a dog; there is no ownership between real friends. That was the only kind of relationship I would ever have with a dog: his friend and caregiver.

When I became a homeowner, my first priority was getting a dog, and I did. My kids grew up with dogs in the home and all the love and companionship they offered. None of them may have looked like Woolie, but they brought us just as much joy and comfort.

Even the severe punishments could never keep my friends and me from carrying out pranks and mischief. We all got blamed for crimes we never committed; so a few small transgressions never bothered our collective conscience.

On some warm autumn and late summer nights after lights out, we snuck out of the dormitory to swipe apples from the orchard. That was one of our favorite felonious pursuits.

It was ironic that we lived and worked on a farm that produced an abundance of food but we still felt that we needed to sneak out to enjoy it. These apple raids were poetic justice in a way—with our labour we grew the apples, so we should enjoy them.

We planned our apple raid days in advance. On the chosen night, we waited until all the other lads and Mrs. Green were sound asleep. Then the three of us quietly snuck from our cots. Our first move was bunching up the blankets and stuffing spare clothes underneath the top sheet to make it appear like we were still there, sleeping soundly.

We tiptoed breathless and bare-footed to the window. One by one, we lowered ourselves down the steel rungs of the fire escape ladder. There was about a five-foot drop from the last rung to the garden below. All of us made the descent smoothly.

But then Brian, the last to go down, missed the last rung

and fell. He landed on a prickly bush with a crash and the crack of breaking branches.

We froze like statues, praying the noise hadn't woken anyone in the cottage.

Brian pulled himself up and could not quite stifle all his grumbles and moans. He had small cuts all over his hands and arms.

We waited. No lights flickered on, no noise or footsteps came from within.

After a minute or two, we let out a collective breath and decided the coast was clear and took off. We imagined flying across the terrain swiftly but silently like the bare-footed Native Americans we often imitated in games of cowboys and Indians.

We made it to the orchard without trouble and climbed the surrounding barbwire fence. Like most Fairbridge kids, we were experts in scaling them by then.

Up the apple trees we climbed, laughing gleefully at each other while stuffing our shirtfronts with the ripest, most delicious red apples. I sunk my teeth into the pale flesh of one beauty with a satisfying crunch. The sweet, slightly tart juice covered my lips; the sweet, sweet taste of a forbidden fruit and the exhilaration of triumph.

Suddenly, we heard the rumble of an engine and the grind of tires on gravel. A car was coming up the main road beside the orchard, and the trees we had chosen were fairly close to it. Our stomachs dropped. We'd been caught off-guard and had no time to get away.

We were dropping our apples frantically, convinced

someone was about to jump out and shout, "Aha! Caught you red-handed and guilty as charged!"

This was going to be a painful trip to the duties master and a long gating. I was sure.

The car came around the bend and the headlight beams fell on us like a searchlight. We must have looked like white-faced monkeys with eyes as wide as saucers clinging to the tree limbs.

But then the headlights slid off us just as quickly as they came. The car rolled onward without stopping. By some miracle, the driver hadn't noticed us.

Lady luck had definitely smiled down on three little rascals that night. But that had been our second scare of the night, and we decided not to test her patience any more. We packed up our apples in a sack and got the hell out of there.

Our speedy retreat went smoothly. We put our bounty in a sack and buried it in the garden. We would dig it up later the next day when nobody was around and feast. We went back to our bunks triumphant.

But unbeknownst to us, one of the senior boys was awake and had witnessed the entire escapade. Even now, it's too painful for me to explain how that son of a bitch indulged in our beautiful, hard-won apples with all his cronies and how they laughed through every last bite.

Summer Adventures

Summer at Fairbridge brought warm sunny days and a break from school. We never got a break from our endless residential chores, though. The summer growing season kept us all busy on the farm tending to the fields. Many times, we younger boys were enlisted to help the older ones in the fields with plowing, sowing, or harvesting crops. We hated it. Fieldwork was back-aching labor and those summer days could get unbearably hot with the sun beating down on us. I would be covered in a thick layer of sweat before too long. On those days, whether I was stoking hay or pulling weeds, I cursed the work over and over in my mind and swore I would never let this be my future.

However, in between our duties and the farm assignments, we still found ways to enjoy having our summertime fun and a few adventures.

Every year, we looked forward to summer trips, traveling the old Koksilah Road in groups to and from the nearest town, Duncan. It was a four-mile trek to town, the unpaved road passing through groves of trees, over open land, and across a river. Most times, we made the trip under the watchful eye of a staff member.

On the rare occasions that we got to go to Duncan unsupervised, most lads would pick up rocks from the road and take aim at the knob-shaped glass insulators atop the telephone poles along the way. Seventy years later, if you dug deep enough in the dirt alongside that old road, I'm sure you would find a ton of glass fragments. My friends and I were no different. Hitting those glass insulators could become a fiercely competitive game among us.

I still have one of those prized glass insulators—an intact one—on my desk. It was a gift from Roy. It makes a handy paperweight, and of course, picking it up brings back many pleasant memories.

In my early years at the school, from around 1941 to 1946, a trip to town was a fairly rare and special occasion. We were not allowed to travel very freely. Other than special events or school-sanctioned activities, the town was off-limits for us.

On a few very special occasions, our cottage mother took us to the movie theater in town. She lined us up army style and led us on the hike down the Koksilah road. We were abuzz with excitement the whole way to see *Bambi*, *Dumbo*, *Pinocchio*, or *Lassie Come Home*.

For me, one movie stood out above all the others: *National Velvet*, about a former jockey who helps a young girl train a spirited horse for the races. It starred Mickey Rooney and the incomparable Elizabeth Taylor, who was 12 at the time. I was 9 when I saw it, and I was amazed. The story was fantastic, and I was completely mesmerized by how beautiful Elizabeth Taylor was. She became my first crush. But besides the incomparable Liz Taylor, I also fell in love with horses after seeing that movie.

I had seen the Clydesdale horses at the Fairbridge barn and in the fields from a distance before, but when I walked out of that theater, I had a new passion for them. More than anything, I wanted my own horse, one that I could train and take racing.

On the hike back to Fairbridge, I rode my imaginary horse, named Pie, just like the horse in the movie. I found a stick in the bushes and made it my riding crop. I was envisioning riding down the racetrack as the jokey. I whipped the side of my leg with the crop and called into Pie's ear to urge him onward: "Giddy up, Pie! We're coming down the home stretch; I can see the winner's circle waiting for us, giddy up!"

I imagined everyone in the stands erupting into cheers as we crossed the finish line. Then I walked Pie to the winner's circle where the dignitaries hung a flower wreath on his neck and congratulated me, the undisputed winning jockey.

No doubt, that movie earned a permanent spot in my childhood memories.

As the days of late spring warmed up and summer approached, we knew swimming season was beginning. Our feet itched for the day it would be warm enough to run down the path that began at the back of the school's central laundry shed and ran past the lower fields and to the Fairbridge River.

Officially, it is called the Koksilah River, but for us that segment of the river that ran through the school grounds will always be known as the Fairbridge River because it belonged to us, the kids of Fairbridge. In the summer months we took every opportunity we could to go down to its waters for a swim. It was our favorite pastime.

On its own, the river was seldom deep enough to swim in, so each summer the staff raised a dam downriver to allow the water to gather and create a good swimming hole.

Every year, we would get impatient waiting for summer to arrive. A dauntless few, unable to wait any longer, went down to the river in early spring for a very cold skinny dip. The water, as we used to say, was "cold enough to freeze the balls of a brass monkey."

However, in the summer the cool water was perfectly refreshing and inviting.

Dense shrubs and tall trees lined the banks on both sides. We cleared the undergrowth from one section to make a beach. It was a rocky beach with no sand, though. It was entirely made of small pebbles and large, smooth river stones. We walked and hopped our way among them barefoot without a problem.

You learnt to swim the hard way at Fairbridge: the big kids threw the little ones right into the deep waters and you'd better start paddling quickly. If you didn't get the hang of it and looked like you were in trouble, someone would come pull you out. It was hardly a method anyone would endorse nowadays, but for us it was effective. The majority of us learnt to swim that way.

I took to the water like a fish. I loved to swim with my head above water and to dive under it as well. I challenged the other kids to see who could swim the furthest underwater before coming up for air. I would swim hard as possible, holding my breath until my lungs were almost bursting for air. I experimented with different strokes. The Australian crawl became my favorite and fastest stroke.

I stayed by the river as long as I possibly could. When I got tired of swimming, I picked a nice stone on the beach to sit on and talked with my friends or just enjoyed the feeling of the warm sun.

The waters of the river seemed to take all our troubles, worries, and strains of living at Fairbridge and carry them away downstream. No matter what happened at school, the farm, or in the cottages, at the river we could be free. Some of my favorite childhood memories were created on its banks, and every time I've returned I can hardly keep myself from its waters.

As the days of June dwindled and July approached, my cottage-mates all grew excited about Dominion Day[4]. I didn't know what they were talking about at first, but soon I learned that Dominion Day was celebrated throughout Canada every year on the first of July, and we would get a special outing to the town of Duncan to enjoy the festivities. It was the biggest event of the year. When I heard that, I couldn't wait for July to come and counted down the days with my buddies.

We all did our best to avoid having our name posted on the punishment list. If you were gated, watching the rest of your cottage mates go off to Duncan would be pure hell and misery.

Then Dominion Day finally came, and we rose early to get to Duncan. I was practically itching with excitement.

When we got to Duncan, we lined up along the main street for the parade. It was a large, magnificent procession, with tons of marchers in their best, flashiest outfits. It was a thrill to see. We gave a rousing cheer when our own Fairbridge Cadet Bugle Band passed as part of the parade.

If we had only gone for the parade, that would've been exciting enough for me. But then, after that pageant was finished, Mrs. Green shepherded us along to the next part

---

4   Dominion Day, marking the date Canada became a self-governing dominion of Great Britain in 1867, is now celebrated as Canada Day.

of the day. We walked along with the tide of other spectators toward the open grounds where a huge town fair was set up.

There were events like logging sport competitions and livestock shows. These were great fun to watch. For us, though, the logging sports were definitely the highlight of the fair. The local loggers competed in various tests of skill, strength, and speed. One event was log rolling on the water, which had two loggers standing on a floating log and rolling it with their feet until one of them fell off. Some of the more skilled loggers could practically sprint on the logs, sending water droplets flying through the air. Other events had competitors sawing or chopping logs in half against the clock and climbing up a spar tree (a tall tree with most or all of its limbs removed) to ring the bell on top.

The last event—scaling the spar—was the most exciting for me. I was amazed by how fast those loggers could ascend the tall pole, and how they would practically fly on the way down. Their speed on the descent was unbelievable. I was gasping and cheering.

After watching all those forestry events, a lot of us were thinking: *To hell with farming, I'm going to be a logger!*

There were also carnival rides at the fair, but we couldn't go on them because we had no spare dimes in our pockets. We just watched the town kids riding the carousel with great envy.

But even with this to put a damper on my spirits, the Dominion Day celebration was even better and more exciting than I could've hoped for. I could hardly wait until next year when we would go again.

MORE FROM SCHOOL
AND SPORTS AT FAIRBRIDGE

After summer was over, we prepared to return to school again. As with many kids, none of us were particularly happy about returning, and I was certainly one of the kids who dreaded it. I struggled in school.

My evaluations ranged from "not very bright" to "above average." Much of it depended on who the teacher was and how patient they were with the children who were slow or had learning difficulties.

Despite my difficulties with academics, I had acquired a deep love of books from my earliest days at Fairbridge. I craved books. The library at the school quickly became my favourite retreat when I was seeking solace. To me it was huge, quiet, and filled with nothing but books. In reality, it was actually quite small for a library, but I had never known one that was bigger. For me, the most important part was that I could find relief from the bullies there and lose myself in a good story instead.

When I had time, I would go there and pick a good book off the shelf and find a chair in the corner where I could get comfortable and dive into the pages. Books gave me a way to escape from the daily pressures and frustrations of living at Fairbridge. I could almost forget about bullies and mean cottage mothers, I could forget about Fairbridge altogether, for a blissful hour or two.

I read a lot of the classics. *Black Beauty, Tom Sawyer,*

Great Expectations, Call of the Wild, and *Gulliver's Travels* were some of my favorites.

Fairbridge never had more than four or five teachers and the Principal at any one time. A couple of them continued to make my life difficult, punishing those of us who were falling behind. But in spite of that, most of the day school teachers treated us well. Mrs. Gray was one of them, and she became one of my favourite teachers in the primary grades. She taught a wide variety of subjects, but I remember her for English composition and art. She was always kind, which earned her our undying loyalty.

Her son George was in our class year and we became friends. They lived in a small cottage close to the Fairbridge property, and George would invite me over occasionally.

I didn't remember living at home before my parents divorced, so going there was my first experience being inside a family home. I came in and was amazed by how pleasant and cheerful it could be, and how I instantly felt welcome.

Mrs. Gray's home reflected her love for art and paintings. She had plenty of them hung up on her walls, most of them showing pastoral scenes. When I arrived, she usually had a neat stack of logs burning in the fireplace, making a pleasant crackling sound. The warmth invited me to take a seat near the grate on one of the cozy, cushioned armchairs. That always felt like a wonderful treat.

Mrs. Gray was quick to offer George and me a glass of milk and some of her home-baked cookies or cakes, which she served on real china plates. Getting to eat off a china plate and drink out of a real glass rather than the scraped and dented metal tableware I was used to was really meaningful to me. At the school they would never let us touch these kinds of cups and plates. It felt like a really special gesture of kindness from her.

As I sat there finishing my cakes and talking with George while Mrs. Gray offered a warm smile, I realized this was what I had been missing out on for all these years—a touch a familial kindness, being in a loving home. I didn't remember living at home with my parents, so this felt like the first time I'd experienced it. When it was time to leave, it was painful to even think about going back to the bare, unfriendly cottage where Mrs. Green waited.

Sports broke the monotony of our daily routines, and so they were a big part of the Fairbridge experience.

Fairbridge kids led a Spartan life, always physically active and living on a very restricted diet. Our meals consisted of lots of vegetables, meatless Wednesdays, fish on Fridays, no special sauces, lots of milk, and occasionally some seasonal fruit. Even our desserts after dinner were not very rich or particularly sweet. Sodas (which we called "pop"), candy, and other sweets were a rarity reserved only for very special holidays like Christmas. Our daily duty schedules included loads of work that was often very strenuous. Therefore, while we may not have enjoyed this routine, it did keep us very lean and fit for manual labor and sports.

At least we enjoyed the sports a lot. Everything from organized sports to casual sporting games among friends in the playing fields, from individual to team sports and school-wide events—we had it all.

For sports teams, the school followed the old British public school tradition of forming "houses," each one titled by colors like the Blacks, Greens, Maroons, and so on. The duty master appointed a senior boy to serve as housemaster for each. This was very much in line with the British system, with rank of seniors, juniors, prefects, house captains, and so on. I competed in the Maroon House. This suited me because maroon was one of my favorite colors, and it still is to this day. In fact, I found out years later that maroon also happens to be the team color for the Edinburgh Hearts Football Club that my Grand-Uncle Hugh Mackay played for in the early 1900s.

The various houses competed against one another and the winners went on to become the Fairbridge school team and compete against the other area schools. One was always proud to make the school team.

One annual sporting tradition we had was the Fairbridge Cross-Country Run. On Easter Mondays, the school held that special race. It was a big event. Most of the able-bodied boys aged seven to fifteen ran the race, and those who did not participate came to cheer on the runners.

The course was five miles long, starting at the main dining hall. It followed the main road through the school, out the gates and onward to Koksilah Road, then to the McKinley Dupe Road. Eventually, we crossed Cedar Bridge over Kevin Creek, which ran through the woods and cow pastures. Along the way, when we crossed a big log spanning the river, we were always tempted to jump down into the cold water of the creek to cool off.

To begin the race, staff members had us form lines. We were divided into age groups with the youngest boys placed in front to lead off the race. Professor Logan gave us a quick pep talk to muster our spirits, and then the whistle sent us off with our feet pounding the gravel.

Of course, the big boys with their great strides would soon scatter the smaller kids to the side of the road in their scramble to get an early lead.

I was not a very good distance runner. I could hold my own on short sprints, but I was never quite fast enough to win any race. Long endurance races like this were even worse. After the first mile or so my lungs would be tired and I would be lagging more than a wee bit behind the older boys.

So guys like me developed a strategy. We would find a buddy to team up with and run alongside each other, trading a few jokes and laughs as we went. Hell, we figured we might as well enjoy ourselves along the way.

I still put all my energy into running a good race. Many of the youngest boys were unable to run the full five-mile stretch and got picked up along the way.

I may not have ever made the winner's circle, but I was always proud to stay in the race all the way to the finish line.

One year I was running with either Brian or Hughie. We were well past the halfway point when we came across a runner who was doubled over on the side of the track. He wasn't hurt, just winded or suffering from a cramp. As we ran past him, we exchanged big grins. This guy was one of the top athletes and brilliant in the school, adored by almost everyone on staff. He was one of those guys who you just couldn't beat in anything, and we'd just passed him in the annual Easter race.

However, he recovered in almost no time and the next thing we knew, he was flying past us. But still, it felt pretty damn great to have overtaken one of the school champions for even a minute.

Another time, I tried to make a deal with Roy before the race. I suggested that we do our best to outrace that top athlete I'd briefly passed last time. I said if we managed to overtake him, we would cross the finish line together as a team.

Of course, I had as much of a chance at beating Roger Bannister to the world's first four-minute mile as outrun the school's champion. It was a fantasy. But in the heat of the moment I decided to just go with it and add one more fantasy of crossing the finish line with Roy and wind up in the winner's circle. Maybe it was just crazy enough to actually happen.

In any event, Roy (wisely enough, in retrospect) made his own decision. As we were coming down the final stretch, he took off and left me in the proverbial dust.

He came in second in our age group, and later he would run second on all groups combined.

With tight lips, I did congratulate Roy on his win. Though I said it was "crappy" that day, he really had run well and deserved his win.

After Roy brought up this tale of my un-sportsmanlike conduct in our later years, I asked him, "Roy, how many months was it before I talked to you again?"

Around age eight or nine, I earned a slot on the school gymnastics team. I enjoyed learning the tumbles, the forward and back flips, the individual and team routines, and all the different aspects of the sport. The most memorable incident on the gymnastics team happened the first year that I was part of it.

Our team was training to put on a display of our gymnastic skills, including the usual tumbles, somersaults, back flips, and so on. One of the highlights was building a human pyramid. As the smallest kid on the team, I got to be the top lad of the pyramid, which excited me quite a bit. I think the pyramid was three rows tall with me standing on the shoulders of Malcolm, the guy below me. I would scramble up there and place my feet on Malcolm's shoulders and he would get a firm grip on my ankles to help steady me. Once the whole team was balanced, I would spread my arms out and hold that position. At that point, the spectators would normally respond with applause.

We pulled it off flawlessly many times in practice, but during the showcase, Malcolm got a cramp as I was climbing into place. As he was tried to shake it off, I wobbled and fell off his shoulders. I landed on cushioned mats covering the floor. The audience gasped and a few of my mates snickered. Other than a blow to my dignity, I was not injured.

I remained on the team for a couple of years and then found myself moving on to other sports, devoting more time to boxing and joining the football team.

The team sports in particular were popular with many kids. In my years at the school, I would try out for and participate in most of the organized sports teams that the school offered, including softball, basketball, boxing, and football—better known as soccer in the U.S..

At the tender of eight, I decided to join the school's boxing team. I did not go out of love of the sport, but out of a desire for self-protection. I was beginning to be fed up with the bullies punching and pushing me around all the time. I figured boxing would toughen me up and teach me some much-needed self-defense skills.

I didn't like it at all at first. After all that bullying, I was reluctant to enter a physical conflict willingly. Normally, I tried to avoid getting into fights whenever possible. When it came time to enter the boxing ring, I was very apprehensive and I would need to muster my resolve before going in.

In my first year of boxing, I was frequently paired with Clifford C. as my opponent because we had a similar build and skill level. At one intramural house match, we were both competing, and again we were set to square off in the ring. This particular match I will always remember as "the droopy shorts fight."

There never seemed to be enough properly-sized shorts for our team to wear, so some unlucky fighter always had to go into a fight with shorts that were too big or too small.

That day Cliff was stuck wearing shorts that were far too large for him. While we sparred around the perimeter of the ring he had to reach down and pull them back up every so often when they sagged.

At some point, I decided to say to myself, "To hell with the Queensbury Rules." I nailed Cliff with a couple of good right jabs when he reached down for his shorts again.

I would discover that what goes around comes around. A couple years later Cliff and I got into a bare-knuckle fisticuffs fight and that fight was one I lost.

But even more ironically, in our first year boxing team photo, I am the one stuck with the damn droopy shorts for all memory.

From joining the boxing team, I became better acquainted with the duties master, Mr. Burns, who managed the team. The duties master, no matter who he was, had always been a figure we looked at with apprehension because he was in charge of discipline. Nobody wanted to be sent to Mr. Burns. That usually meant we were really in trouble.

When I got to know him more through the boxing team, we discovered a shared heritage. He was also a fellow Scotsman, so we developed a friendly connection. I grew to like and respect this man. I knew in his role as the duties master, he doled out the punishments as he had to, but he wasn't excessive or cruel.

But soon, he started showing me a little favoritism because of our connection. When he came into our dormitory to administer the strap on the unlucky lad who was on the list, he would greet me kindly.

It was only a small greeting. Just a nod and a, "How are you today, Roddy?"

Still, it was enough for the bullies in the cottage to notice. We would all be standing in the dormitory beside our beds to watch the strapping, so all the boys would see Mr. Burns offering that small greeting. It gave the bullies yet another reason to torment me. I found myself wishing he would stop acknowledging me in the first place.

Overall, my first year of boxing was pretty disappointing. I didn't see the results I wanted and the bullying was still an issue. But I stuck with the sport, determined to learn how to protect myself from the bullies.

One of the reasons I decided to stay on was because I was inspired by one of the Duncan boxing coaches, Edward Heppell, who went by Ned. I had begun to admire him.

Ned was an expatriate born in London who served in the British Army's 7th Lancers regiment in Palestine and India in 1908, where he had been a champion boxer in the army. He immigrated to Canada in 1930 and worked for a while as a logger on Vancouver Island. He had the looks and conduct of an old-time fighter—very lean but strong as an ox. He could reportedly pull good-sized stumps out of the ground. In the prime of his life, he must've had the strength of a mule.

When I fought, I entered the ring nervous and more than a bit scared. But Coach Ned had a way of building up my self-confidence so that by the time the bell rang I was revved up to go. Once the first couple jabs fell on me, my nervousness slid away and I was in full boxing mode.

Coach always reminded me to tuck my long jaw into my left shoulder and keep the left jab going. The more I fought, the more comfortable I became in the ring, thanks to Coach's encouragement.

While we are on the subject of activities that took place in the school gymnasium, there was one other, more nefarious activity that took place there. Certain members of the Turdy Town mob devised a way to spy on the girls during their hour in the gym.

We'd discovered there was a large storage space for benches and chairs underneath the stage. The stage floor had wooden access panels that would slide out to get the benches and chairs in and out of the gym easily. These access panels had drilled finger holes that allowed janitorial staff members to easily slide and lift the panels in and out. We used them as peepholes.

When the girls had their hour of exercising in the gym, we would sneak through a back entrance of the gym and crawl through an opening to the storage area. Then we each picked a peephole to use to see the action-taking place on the gym floor.

Back then, the girls did not wear the tight or revealing gym clothes that are more common today, but their gym uniforms were more revealing than their school uniforms. I think you can imagine what we raunchy lads had in mind, with eyes glued to the peepholes. We got quite a show. This wonderful scene of the girls performing their stretching exercises brought on some heavy breathing and made our hormones go wild. Yes, I realize that sounds like mild stuff for today's youth, but for the 1940s, at a place like Fairbridge, it was pretty hot stuff for us.

It didn't last, though. One time, one of the boys tripped over a stray chair and the noise alerted the girls something amiss was going on under the stage. Most of us pulled a hasty retreat out the back door, but the clumsy lad was not as quick. He remained glued to his peephole and got his just reward when a girl's finger connected with his eyeball.

THE NOTORIOUS DEMON

By the time I reached seventh grade, I found myself spending a fair bit of time standing outside the principal's door because I'd been sent there for discipline or for having too many tardies. Almost always, there were one or two other schoolmates to chat with while I waited.

I could almost bet my one-cent weekly allowance that one boy in particular would be there pretty much every time: Dennis, nicknamed "Demon" for his daring exploits. He would be leaning against the wall, waiting coolly and casually for his turn to see Mr. Grant.

Demon took each school rule as a personal challenge. He broke the rules as though it was his hobby, so he was always getting in trouble with the staff. Punishment only seemed to encourage him to pull bigger stunts. The rest of us practically revered his audacious feats of rule-breaking and troublemaking. He seemed to be a bit on the weird side but was still a likeable lad. After all, he provided us many laughs since his pranks were mostly aimed against staff members. He was never mean-spirited to any of us.

I may have been a bit wild myself, but I was not nearly bold or dumb enough to attempt anything even close to Demon's crazy stunts.

We traded stories about Demon. They took on some embellishment as stories tend to do, but his adventures were already so incredible that we couldn't add much more to them.

One of them related an incident that happened during school hours. Demon was up in the library, supposedly studying with a few others when he found something more entertaining to do than schoolwork.

There was a small door at the end of the library that led to the attic. On it was a sign reading, "Absolutely No Students Allowed Past this Door." Of course, Demon took such warnings as a dare.

Without hesitation, he opened the door and began to crawl along the rafters. But he got lost in the darkness and decided his best bet was just turning around and going back out the way he came. Spinning around on the narrow beam, he wobbled and lost his balance. As he stumbled, one of his feet broke through the plaster below and went right through.

Of all the rooms that could've been below, he happened to find the Principal's office. Mr. Grant was sitting at his desk enjoying his lunch, when suddenly he heard a loud crack, and pieces of plaster and white dust rained down on his food.

His eyes shot upward and, lo and behold, a wriggling boy's foot and leg was sticking through his office ceiling.

Rest assured, the Demon left school that day with painfully sore hands or a very sore ass. Possibly both.

Another time, I got to witness one of his brazen moves firsthand.

One Sunday at church service, Demon was assigned to collection plate duty. With the other collection boy, they solemnly collected everyone's offerings.

He made his rounds up the aisle, not paying much

attention to the plate until someone dropped an unusually large silver coin in it. It made a resounding clang as it hit the dish. Demon's head perked up. His eyebrows shot up toward his hairline and his eyes lit up like a Borealis sky. The coin was a large, shining dollop of pure silver, bigger than any Demon had seen before. It caught the attention of many other kids as well, who craned their necks to catch a glimpse of it.

Demon's eyes remained fixed on the precious coin all the way up to the front altar.

Two boys approached, ready to pass the plates to the Reverend for his blessing. The altar boys bowed their heads toward the minister as he prayed the blessing.

Suddenly Demon did a hasty half turn away from the minister and snatched the coin. This time he was not as smooth as he usually was.

He may have turned away from the minister, but then he was facing the rest of us in the pews. The whole congregation had seen his heist, not to mention God himself.

After the service, he explained to a few of his close cronies that he couldn't do it while facing the minister, so he had turned around. He believed that if the minister witnessed him, he would've been struck dead on the spot, his soul sent straight to hell. Apparently he didn't have it on his mind that while the minister may not witness his dastardly deed, God would.

That threat seemed more fearsome to him than the strapping he would receive from the duty master.

Like Demon, I had a healthy fear of God, but it didn't

prevent me from being stubborn and acting out. Most of my pranks were more subtly subversive, not outright in the faces of the staff.

After his time at Fairbridge was up, Demon was shipped back to England. I don't know what happened to him after that. God only knows what kind of life he led after such a troubled childhood at Fairbridge.

Turdy Town and the Bench Lands

Imagine our excitement when one day my friends and I were exploring the woods on the outskirts of Fairbridge, beyond the playing fields, and discovered a cluster of abandoned little forts.

They were built out of salvaged pieces of wood and scrap metal and tarps, clearly the work of some enterprising lads like ourselves. They looked like they had been there since the early years of Fairbridge and possibly built by the first groups of kids who arrived from overseas.

We could not wait to get back to the cottage and share our discovery with the rest of the gang. But we agreed that this would stay within our trusted circle: Brian, Roy, Coop, the brothers Leon and Louis, and I.

The six of us were always eager to find new ways to escape our crappy daily routines and the bullies. So this discovery quickly grew into an idea: we would build a little town in the woods for just ourselves.

This construction project became our biggest and most memorable endeavor.

First we cleared a small space deep in the woods. We tore down some of the old shacks we'd originally found for materials and started rebuilding them in our new location. We scrounged around the residential area for abandoned old pieces of lumber, boards, parts of old tin roofs, whatever else we could use to build our town. This was no easy task since there wasn't an abundance of building materials lying around. Sometimes we had to swipe things from buildings within the school area. Part of one abandoned metal shed became our backside wall, fortunately for us, none of the staff members noticed.

Slowly but surely, our little town came together. We named it "Turdy Town." The bigger guys were constantly calling the six of us "turds", so we quite proudly reclaimed the title and gave it to our town.

The shacks of Turdy Town looked resembled the homes in India's slums as depicted in the film *Slumdog Millionaire*. They were just as ramshackle and rickety as viewed in the film.

Each citizen of Turdy Town was sworn to strict secrecy. If the staff ever caught us in our little town schemes, the punishment would've been severe. We would've been gated *for life*. Thankfully, we were never discovered.

To furnish our shacks with the comforts of home, we snitched food, dinnerware, and whatever else we could sneak out of the cottage area.

We really did not feel guilty about stealing or lying because by now we learnt that honesty did not always pay off. We could get punished just the same, whether or not we followed the rules and told the truth. I amended my own personal code of ethics shortly after I had to confess to a couple of misdemeanors when I had been completely innocent. My new feeling was "screw them with their phony hypocritical honesty shit." If they punished us for being honest, then I may just as well lie and take some benefits where I could.

Our honour code was simple: We never stole anything; we *swiped* the items we needed. We didn't think swiping was criminal; it was simply claiming something to share with mates for our own enjoyment. Anything lying around abandoned or belonging to staff members was fair game for swiping, but our golden rule was never to take from a fellow schoolmate. That would've been stealing and a sin.

If a staff member asked us whether we stole that, we could look them in the eye and answer with an emphatic "No!" and know we weren't lying. Stealing and swiping weren't the same thing in our code of ethics.

On the other hand, if they had asked, "Did you *swipe* it?" then that would have presented a dilemma. Good thing none of them did.

Upon the completion of our building project, we elected Brian the Lord Mayor of Turdy Town. Brian, unfortunately, also had the nickname "Bonehead," which was hardly appropriate for one holding the exalted title of "Lord Mayor."

Fairbridge kids were always giving out nicknames. Few of them were complimentary. No one was spared, especially if they had some physical blemish or trait that stuck out. Roy got "Smonkner" because he was small like a monkey, and Leon, who had teeth that were slightly protruding, was "Tusky." Another kid became known as "Clapper" for his large lips. For a while, I was stuck with "Schweinhund." My head has always been slightly too large in proportion to my body, and having a square jaw made me a natural choice to play the part as a German soldier in various role-playing and re-enactment games. Hence, I was stuck with a crappy German nickname.

As the Royals would say, I was not amused. These were the early 40s, and we were still at war with Germany. We knew the bad guys always lose, so I didn't really enjoy my assignment of Ober Lieutenant Fritz in war games. One of the guys suggested that with my jaw. I could be able to handle the role of Mussolini. To that I responded, "Yeah and get hung naked in some Italian town like he did." For all that, I did get a lot of practice on a German accent.

I served as Chief of Police of Turdy Town for a short term. Short because the citizens of Turdy Town did not appreciate our legal system. Citizens found guilty of misdemeanors would go before Brian—who served as Judge as well as Mayor—and he would fine the accused a certain number of their marbles, or as we called them, "miggies." Of course, Judge Brian thought it perfectly legal and fair that the miggies became property of the court and remained in our custody. The citizens thought differently.

I gave up the position after a while. Nobody else wanted to be a cop, so we eliminated the position entirely. The experience did serve as an early lesson in how some governments operate for my future studies in Civics.

So we acted out our make-believe dramas in Turdy Town.

When President Franklin Roosevelt died, Turdy Town held a special memorial service. We purloined a bed sheet from the laundry to create a flag, especially for this somber occasion. We cut it into the proper shape and produced the American stars and stripes on both sides. It looked quite authentic fluttering over Turdy Town before we ceremonially lowered it.

His Honor the Lord Mayor Brian, a bugler in the school's cadet band, played his bugle while the flag was lowered.

Afterward, I faked playing the bagpipes to the tune of "Scotland the Brave." My method was to hum while pinching my nose and gently striking my Adam's apple with the flat edge of my hand. It was a rather good imitation.

We staged mock battles using Turdy Town as a city to be captured or defended. We fought frontier battles with imaginary Canadian Indians, where our Indian braves used bracken stalks for spears. Other times we would be soldiers fighting in World War II. Brian and I kept up our competition over who could do the better impression of Winston Churchill's speeches. I think Brian had the edge on me, but I continued to spout off my own renditions during these games of make-believe. "We shall fight them on the beaches…" was my favourite.

I would soon learn other kids at Fairbridge had also built shacks for their private use. It seemed that the woods surrounding Fairbridge had been concealing shacks like ours since the first groups of kids at Fairbridge started coming into the school in 1935. New arrivals would then take over the old shacks or build their own from salvaged materials.

Another of our favourite fun escapes was to an area in the north part of the school property that we called the "Bench Lands." This was a popular place for Fairbridge kids to hang out, second only to the banks of the Koksilah River in the summertime.

To get there we had to walk about an eighth of a mile down the road that led to Duncan. We climbed a small hill and then on its other side, where the land dipped down, there was a large pond. When we reached the shores, we'd arrived at the Bench Lands.

In the early years, we had to get permission to go anywhere other than the residential area, but later those restrictions eased up a little. We could go most anywhere on the Fairbridge property fairly freely, but we still needed permission to leave the school site.

Since the Bench Lands were on school property we were usually free to go there, unless we'd been gated. If we had been gated, we had to wait for a window of opportunity to open up when we could sneak away for some great-unsupervised fun.

During the spring and summer months, we would build rafts out of scraps of lumber and old logs tied together with rope and go rafting on the pond. Sometimes I would imagine the pond was an ocean, and I was the young lad Jim Hawkins from *Treasure Island*, searching for the pirate Long John Silver and the treasure.

One day, I jumped on one of these rafts barefoot and felt a sudden and tremendous stab of pain. I yelped loudly. I landed right on an upturned rusty nail. The nail went right through my left foot.

Even worse, that day happened to be one the many that I had been gated to the cottage. I wasn't supposed to be out here. But Mrs. Green had gone into Duncan, so I decided to hell with the woodpile and joined my pals heading for the Bench Lands.

There was no way I could report this injury without admitting I had snuck out. So I knew I couldn't say anything, nail or no nail. I would have been strapped or given an even longer gating sentence. I hobbled back to the cottage with my foot wrapped in an old hankie and acted like nothing had happened. Several days later, my foot became so painfully enlarged that I could barely put my shoe on. I also felt a swollen gland in my upper groin area.

Sunday morning arrived, so it was time to go to church. The pain in my foot was horrible, but in spite of it I put on my shoes and lined up with my cottage mates.

Mrs. Green asked me why I was limping. I lied, saying, "My shoe is too tight."

I made it to church but halfway through the service I began to feel sick and dizzy. I collapsed.

The next thing I knew they had me in a car, rushing me to the hospital in Duncan. The rusty nail puncture had caused a severe infection in my leg.

When they asked me how it happened, I was still too afraid to tell the doctors about sneaking out. I was sure that if I did, it would come back to Mrs. Green, and then I would be in even worse trouble. I simply said I had accidentally stepped on a board that had a big nail sticking up, which wasn't a lie. Somehow I scraped through the incident without additional punishment.

THE SCHOOL HOSPITAL

After my initial stay at the school hospital, I had it imprinted on my mind as a safe haven. I would do just about anything to get back there to escape the bullies and the cottage mother. However, I was not a sickly child, so I had to conjure up and fake symptoms of illnesses such as the common cold or an upset stomach.

The adults were always telling us to come in from the rain, or we'd catch influenza. So I purposefully tried staying outside during showers and downpours. I even planted myself under the gutters and let the streams of cold water soak my hair and run down my shirt. *Please let me catch influenza, or whatever other diseases are out there;* I thought to myself. Much to my dismay, the only thing I caught out there was disappointment. I was left hopeless, soaking wet, and cold.

On those rare occasions when I was genuinely sick, it was very unpleasant. My earliest bout was an episode of tonsillitis, and I had to suffer through the misery of getting a tonsillectomy in the 1940s. It was a horrible experience. I was sedated with ether, which didn't knock me out cold immediately. Dazed and only semi-conscious, I remembered feeling the terrible gagging sensation as they stuck cold metal implements in my mouth before I eventually succumbed to the ether. When I came to, my throat was raw and painful. I could hardly swallow anything for days.

My next hospital visit was for a ruptured appendix. They rushed me to the hospital in Duncan for the surgical procedure. I later learnt that I was lucky to have survived.

Once I was on the mend from the appendectomy, life as a child patient in the hospital was fun. The nurses, hospital staff, and especially the adult patients in Duncan were very nice to me. Several of them gave me sweets and bought me comic books. One young logger in our ward would push me around in a wheelchair up and down the hallways. I was soon begging him "Faster!"

With all that unauthorized activity, I ended up with a bout of pneumonia. In the ensuing delirium, I dreamt I was in some kind of heaven on earth.

The doctor, who was not at amused, gave strict orders: "This lad is to be confined to his bed until I give further notice."

I did recover and they eventually released me to the school hospital for my final days of recuperation.

The school nurse, Miss King, was very pretty and a kind lady. She was likely the inspiration behind a particular affection I held for nurses most of my life.

During the sick call, she took our temperatures. The moment she turned her back, I took the thermometer out of my mouth and held it close—but not too close—to the heater mounted on the wall in hopes of raising the temperature reading. I put it back in my mouth before she noticed.

When she removed the thermometer, I immediately started coughing and hacking away as loudly as possible. I was desperate to stay hospitalized. If it took an Academy Award-winning performance to prolong my stay, I was going to give it my best shot.

Now, there is little doubt on my mind that Miss King knew what we were up to most of the time. I'm also fairly certain that she knew about the ill treatment many of us suffered in the cottages, so if there were spare beds, she would admit us anyway, sick or not.

Once I was in, I could relax. It was like taking a temporary holiday from the cottages. The beds felt even softer than I remembered, and I could sleep in and happily spend the day reading or chatting with my fellow patients or pulling out the board games.

Late in the afternoon, Miss King would pull the ward curtains closed. This was our daily rest period. No playing or talking allowed.

Sometimes during our rest period, Miss King would leave the hospital to run errands. When we heard the front door close, we knew exactly what it meant. We had a precious half-hour or so all to ourselves. We could not contain our gleeful smiles and immediately sprang into action.

The hospital's long, shiny, and slick linoleum corridor was perfect for running and sliding in our stocking-clad feet; we evolved this game a little further.

We took blankets off our beds folded them up to use as a soft pad so we could slide on our bellies.

Holding our blanket pads close to our chests, we took turns hurtling the corridor at a run to build momentum. When we'd run a quarter of the way down the hall, we leapt down on our pads. And voilà—we had an indoor sledding run on the glossy floor. It was delightful.

One time, though, a botched blanket slide left me with a

chipped tooth. While I was running at full speeds for takeoff, I tripped on the dangling end of my blanket and fell forward. My front tooth was the first part of my body to meet the hard linoleum floor.

The shot of pain came immediately. I clutched my mouth as the others rushed over to see if I was OK.

If the hospital were still standing today, (it's long gone) one of its hallways would l have a small gouge in the floor, courtesy of a rambunctious lad who was not really that sick that day?

My chipped tooth stayed chipped for decades afterward until in 2008, at the age of 73, my dentist repaired it. Later, I wished she had left it alone. I missed running my tongue against the edges and feeling the gap there like a little road bump. When I felt it, it would immediately bring back a happy memory of those wonderful days slipping and sliding down the corridors of the Fairbridge hospital without a single care in the world.

During one of my visits, I struck up a friendship with one of the older boys, Eric Lewis. Eric suffered rheumatic fever and spent over two years at the hospital.

When we were stuck lying in bed, we passed the time by playing the game "I spy with my little eye."

Eric was a particularly sharp and perceptive lad. He was not necessarily academically successful during that period, but he was very clever. During his long convalescent hospital stays, he spent a lot of time bedridden and alone, and he had to find ways to keep his mind occupied. Whatever he did;

it ended up honing his mind for a very successful business career as an adult.

He particularly excelled in the little game, of "I Spy." He constantly had me stumped and frustrated, while he guessed my riddles rather quickly. I finally figured out he had a strategy: he would identify multiple things in the room that all began with the same letter, so when he used that letter, it would be much more difficult for me guess what the answer was. I had to admire that kind of sharpness. He seemed like a great person to have in my corner.

When we weren't playing our little games, we were talking and sharing stories. Eric had some great tales to tell. One of them was about the forts. The forts were a cluster of shacks in the woods, much like Turdy Town. Eric's group of friends, including the notorious 'Demon,' built theirs only a few years before we erected Turdy Town.

Eric told me how one time how Demon was bragging about his illegally-constructed forts in front of a couple of cottage mothers—his cottage mother and her friend. Naturally, they asked him to show them where these forts were.

The women must have figured that once Demon had led them to the forts, they would have irrevocable proof and then have him and everyone else involved sent to the duty master for a good whipping. Otherwise, it was just another false tale by a boy who was known for telling tall tales.

A couple of the boys overheard Demon spilling his guts and were about to take him apart for betraying them.

Demon was cool and unruffled. He told them not to

worry; he had a better plan in mind for the cottage mothers.

So Demon proceeded to lead them into the woods. However, he picked a path going far from the actual forts and much deeper within the darkening forest. After a good hour of hiking through bushes, climbing over logs, and beating back branches, the cottage mothers became exhausted and sat down for a moment to rest.

Demon, leading the way, simply snuck off and abandoned them. He was much more familiar with the layout of the woods than C Mothers were and easily doubled back to where his pals were waiting.

It was already late in the day when the women realized they were alone. They stumbled around looking for a way back. Then it started to rain, night and the darkness of the forest was coming fast. Frantic screams from the women of "Help, we're lost!" could be heard emanating from the dark forest.

Demon and his friends were laughing so hard they could barely breathe and clapped their intrepid mate on the back. As the weather got worse and the sky darkened, they decided someone should go rescue the poor women.

So two of the boys, looking just like brave and innocent Boy Scouts, went in and rescued the cottage mothers—to much praise and gratitude, of course.

The next day, word of the Demon's dauntless deed spread like wildfire throughout the cottages. Everyone fully expected him to get a public flogging. That was a rare sentence for someone who had *really* screwed up, and it would be a spectacle for all to witness.

The intrepid Demon surprised us yet again. He came up with a simple fabricated story. With a straight face, he quite innocently explained how he had gotten separated from them and lost his way. Once he realized what had happened, he spent a couple of hours searching frantically for his dear cottage mother and her friend in the rain with no luck. He said he'd been so relieved when he heard that they had been rescued. He'd been ridden with guilt and worry.

The cottage mothers bought his story and even sympathized with him. He got off without so much as a dock in his allowance, that glorious one-cent.

I was riveted by this story. I couldn't believe Demon had gotten away with it. After he finished the telling, Eric and I agreed that Demon was not only one hell of a troublemaker, but a far more intelligent kid than most people gave him credit for.

CHRISTMASTIME AT FAIRBRIDGE

As the summer faded away and autumn turned to winter, we started anticipating the coming of December and with it, Christmas.

Winter brought a stark change to Fairbridge.

Soon, a glistening pure white blanket of snow covered the football fields. It settled on the boughs of the majestic Douglas firs bordering the fields nearby and magnificent cedars a little farther in the distance. It was a picture-perfect scene fit for a Hallmark Christmas card.

From our frosted dorm windows, we could see the snowy mountains, in the distance, and several lumpy-bodied snowmen that we'd built standing in the playing fields. Many mornings in the early dawn I spotted several deer prancing nimbly in the snow at the forest edge. When I saw them, I grew very still, transfixed by their gentle movements.

This beautiful winter scene at Fairbridge is one I will never forget.

When the snow began to fall, it meant we had to add shoveling duties to our roster of chores, but the fun of snow far outweighed the work factor for us. We took to it headlong, starting snowball fights and building snowmen. Sledding down the hills was our favorite winter activity, though. We crafted our own toboggans out of old scraps of wood, and rounded barrel staves. A garbage lid or a discarded sheet of metal would also work in a pinch.

The pond by the Bench Lands froze over and became our ice-skating rink. Skating was a rare and thrilling luxury, but we only had one pair of skates to share among all of us. I have no idea where they came from. Most likely, one very enterprising Fairbridge kid swiped them from one of the local Canadian kids.

They were not your typical lace-up, boot-style skates; they were a pair of the old-style skating blades that you would tie to the bottom of your boots. We could all share them without ever worrying about shoe size, since we only had one pair, we inevitably ended up with lines of anxious, ill-tempered kids losing patience as they waited to use those highly-treasured blades. The longer and more frustrated the line was, the fewer laps we could take on the skates when it was our turn.

It was well worth the wait when I finally got on the frozen pond. Skimming across the ice was exhilarating. It the closest I could get to actually flying. I raced faster and took my corners sharper, imagining that I was a hockey player for a couple precious minutes. Then I had to hand off the blades to the next clamouring customer.

I also fondly remember mornings after completing my dairy barn duties racing to the bunkhouse. There the Irish cook would break regulations and toss us hot pancakes through the kitchens back window. Nothing was better on a cold winter day than the warmth of a couple of illicit pancakes tucked inside my shirt, scurrying home to my dorm where I could eat them safely.

As December came, we were all anticipating the coming of Christmas. The first signs heralding the holiday appeared during our day school classes.

In art class, our teacher, Mrs. Gray, had us doing holiday

crafts. She showed us how to make our own Christmas cards out of construction paper. We made twisted streamers out of rolls of red and green crepe paper. We also went out to the forest during class and cut the lower boughs from the evergreen trees to make fresh wreaths.

I had never been a big fan of art classes, but when the time came for these annual holiday crafts, I suddenly found myself looking forward to it.

Drama class, a year-round favourite of mine, began preparations for the annual Christmas play. I had become quite good—after all, perfecting the art of lying when threatened with unwarranted punishment does require a certain amount of theatrical skill.

One year our drama teacher, Mr. Chappell, cast me as Scrooge in the adaptation of the Charles Dickens classic *A Christmas Carol*. As usual, I diligently memorized my lines and played my part in the ensemble. We even learnt an old English country-dance known as the Sir Roger de Coverly to perform for the play.

To this day, one of my lines as Scrooge still sticks in my mind. It comes when two business gents, soliciting donations for the poor, approach old Scrooge. They plead with him to give, saying many poor people will die if he doesn't. Scrooge replies, "Tis better they die and thereby decrease the world surplus population; this is not my business. Good afternoon, gentlemen!"

This is how I imagine the rich bigwigs in the British government responded to calls to assist poor kids like me. Instead of helping, they shipped us off to an uncertain future and decided it was none of their business what became of us. We were just the surplus population, after all.

Every Christmas season I always look for whichever productions of *A Christmas Carol,* I can find on television. I prefer the old black-and-white film versions because I think they create a more realistic portrait of what life was like, particularly for the poor, when Dickens was writing. The movie starring British actor Alastair Sim stands out as the finest production I have ever seen.

Once we were released from school classes for the Christmas holidays, it was time to trek out to the surrounding forest and pick out a Christmas tree for the cottage. We went out as a group to the woods and got to cut it down and drag it back to our cottage. One group of senior boys was also assigned to bring the huge 30-foot tree for the main dining hall.

Decorating in the cottage began, in earnest, then. We put the tree up in the dining room and made the cottage look more festive with streamers and a wreath on the door.

Around the same time, each cottage received a catalogue from one of Canada's two main department stores, Eaton's and Hudson Bay. We leafed through the pages looking for the Christmas present we wanted that year. We were allowed to ask for anything, as long the total cost came out to exactly one dollar or less. That was Santa's limit, our cottage mother would tell us. In reality, that was all the school administration would allow.

When each of us had made our selection, we would write our letter to Santa. Our cottage mother reminded us to make our requests politely and assure him that we'd been good that year.

That always struck me as a bit ridiculous. We were all guilty of our minor trespasses, and who was going to write, "Hi Santa; this is Billy here. Please send me a really big Lionel train set. And oh, by the way; I stole some biscuits last night and lied to my cottage mother about it, but I'm sure you will understand."

We all dutifully wrote our letters and just as dutifully left out certain less-than-savory details that he didn't really need to know.

Every year my friends and I would hold a contest to see who could make the most of our lowly one-dollar limit. One year I came out with a shrewd strategy: I picked three different, less-expensive items. Chief among them was a cheap toy revolver. I also asked for a pair of cowboy cuffs, made of cardboard, no doubt, and lastly a roll of caps that went *bang* when you pulled the trigger on the toy pistol.

We looked up to our cowboy heroes like Gene Autry, Roy Rogers, and Tom Mix back then. They sometimes wore these fancy gloves, and their cuffs were elaborately embroidered.

Finally, after weeks of impatient waiting, Christmas Eve arrived—only one more day to go. That evening, each of us hung a stocking on the end of our iron bed frame, and felt almost too restless with anticipation to sleep.

On Christmas morning, we were awake, bright and early, checking the goodies in our stockings. They never varied— always a tangerine, a few walnuts, a piece of candy, a pocket comb or some other small personal item. Sometimes the big guys forced the little kids to hand over their candy. Most times we simply traded the treats among ourselves.

Then it was time to wash up, have a small breakfast, and go to church for the special sermon on Christ's birth. The choir finished the service off with Christmas carols. Normally, we all enjoyed singing the carols even more than the other hymns, but today we couldn't wait to get to the final verse. We were all imagining the twinkling, brightly decorated Christmas tree and the presents under it waiting back in the cottage.

As soon as the service was finished, we all burst out the front doors of the chapel and raced up the path back to the cottage.

It was a mad dash to get up the hill to our individual cottages. All of us, the younger and older kids, the boys and the girls, all ran together up to the chapel road like a herd of reindeer.

My group made it to S Cottage and tried to find a good view through the dining-room window. The cottage mother kept the room with the Christmas tree locked that day. The only way to get even a little glimpse inside was to climb to the top stair of the outside balcony and crane our necks. All fifteen of us boys would be pushing and shoving each other to get up there. Some boys hung from the balcony railings for a view, risking a two-story drop if they fell.

But if we got just the right angle view through the window, we'd have a small glimpse of the Christmas tree and presents nestled at its base.

We picked out the biggest gift, and our eyes locked onto

it. What could it possibly contain, we wondered? All of us ardently hoping, could it please, please, be my present?

From that distance and that angle, it was impossible to read which present belonged to whom. We would have to find out later which lucky lad got the big one to himself.

Still, we loved every moment of it. Even the pushing and elbowing. It was all part of the yearly ritual.

Then, later, it would be time for Christmas dinner, the main event.

We all gathered in the main dining hall. In the middle of the hall stood the huge, fragrant tree from the forest, all decorated with tinsel and hand-made ornaments. Brightly colored twisted streamers snaked among the crossbeams above.

We took in the festive surroundings as we made our way eagerly to our seats.

At each spot, we found a paper Christmas cracker—a British holiday tradition. They were cylindrical rolls about six inches long wrapped in brightly colored paper. They looked a little like oversized candies in wrappers with twists at both ends. The Christmas crackers are a tradition that I have continued every year for my family.

We paired up with another lad sitting next to us, and each tugged on one end of the cracker until it broke open with a small pop and the pocket-sized prizes, like a toy car or a whistle, and the rolled up paper hat fell out on the table.

We promptly unfurled the Christmas hat, which looked a bit like a crown, and put it on our heads. It was a tradition to wear them for the rest of the evening.

The table would be full of giddy laughter, chatter, and the pops of crackers. It was all good fun, setting the tone for the evening. Oddly enough even the witch of a cottage mother seemed to be less mean and participated in the spirit of Christmas Day.

Soon the dinner arrived. We had the traditional British Christmas dishes: turkey with dressing, mashed potatoes, and Brussels sprouts for the main course, and steamed pudding for dessert. Unlike our other meals in the dining hall, this was one supper nobody complained about. It was rich, tasty, and satisfying.

Throughout the meal, the headmaster read fake telegrams informing us of Santa Claus's progress: "Santa and his reindeer had been spotted flying over the Yukon and estimated time of arrival will be one hour."

The younger boys were riveted by his words, imagining Santa's sleigh full of presents zipping across the snow-covered landscape. Some of the older boys scoffed and tried to burst their bubble.

Our excitement was building through the main course. By the time we finished our steamed pudding, it was reaching a fever pitch. We could barely sit still. The youngest children—the ones who hadn't experienced Christmas at Fairbridge yet—were wide-eyed, feeding off our enthusiasm, unsure what to expect.

Finally, the climactic moment arrived.

The great fat jolly man in a red suit and white beard burst through the big front door of the hall with a "Ho! Ho! Ho! Merry Christmas!"

We instantly recognized that Santa had a marked Lancashire accent. Moreover, the only staff member missing from the party was Mr. Bullcock, a Lancashire native, so there you have it.

But none of us were ever daft enough to say his name out loud. That could easily have led to receiving no present that year.

We couldn't really be fooled, yet none of us wanted to spoil the festive spirit.

Santa ushered us back to our cottages where we could finally open our long-awaited presents. Our joy could hardly be more complete.

Most of us only got one present, the one we'd selected from the catalog. Some kids were lucky enough to have godparents, wealthy British Columbian citizens who sponsored them financially (donating $150 annually per child for their daily care) and might send them nice, more expensive presents.

Occasionally, one or two kids in the school received a store-bought sled from a godparent. Such a gift became the envy of everyone riding down hills on their homemade contraptions. The lucky recipients found themselves surrounded by a throng of boys and girls who suddenly wanted to be their best friend.

For some reason, our party of 1941 received support from godparents who were mostly part of British Columbia's lumber industry. Brian's godfather just happened to be one of the biggest, richest lumber tycoons of all Canada: Mr. Bloedel of the HR Macmillan & Bloedel Seaboard Lumber Company.

Every Christmas, Mr. Bloedel invited Brian and a friend

to visit him in a beautiful cabin on Sprout Lake near Port Alberni, one of many homes he owned. One year, Brian picked me to get the lucky ticket to go along.

It wasn't a rustic cabin in the woods. It was a large, luxurious residence that happened to resemble a log cabin on the outside. Inside, it was filled with expensive furniture and every comfort a person could ask for. The spare bedroom we slept in had a ceiling covered with dollar bills. It looked like someone had thrown a sack full of bills up at a ceiling covered in glue, and they stuck there and never came back down.

Brian and I marveled at the sight; we had never seen that much money in our lives. We lay in our bunks at night wishing one or two bills would come fluttering down on our beds.

Every morning we woke up to a heaping breakfast of bacon, eggs, and pancakes—to any Fairbridge kid, that breakfast would seem like a feast fit for a king.

One year at the age of 10 I received a pair of long trousers from my godfather, Mr. Edwards. I was overwhelmed and marveled at them. These were trousers, reserved for the senior boys and adults. I felt so lucky.

The school rules stated that boys under the age of 15 were not allowed to wear trousers in that style, but I figured since this was a present from my godfather, Mrs. Green might make an exception and let me wear them for special occasions off the Fairbridge property.

Unfortunately, my joy was short-lived because within days that bitch of a cottage mother cut the legs of those pants. They looked ridiculous afterward. As if that wasn't bad enough, she forced me to wear the cut-off trousers for Sunday church services. Of course, this made me the target of many a smart-assed remark from certain schoolmates.

Aside from the trousers, I don't remember ever receiving a big present in all my years in the school. This was not something that I felt bad about, as this was the case for all my schoolmates.

Most of the gifts given at Fairbridge were pretty modest, nothing elaborate and below the one dollar mark. Though they were small, we were always thrilled by what we received.

Over the years, like so many parents, I went to the malls and scoured the stores madly and bought far too many toys and gifts for my kids as they were growing up. I was always happy to do it and keep the magic of Christmas alive for my kids.

Nevertheless, too many times I felt that I was witnessing my kids and other kids tearing open present after present with a look of feigned pleasure to hide their disappointment over what they received.

Then I think back: surely, we too must have wished for more when we unwrapped our gifts. It seems to me that we were far happier with our meagre haul than most kids are today. For us, even the smallest present was worth a lot.

It was not only the presents; the gift of Christmas for us was a break from our drab daily routines. We cherished the season of Christmas, every day of it.

The Final Years in "S" Cottage

As I got older, life in S Cottage improved marginally. I was beginning to pick my own battles and hold my ground against the senior boys and the boxing training helped. I remained on the team and gradually honed my skills. The two worst bullies had also left the school by then.

I had also developed an innocent, puppy-love crush on one of the day school teachers. Her name was Miss S., but to us she was fondly known as Mimi. She was the most popular teacher on the day school staff. She also lived on site in one of the staff cottages, so we saw more of her than the teachers who took up residency in Duncan.

Mimi was young and pretty, not that much older than a few of the senior students in the school. Her warm-hearted personality was her best feature. She was always wearing a cheerful smile whenever I saw her. Unlike most of the staff, she would greet students with sincere kindness and a "Good morning" or a "Good afternoon." Even if we were not in her classes, she might take a moment or two to talk to us and ask how we were doing, and you knew that she cared.

Because she was so young, one or two of the senior boys even asked her out on a date, but she politely turned them down. She taught the junior high grades, from 7th grade and up, and I hadn't reached that level yet. I liked, actually loved it when she greeted me in the halls with her warm smile.

At the ripe old age of 10, I sent Mimi a love letter. She thought it was cute. Unfortunately for me, she thought it was endearing enough to discuss it light-heartedly at the staff dinner table.

It did not take long for word of it to reach Mrs. Green's ears. When she heard of it, she hauled me in for a very severe tongue-lashing. She twisted my innocent puppy-love sentiment into the filthy lust of a sex-crazed boy. She sentenced me to a gating and threatened to send me to the duty master if I ever sent anything of the sort again.

After that I felt a little sheepish whenever I passed Mimi in the day school building. I looked at her with shy glances and hurried on my way.

Nowadays, Mimi is still alive and living in Victoria. The years have not dimmed her radiant, cheerful personality. My wife and I greatly enjoy visiting her whenever we are in the city.

When I was 11, I joined the Canadian Boy Scouts. I saw it as a great opportunity to get out of Fairbridge and meet a different group of boys. I took it gladly.

The first thing I had to learn as a scout was how to wear my uniform properly and keep it clean and pressed. Our uniform consisted of a khaki button-up shirt, matching shorts, and a neckerchief, all of which had to be cleaned and pressed seamlessly. Long socks, brown leather shoes, and a hat peaked in the Royal Canadian Mounted Police style completed the ensemble.

Every article in my uniform was brand new, and I accepted it with a little awe.

I took great pride in washing and pressing it. I felt like

it was something special that had been entrusted to me, a symbol of pride, and I wanted to take care of it properly. I took extra time pressing the creases in my scout hat to make sure they were razor-sharp.

As I admired my work, I imagined a commissioner of the Royal Canadian Mounted Police spotting me on parade and noticing my handiwork and dedication. Surely he would take note, and that would lead to a career with the famous Mounties. They are easily recognized everywhere for their cardinal-red jackets and flat-brimmed, tan peaked hats which look much like U.S. Ranger's hats.

After learning about our uniforms, we had to memorise the scout pledge. I took the duty to heart and can still recite it word-for-word today. Our motto, "Be prepared," has served me well throughout my life.

With this solid foundation established, we could go out and do the various scouting activities and rites of passage. We went out hiking. We learnt how to navigate in the open using a compass and perform first aid and identify animals and plants. In the summer months, we went camping in the woods. After a long hike, we found a good spot and learnt how to prepare a campsite. We erected old-style canvas tents using rope line and stakes, which were far more difficult to master than the simple modern pop-up tents. A few times we even tackled mountain climbing in the Cowichan area. I came back from those excursions feeling empowered.

We received merit badges when we accomplished tasks and passed certain tests. I worked hard to earn badges and added them one-by-one to my uniform sleeve. Soon I accumulated a nice, brightly coloured collection that I wore with great pride.

Eventually, I earnt enough badges and the respect of my scoutmaster, and he promoted me to Patrol Leader.

It was my first experience being in a leadership position. I didn't really know how to give orders, and even though I had the power to do so, I was hesitant.

I was more worried about losing a friend than being a leader and bossing people around. I became very close with my troop-mates. I had learnt at an early age just how important it was to have good friends. We got through all the difficult times together by helping each other and leaning on each other for support. My troop-mates were no different.

Protecting friendship rather than overexerting rank became my leadership philosophy, and it never really changed as I got older.

When we traveled to Duncan or the towns beyond for Boy Scout meetings and school sporting events, Mr. Bullcock drove us in the school truck, which was rigged up with a canvas-covered bed and benches like an army troop carrier.

Quite often on the way back to the school he would stop at a little country shop to pick up his cigarettes. Sometimes he let us go inside with him.

We rarely had a nickel between the six of us to buy anything. All we received each week for an allowance was two cents, one for the chapel collection plate and one to keep, and often that second coin would be taken away. The shop owner, like most in the area, could recognise a Fairbridge kid as soon as one of us walked in.

As usual, he didn't look especially pleased to see us. There was no profit in dealing with us, since we had no money. Our young, innocent faces didn't give him any sense of security either, but we tried our felonious routine anyway. We had it perfected by now. One of us walked up to the counter to distract him with some dumb questions.

"Uh, sir, how much is that toy car on the top shelf behind you?" my friend Brian began, and that was our cue.

The rest of us skimmed over the shelves, taking stock of the candy and comic book inventory.

Then I saw them: Mackintosh toffee bars—bingo! My favorites.

Big ones cost five cents, but I made do with the smaller one-cent bars. They were easier to grab and fit in a pocket.

We swiped what we could quickly.

Soon enough, Mr. Bullcock was calling out, "Right, lads, time to get 'tharse' to the truck, now!"

At his command, we put on our most innocent, disappointed looks that only kids can muster and rushed to the door.

We ducked back under the canvas roof and settled down. As the engine started to rev we reached for our loot.

"Voila!"

Assorted candy bars popped out of pockets. Beside me, my friend Cliff pulled a comic book from the front of his shirt.

This would've been small stuff for mobsters like Al Capone, but our operation was every bit as professional with no violence involved. That is, except for the occasional scuffle among ourselves that broke out while we debated how to split the spoils.

Of course, we refrained from shop snitching in our Boy Scout uniforms—that would have gone against our scout creed, and I took my scout creed very seriously.

After being shipped off to Fairbridge, I more-or-less lost contact with my entire family, but I did correspond occasionally with my father. The letters were typical of estranged father-son communications and they could be stiff and awkward sometimes. Most of his letters focused on giving me advice, and he often expressed his displeasure with my lackluster school reports. He never really wrote to praise me or reassure me. In an attempt to gain some sort of approval, I bragged in my letters about any accomplishment I could come up with. Praise from my favorite teachers, boxing victories, those scouting awards and my patrol leader promotion—anything that was worth mentioning. It all went in those letters.

Even when my father acknowledged these accomplishments, his letters always seemed to dwell on my shortcomings. He offered no encouragement and little praise, and very seldom mentioned my strengths. Paradoxically enough, other family members would later tell me he was always quite proud of my achievements. It simply didn't show in his letters. That's why the praise and affirmation from my scoutmaster, my coaches, and a few teachers meant so much to me. I still had a lot of self-doubt, but scouting and boxing was making a difference.

Assigned to a New Cottage

I cannot count how many times over the course of the four years I spent in S Cottage that I would lie awake in my bed and pray, "Dear God, please send this cruel, vicious woman and the bullies all to hell."

For those four long, miserable years, until the age of eleven, I endured the hell of living under Mrs. Green's thumb. Then one day my salvation finally arrived.

Mrs. Green was leaving Fairbridge.

I was overjoyed. The day I found out, I laughed in relief and astonishment until tears began streaming down my face. I said to myself, "Yes, there is a God in heaven after all."

I was praising him for this news. I had never been more grateful for anything before. Finally, my life was about to change for the better.

Immediately after she left, four of us were transferred to a new cottage: J Cottage. I didn't particularly care. I was glad to be rid of that miserable cottage as well. Anything would be an improvement over where I had been.

I didn't know who would be my new cottage mother, but I figured no one could possibly be worse than Mrs. Green. I would soon learn not to make such quick assumptions.

In J Cottage, we met Ms. Bates[5], the new woman responsible for our well being. For some strange reason, she took an instant dislike to the four of us who had been transferred from S Cottage. She eyed us disdainfully, looking us over like we were a group of dirty guttersnipes that she

---

5 Her name has been changed.

would have to deal with. On arrival at her cottage, she gave us a harsh lecture and warned us that any disobedience on our part would result in punishment. We couldn't understand her hostile attitude. After what we had endured in S Cottage, we were as docile as sheep, but the contempt in her expression was unmistakable.

Later, I would learn there had been an intense rivalry between Ms. Bates and Mrs. Green, hence her immediate scorn. What luck … the four of us escaped one tyrant for another with Ms. Bates.

Ms. Bates was a short, stocky woman with a close-cropped butch haircut. She was a heavy smoker. Her upper lip sported a brown tobacco-stain moustache. She had no trace of soft motherliness in her appearance; she was all harsh edges and angles.

What was more, her personality matched her looks?

Our cold initial reception was followed by a taste of her numerous snide remarks as she showed us our beds and assigned us cottage duties. She emphasized that she would not tolerate any misbehaviour or disobedience of her cottage rules. I half-expected her to read us the "Ten Commandments" next.

I naively thought I could win her favor. I knew she was a Girl Guide commissioner, so I thought my early success in scouting might impress her.

However when I told her how I had earnt my rank, she just sneered and remarked, "How on earth did they ever make you a Patrol Leader?"

That deflated me. My promotion was the first measure of approval I'd ever gotten from the adults.

I still tried to curry favor with her. I employed all the old tricks of "brown-nosing." I acted excessively polite around her, which was not difficult because Mrs. Green had thoroughly whipped politeness and manners into us. I addressed Ms. Bates as "Mum" without being prompted to and tried my best to sound sincere and devoted when I said it. I made valiant attempts to keep my socks pulled up at all times. I was overly conscious of my table manners said "please" and "thank you."

Still, all my efforts to get her off my back made no difference. The disdain, nagging, and exceptionally sharp-tongued sarcastic remarks continued. Her unrelenting criticism did nothing to help my already low self-esteem.

Fortunately, I got along better with my new cottage-mates. Most of us in J Cottage were close to the same age. There were no huge disparities like there had been in S Cottage to give older boys an unfair advantage. Besides, the senior lads in J Cottage were not the bullying type. And at age 11, I had finally grown stronger and was beginning to fight my own battles.

I quickly learnt that Ms. Bates played favorites with the boys, and the four of us from S Cottage were decidedly not included. The ones she liked received good treatment and all the privileges of the day. We, the S Cottage boys, got the brunt of the blame and the punishment for incidents that often had nothing to do with us.

Thankfully, Ms. Bates did not reach for her strap to discipline us. That was a great relief physically. I could wake up without feeling sore in the morning from my bruises. Instead, she preferred to sentence us to a gating as punishment. For the slightest infraction of her rules, she would gate us for a whole week or longer. She especially delighted in doing this when we had a fun, special event scheduled.

So while the other boys in the cottage would be off playing miggies, swimming, running across the football field, or attending a school dance, we would be stuck stacking wood, scrubbing down cupboards, shining the wood floors, or washing windows. I decided that I would rather take the strap than a gating most days. Problem there, it was not as if I had a choice.

This prejudice against us only fueled my growing rebellious attitudes. As I was growing up, I was getting increasingly fed up with our treatment and more inclined to talk back to her and certain other staff members.

It was all I could do to rein in my tongue. Many times I just went ahead and let Ms. Bates, and the day school teachers know what I was really thinking.

On one occasion, Ms. Bates sentenced me to a gating that included working on the woodpile for some chicken shit incident. I was really pissed off as I watched all my cottage mates grabbing their swimming trunks and laughing as they ran barefoot toward the river. I loved going down to the river more than practically anything, and she knew it. This was her way of rubbing my punishment right in my face.

As I fumed while stacking the wood, I started to sing. It was less of a melody and more of a shout at the top of my lungs aimed right at the cottage. I wanted her to hear me as I bellowed out the words, "If I had the wings of an angel, these high prison walls I would fly!"

She screamed back in her trademark caustic tone from the window, "Patrol Leader Mackay, report to me immediately!" She laid a heavy emphasis of sarcasm on the title "Patrol Leader."

My anger overpowered all fear of punishment. I yelled from the top of my voice, "Coming, Guide Commissioner Broad-Ass!"

I came face-to-face with her, defiance evident in every inch of my stance to show her I wasn't afraid of her.

She snarled, "For that insolence you will report to the duties master for discipline right now!"

I nodded my head, but my expression didn't waver. I turned and marched. When I was out of her sight, I aimed a kick at her dog, named "Bitey." I did love dogs, but at times a few of us would take our frustrations out on her poor dog. It was cowardly as hell, and I'm ashamed of it then and now.

Ms. Bates frequently would leave her cigarette packs out on the kitchen counter. When she did, I often found myself looking at them curiously, wondering what it was like to smoke. How would a cigarette taste in my mouth? So many adults seemed to love them. I'd seen a few cowboys lighting up in the movies and images of Native Americans smoking pipes. I wanted to see what it was all about. There were also a few other staff members, like Mr. Bullcock and Mr. Brown, who smoked.

One day, temptation and the opportunity arose; there was

a pack of cigarettes lying on the kitchen table and it seemed to be beckoning to me. Cautiously, glancing around making sure no one would see me, I peered inside the pack, still not daring to take one. Then one day my burning curiosity overcame my fear of getting caught. I simply had to try one for myself.

Making sure Ms. Bates was not around; I picked up her pack up and slid a long cigarette out, rolling it between my fingers experimentally. The paper felt so smooth.

I took my prize outside where no one would see me, crouching under the cover behind the bushes by the frog pond that was behind of the cottage. I struck a match to light it as I had seen smokers do countless times and began smoking, taking deep puffs in and out. Within a minute, I was throwing up and wishing I had never touched that bloody thing. It was awful.

I spent the next several days feeling sick with fear that she would discover someone had stolen one of her cigs. Every time she came across the room, I thought, "This is it; she knows. She will find me and I will be gated for the rest of the summer."

I had no idea that smokers like her rarely had any idea how many cigs were left in their packs. The cigarette I took was never missed. After a week passed without incident, my fears calmed down.

Summer brought a rare treat in outings to pick blackberries. Ms. Bates brought out her Model A Ford and told us to get in. Our spirits lifted immediately when we heard, and we jostled among each other to see who would get to sit in the back rumble seat.

We drove out of Fairbridge, and down the unpaved back roads of Cowichan country where the evergreen trees grew tall and wild until we found a nice patch of blackberry thickets. The rambling, thorny bushes grew plentifully out there in the clearings by the roadside, and for a month during the summer, they would be heavy with plump, luscious berries practically bursting with juice.

Ms. Bates gave each of us a five-gallon brass pail to fill and let us roam. We navigated nimbly around the thorns and stuffed our mouths with sweet berries and plopped handfuls of them in the pails. Our fingers were quickly stained dark purple; bare arms took occasional light nicks from the thorns.

When her back was turned to us and our pails were full, we took to throwing berries at each other and then our clothes would be stained in purple to match our faces and hands. We laughed until our sides hurt and chased each other and never wanted those afternoons to end.

LIFE IN "J" COTTAGE

During the cooler autumn and winter months, sometimes we had to work in the furnace room to make sure our cottage stayed heated. Every two cottages shared a furnace room between them, and took alternating two-week shifts of tending to it. Most of us actually enjoyed these duties because the furnace room was a safe haven from the watchful eye and sharp tongue of the CM upstairs. Yes, we had to haul wood and stoke the furnace, but we also got a rare chance to enjoy some extended camaraderie. We sang the latest cowboy songs we heard on the radio, told stories, bragged and told a few lies, and cursed various staff members and boys we didn't like. We planned diabolical pranks against pals who weren't there. And we could do all of it without fear of being overheard or interrupted.

The furnace room was our space that we claimed for ourselves. It was our retreat. We penciled in and carved messages on the walls there as a testament to our past presence, fairly confidant the cottage mothers would probably never find our graffiti there. We left our names, wrote out who loved or hated whom, which staff members were on our shit list.

My good friend and *Bayano* crewmate Mitch had a hobby we both loved: music, particularly cowboy songs. We spent many winter hours in the furnace room enjoying the warmth and comfort there and singing together. Mitch added notes on his harmonica to our renditions of Hank Snow or Hank

Williams songs that we'd heard over the radio. Mitch had a good voice in addition to his skills on harmonica. There were a few times when we both felt destined to be singing those songs on the same stage with our Hank heroes someday. At least, I did because in spite of all the bad times, I had become one of those dreamers.

A couple of reunions back, I gave Mitch a harmonica. He looked at it as if to say, "What do you want me to do with this?" I reminded him of our old furnace room and the music sessions, and asked him to play it. He protested, saying he hadn't played in years, but I pressed him: "Come on Mitch, play it for good ol' Hank and those memories of the old furnace room in J Cottage."

Finally, he lifted it to his mouth and started to play. The notes came out just as sweet as they used to in the furnace room. After all those years, his skills were still intact.

Because it was so secluded, the furnace room also made a good place for other secret activities and schemes. I decided to kick-start my bodybuilding career there.

At the time, bodybuilder Charles Atlas was one of my biggest idols. We pored over his adverts in local newspapers and magazines that were often lying around. He was always portrayed as this handsome, well-built guy with one arm wrapped around a gorgeous girl. Next to that, picture would be another one where some bully on the beach was kicking sand in the face of a little scrawny kid. The caption read, "Does this happen to you? Then take the Charles Atlas course now."

I decided I wanted a physique like Charles Atlas. The very

thought of attracting pretty girls, making my opponents back off seemed quite appealing to me.

To that end, I resolved to build some weight-lifting bars to build those muscles. I would hide the weight bars in the furnace room where Ms. Bates wouldn't find them. It was quite the amateur metalworking project. I found some old jam tins and filled two of them with scrap lead that I melted in the furnace. Before the lead had cooled I stuck a short iron bar in the middle of the cans. Then, for some reason—I forget why—I had to pound the cans with the blunt end of an axe. While I was pounding away vigorously, I smashed my left forefinger, splitting it open.

I stifled a scream of pain as my eyes watered. I dropped the axe and I certainly didn't pick it up to try again. That was the end of my bodybuilding venture. I also avoided muscular guys on a beach from then on for good measure.

At some point in those years, Reverend Hipp replaced our old Reverend Hughes. Like many of the staff members, Rev. Hipp was an Englishman. Unlike many of the other staff members, he took a genuine interest in us children. He would frequently stop to talk with us or ask how we were doing. He never talked down to us, and we appreciated that. He also had a family and often invited us to visit at his home, a staff member cottage.

We liked the good Reverend for all those reasons, but we admired him all the more for his unique pet: a wild fawn that he rescued. The deer followed him everywhere he walked, and often nuzzled his pockets in search of food. Sometimes he let us feed the fawn from a bag of sliced apples.

We respected and loved Rev. Hipp because he was such a kindly character, and we were all saddened when he left Fairbridge years later.

Quite often, he would supervise the boys' playing soccer. On one occasion, a couple of lads started a farting contest, and he halted the drill practice.

"Now boys, breaking wind is not only disrespectful but also very un-sportsmanlike conduct. Even in sports we must conduct ourselves like gentlemen." He said this quite seriously.

One of the lads muttered, "The good Reverend must think we are playing cricket[6]."

Of course, that only encouraged us to humorously quote the good Reverend whenever one of us farted in public. That happened often because cabbage was one of the vegetables we were served often. We staged great farting contests in the dorms. The heavyset lads tended to win. I guessed it was because they ate more of the cabbage.

Another time, Rev. Hipp gave us a short homily on gardening. Each cottage had its own garden plot, and the kids were allowed to use a section of it to grow their vegetables. The staff even held contests over who could grow the biggest watermelons or pumpkins.

The Reverend told us when we seeded our gardens with flowers; we should kneel down to the flowerbed and smile. This simple act of kindness would make the flowers blossom sooner, he claimed.

Most of us were a bit skeptical about his theory, but Roy

---

6   Cricket in those days was definitely considered a gentleman's sport.

seemed pretty convinced. He was out there every day on his knees beaming at his flowerbeds.

Interestingly enough, his flowers flourished while most of our plants barely bloomed. We couldn't believe it had actually worked. Too bad "Miracle-Gro" was not around in the 40s.

Then our expert gardener, 'Daggy,' pointed out that Roy watered his flowers regularly, but the rest of us did not.

As mentioned before, we gave nicknames to each other, and they were rarely flattering. Unfortunately, most nicknames chosen were based on the individual's fewer flattering features or characteristics. This undoubtedly happened most often with the ones who didn't fit in or didn't want to. Victor R., known by us as Daggy, was a prime example.

As nicknames go, "Daggy" is about the most degrading you can get—it's an old British sheepherder expression for the dirty balls of wool that cling to a sheep's anal area.

He was bullied pretty badly. The fact that he wore glasses didn't help him. In those days, glasses practically guaranteed teasing.

I did not know Daggy very well. We didn't cross paths very often. All I knew was that he looked a bit awkward and acted strange. By all accounts, though, he was actually a very bright boy. One thing he really loved and excelled at was gardening.

Daggy simply loved plants. He saved hundreds of seeds, which he kept organized in different empty bottles and jars. He stashed them in his fort in the woods, where he had row upon row of jars full of seeds sitting on a home made rickety table. When the staff held gardening contests to see who could grow the biggest pumpkins or watermelons, Daggy dug right in.

Some of the kids put together a specialized watering system to give their pumpkins and watermelons an advantage. They dug a sturdy stake in the ground with a tin filled with water attached at the top. Then they took a piece of string, dipped one end in the water tin, and tied the other to a nail that they stuck directly into the body of the growing pumpkin or melon. The water slowly trickled down the string and into the vegetable, and we figured that would feed the plant.

We watched our melons or pumpkins grow larger by the day, but still, none of our plants could beat Daggy's. He tended to his plants meticulously and lovingly every day. He checked on them at every opportunity he could get. They grew the biggest, and he won the contests. He was always very proud, beaming as he showed off his produce.

The others grew jealous of him. Some of them took a penknife to Daggy's plants and cut the roots in the ground. It either killed the plant entirely or stunted its growth. This left him very distraught and frustrated when he couldn't figure out what was wrong.

The poor kid not only suffered the endless taunts from his peers, but certain staff members also made his life miserable. He was one of many kids who had a bedwetting problem. His cottage mother humiliated him by making him sleep in the wet sheets.

Perhaps some of the cottage mothers thought these punishments would discourage bed-wetting. In reality, though, it made the problem worse[7]. The constant beatings he suffered only drove Daggy to become rebellious and act out more, which in turn brought more punishment.

When I had been living with Ms. Bates for over two years, and I was around 13 or 14, a couple of us were wrestling in the basement as we sometimes did. In the heat of our hand-to-hand battle, we threw out the occasional cuss words and oaths.

My opponent had grabbed my arm and twisted it behind my back. He was twisting too hard; my shoulder felt like it would pop out of its socket. The pain was terrible, and I was shouting some choice curses to get my opponent to release me.

He finally let go of my arm, but my relief was short-lived. Almost immediately a sharp slap landed on the side of my head, leaving my ear ringing deafeningly. A stab of pain had me enraged like a bull I whipped around, unleashing a good right jab to an unknown opponent, as I had no idea who had slapped me in the ear. It was Ms. Bates standing there, only now doubled over and heaving, with the wind knocked out of her.

I froze. Realization hit: I'd just physically assaulted a staff member. The rush of emotions—a sense of power, a trace of triumph, but on top of it all, a deep, mortal fear of how she was going to punish me for this overwhelmed me.

She collected herself again and hissed at me with

---

7   David Hill in his book *The Forgotten Child* cites incidents of children with bedwetting problems receiving the same harsh punishment in the Australian Fairbridge Farm School. One cottage mother even forced a girl to put her head down the toilet.

extra venom, "Mackay you will report to the duty master immediately!"

The whipping I received that day was well worth it. For starters, though Ms. Bates continued to hassle me, she was far less threatening about it. Her sarcastic remarks lost a little of their edge. I could tell she had my right hook in mind whenever she dealt with me afterward.

I also gained a good measure of respect from a few of my cottage-mates, much like Roy had when he took the strap out of Mrs. Green's hand.

Of course, I never let on to anyone that I hadn't known it was Ms. Bates behind me when I threw that punch, and that if I had, I probably wouldn't have done it.

THE BOYS AND GIRLS

At one point in our adult years, Hughie described me as always being "a lady's man" in apiece published in our *Fairbridge Gazette*. I had a good chuckle when I read that. I may have acted out the lady's man role but believe me; it was all bluff. I was no Casanova in either looks or skills with charming the fairer sex. I was certainly very attracted to the lasses and kept a special eye out for them, but I had to work harder to attract them. Winning their hearts did not come naturally to me. I compensated by acting confidant and making every effort to be a gentleman around them.

At Fairbridge, the sexes were kept strictly separated. The girls' cottages stood some distance away from the boys' cottages on the other side of the residential area of Fairbridge. As such, romantic meetings were extremely difficult to arrange.

In my early teenage years, my active interest in girls was starting to develop.

Around age nine, I joined the school choir for a brief stint. I became very distracted during practice by all the lovely lasses who were also in the choir. My gaze drifted to Mary and Irene in particular. I kept trying to catch their eyes. I was flirting with one of them at that point. The choirmaster eventually dismissed me, not because I lacked ability, but because I was so preoccupied with the girls.

I was saddened when I had to leave the choir because I truly loved to sing.

Among all the other stories we traded in the furnace room at the cottage, we also loved talking about the swell girls whom we had our eyes on and boasting about made-up sexual activities we'd done. Most of the time, we would elbow the bragger in the ribs and say, "No way that's true!"

With the strict housing arrangements separating the boys' cottages from and girls' cottages, even mild romantic meetings were extremely difficult to arrange. So most of the affairs we discussed were made-up fantasies with Irene or Mary, or whoever else we had our eyes on.

One night, a group of us decided to sneak over to the girls' dorms on the other end of the school grounds for some mild sexual encounters.

We made good use of our experience raiding the apple orchards. We climbed down the fire escape ladder like old pros.

As we got closer, proceeding very stealthily, we got into a whispered debate over precisely which dorm we should tackle. Each of us had our own special choice girl, but we soon realized we had one major problem: the girls who would go along with this romantic dorm raid would be greatly outnumbered by girls who would immediately run down to get the cottage mother. Then both, our paramours and we would be sent to the dreaded duty master faster than you could swing a conker.

So we turned back around and slunk home to our cottages like dogs with tails tucked between their legs.

As miscreant teenagers, we added another activity to the list of things to do when we went to the river in the summer. We dared each other to sneak peeks at the girls while they were changing into their swimsuits. They had a small spot cleared for them apart from the main beach, well hidden by dense bushes. We stalked carefully through the shrubbery for a glimpse. When that didn't work too well, we climbed to upper branches of trees to try to get a better view. We moved among the branches like agile monkeys in the jungle.

Every now and then, some dunderhead clumsily broke a branch in his haste and eagerness. The girls whipped their heads around at the loud snap from above, saw us peeking, and immediately began screaming. We knew we had to get the hell out of there and fast. One of the staff members or one of those despised senior boys was already rushing over.

We scrambled down those trees as quickly as we possibly could, knowing full well the consequences we faced if we got caught. As soon as our feet hit solid ground again, we ran. We didn't stop until we reached a safe distance far from the river. Then we flopped down in the tall grass of the fields. When we caught our breath, we began chattering excitedly.

"Geeze, guys, did you see Mary's bare ass?"

We had some stories that day that would have put Huck Finn to shame.

Sex education was nonexistent in our school curriculum, so we were left to figure those things out on our own. I got a little help from reading the classic erotic D.H. Lawrence novel, *Lady Chatterley's Lover*.

One of my most painful and humiliating moments in the day school took place during one of Mr. Grant's history classes when I was sneaking more time with the Lawrence novel.

Mr. Grant began the class as usual with a short introduction to the day's topic: the Roman Empire. Then he gave us a reading assignment to complete and took a seat at his desk while we worked. He graded our homework, his eyes occasionally flitting upward to check on us.

I surreptitiously pulled the novel from my bag and hid it inside my open history book.

My desk was second row to the back of the class, and I felt well concealed from Mr. Grant's view while I devoured the pages. Soon enough, the lad behind me started poking me in the back, whispering, "Come on, Mackay, gimme the book. It's my turn." I brushed him off.

This tale of love and passion had me so completely absorbed that I let my guard drop. The scene riveted me where the gardener and Lady Chatterley were admiring each other's naked bodies in exquisite detail. I could practically picture the scene. I didn't notice that Mr. Grant had left his desk and quietly strolled to the back of room, where he could clearly see the illicit book that had me so deeply engrossed.

The slap hit me squarely on the ear with the force of a cannon. Both books fell to the floor, their pages crumpling under their covers.

My passionate reverie was shattered. My ear was ringing deafeningly, just as it had in the earlier episode with Ms. Brady. I looked up to see a purple-faced Mr. Grant standing over me.

He reached down, grabbed the same injured ear with a vice grip, and dragged me from the classroom while I yelped from the pain.

There was no question as to what punishment I was about to receive. Yes, I was in for an exceptional tongue-lashing followed by about twelve lashes of his strap on each hand, topped off with a humiliating return to a classroom full of sniggering kids.

The teachers, cottage mother, and other staff members never let a word on that taboo subject of sex education escape their mouths. The older boys might surreptitiously give the younger lads a limited and crude description of what sex was all about.

I have no idea when I first became aware of that sinful sex activity, masturbation. At Fairbridge, this was referred to as "wanking-off."

Quite often, someone would catch strange bed movements in the middle of the night and look over to see a shaking, tent-like mound on another boy's bed. The cottage dorm was definitely not the best place for that activity. We all knew that "the old bed mound" was a clear indication a lad was wanking-off. By dawn, every other lad knew. Then all hell would break loose.

The entire dorm would turn on the poor culprit, calling him a sex maniac and several other nasty epithets. Even your best pal would join the mob razzing you mercilessly. If a boy was ever caught wanking off, no matter where, he would get taunted about how his 'self-abuse' would lead him to go blind, grow hair on his palms or become feeble-minded.

In 1971 Arthur Sanger, a former duties master hired by Mr. Logan in 1940, wrote *It's in the Book: Notes of a Naïve Young Man*, where he recorded his impressions during his time at Fairbridge. The relationship of the sexes was a delicate subject among the staff. He writes:

"I became increasingly concerned about boy-girl relationships, believing the separation of the sexes far too rigid. At a meeting of cottage mothers, the matron complained about older boys walking home with girls after swimming periods and loitering outside their cottages in the evenings, and she demanded stricter restrictions. Much to her ire, I argued for more rather than less freedom, going on to suggest that parties and dances be organized to put these awkward teenagers more at ease with each other and to foster normal healthy relations between them. This was vetoed, but I sensed that most of the cottage mothers agreed, though they were not willing to challenge the domineering matron. They were delighted as I was, when three weeks later she resigned."

During Sanger's tenure at Fairbridge, two cases of homosexuality were discovered. Professor Logan insisted that these were isolated cases, not the norm in the cottages, but historically, homosexuality was quite prevalent in British boarding schools in that time period.

The boys were dealt with harshly. In the first case, the assistant headmaster gave them "a walloping," and on top of that a strongly worded lecture on the subject and a load of extra work. The second time, Sanger was called in to do the deed, but he found that he couldn't bring himself to punish them. He writes:

"Shocked to the core, I sat the boys down, and though ignorant on the subject, gave them a talk on the harmfulness of sexual perversion. I decided not to whip them as their wrongdoing was beyond correction by corporal punishment, and I promised not to report on them, providing they promised to cease the practice forthwith. They did so solemnly, we shook hands, and they departed much relieved."

While the boys left counting their lucky stars, Sanger left the room with his faith in Fairbridge shattered. He questioned whether homeless children were truly better off at Fairbridge than back in England in a foster home.

Sanger left Fairbridge disheartened, feeling that the school was falling far short of its noble ideas laid out by Kingsley Fairbridge. He also felt that he personally had failed. I think this was because he could not reconcile his ideals with an organization that felt the only way to correct a child's misbehaviour was by punishing them severely to the point of child abuse. He couldn't stomach it. Sadly, this kind of conscientious man was exactly the type of person Fairbridge sorely needed on staff, unlike the pervert they hired during my time.

That man was Mr. Rogers[8]. Mr. Burns, the Scotsman and boxing coach whom I respected, eventually replaced him. Yes, my Scottish blood must have factored into judgement of Mr. Burns. On one of several occasions, a lad was sent to the perverted Mr. Rogers to receive his punishment. Following the usual verbal admonishment, the lad was ordered to drop his trousers. He braced himself for the first whack of the strap on his bare buttocks.

He waited. A minute or two passed, and nothing happened.

---

8   His name has been changed.

Finally, the kid nervously glanced around to see what was going on. He was completely shocked and scared by what he now observed. Mr. Rogers had dropped his trousers and was standing there masturbating.

Stricken with fear and disgust, the lad yanked up his trousers and didn't even bother buttoning up before he flew out of the room and ran from the building while tears streamed down his face.

One of the adult farm- hands found the lad hiding in a stall in the horse barn, still shaking and crying. He was terrified, and it took a good bit of coaxing before he told his story. He blurted out what had happened in between sobs.

Justice did prevail, to an extent. The Headmaster dismissed Mr. Rogers, and the legal system sent him to prison. However, there was no counselling offered to the lad who had been driven in fear to hide in the horse barn, nor to the other victims.

Mr. Rogers served a short prison term, and after he was released, the kindly headmaster was willing to give him a second chance. He believed that Mr. Rogers had sincerely reformed and rehired him.

Of course, if you put the wolf back in the chicken coop, the slaughter continues.

Mr. Rogers continued performing his filthy acts to the children. He was unable to keep his perverted hands off the kids and was arrested and locked up again, never to return.

Mr. Rogers was not the only pervert. Stories circulating with many of the older students indicate at least three others, including one cottage mother had been guilty of seual offences. Who knows how many others were out there, how many former Fairbridgians never spoke out about their abuse, never received counseling or help, and took the secret to their grave.

Fortunately, none of the duty masters abused me in such a perverted way. Most times when I was sent to the duties master, one or two other kids were waiting in the room for their punishment and would have been witnesses if he'd tried anything foul.

My first encounter with sex happened when I was 12 or 13. I was very naive and innocent at the time, so it was more laughable than serious. I was sitting in the backseat of the school car on our way to see a doctor in Victoria. Mr. B., better known by us as "Mousy," the assistant duty master was driving. Sitting next to me in the back was a girl, who shall remain anonymous. She was around my age and I was quite attracted to her. It was not only me; several of the guys had a crush on her—she was pretty, quite flirtatious, and had a bit of a reputation for being hot stuff. Out of respect, my lips are sealed as to her identity.

The trip to Victoria took a couple of hours each way back then, so we were riding in this car together for a long time. When we were about the half way to Victoria, I felt her hand coming to rest on my bare knee, her fingers curling around it. I reciprocated the gesture, placing my hand on her knee. I was hoping, praying, that this was what she wanted. One look at the grin on her face assured me it was.

Her fingers began searching their way up to my leg and sneaking under the hem of my shorts. I was steamed up. I nervously kept one eye on Mousy in the front to make sure he wasn't seeing any of this. Gratefully, he kept his eyes on the road rather than the rearview mirror.

The girl continued reaching her hand up the leg of my shorts. When that proved a bit too clumsy, she withdrew and went for the direct approach; she began to unbutton the fly of my trousers.

This made me extremely hot and nervous. I was sweating and breathing quickly; it felt like the temperature inside the car had skyrocketed to over 100 degrees.

Mousy was still looking calmly at the road, his eyes not flicking back to see us in the rearview mirror. I took my chance. I was too wound-up not to.

I swiftly fingered my way up to her skirt to her knickers, and then beyond. And I was there. I nearly panted aloud, "Eureka!"

The stirring of my loins as she was feeling me was unbearably delightful.

Somehow, I felt this must be the sinful forbidden fruit we were warned about at church. But if this was so sinful and wrong, how could we be getting such great pleasure from it?

That was as far as we went in that car, though. To pursue any more passionate moves would have been sheer madness. Unlike the gardener and Lady Chatterley in the book, making love in the back seat of a car driven by the school duty master was hardly going to be a passionate tryst.

I was anxious throughout my whole medical examination that the doctor would ask me to drop my pants. Fortunately, he didn't.

On the return journey north, Mousy separated us as we entered the car. He asked her to sit in the passenger seat up front while I stayed in the back. *Damn it!* I thought.

Maybe on the way up to Victoria, he had glanced into the rearview mirror or heard our excited breathing and suspected something unusual was happening. If he did, he never said a word. He was just as silent during the drive back as he was on the way up.

He was, however, kind enough to stop and buy us an ice cream cone at the Malahat Lookout Café. Maybe he figured the frozen treat would cool the seeds of our ardour. When we resumed driving, the mountainous, winding road of the Malahat gave me an upset stomach. I tried to hold down the queasiness but I up-chucked the ice cream all over his bald head.

I was immediately sick with worry. What if Mousy thought I decorated his head out of revenge? Fortunately for me, a very chagrinned Mousy simply wiped his head off and continued driving the rest of home without comment.

Moral of this story: ice cream is no substitute for one's first sexual encounter.

Joining the Boxing, Basketball and Football Teams

As mentioned before, sports were a major part of life at Fairbridge. They were a source of much-needed fun to break the drudgery of our daily lives.

With experience, I began to enjoy boxing more and more. I started winning more bouts. One of my advantages was that I was small for my age, so quite often I was paired with opponents who were a year younger, giving me an extra year of boxing experience over many of them. Coach Ned worked me over before each bout and reminded me to tuck my long jaw into my left shoulder and keep the left jab going.

At age 11, I was in the 61-70 lb. class and doing quite well. Our local newspaper, the *Cowichan Leader*, mentioned me in a news article covering the annual boxing championships that included other local teams: *"Roddy Mackay (F) eliminated Dick Townes in the elimination bouts, then went into the finals with Brian T.. Mackay defeated his opponent in a bout of light dancing interchanges, interspersed with hard-hitting, two-fisted exchanges. Mackay was awarded the Arthur Mann trophy in that weight division."*

I was slowly amassing a small collection of trophies from boxing.

Once again, the *Cowichan Leader* covered those Championships in 1947, when I was 13. It wrote: *"Fairbridge captures five of ten classes in the Kinsmen's Annual Boxing Tournament. In the 81-90 lb. class, two Fairbridge lads, Hughie*

[T.] and Roddy Mackay, brought shouts from the fans as they battled on and off the ropes, both disporting themselves like veterans. Mackay was the winner."

That year when I won the Kinsmen's Tournament, I took home a special Kinsman Club championship jacket. All the trophies I took home did not impress me nearly as much as that very special prize. It was one swell-looking jacket. I must confess there was a certain amount of what we used to describe as being "swell headed" in my attitude at the time. I thought I was hot stuff, like an early version of the Fonz of the TV series *Happy Days*. The next time I went to hang out at one of Duncan's two local soda fountains, the Greenhaven, I sported that jacket smugly. I kept one eye on the door, and when a group of pretty girls came in, I ostensibly adjusted the jacket over my shoulders, thinking, "Just wait until those girls see this flashy championship jacket; they'll be all over me."

Much to my disappointment the girls did not react quite as enthusiastically as I hoped. They walked past me not paying much attention at all. That put my ego back in place where it really belonged.

In my last two years of boxing in the Duncan events at age 16 or 17, I fought the same kid in the finals for the title in our weight division.

The second time I faced him, I was nervous as hell in the minutes before the fight. Never mind that I had already beaten him the year before. He had grown a bit bigger than I had since then.

Coach worked me over, doing all he could to build up my confidence before the bell.

The fight started, and he nailed me with a couple of good jabs in the face. As usual, that was all I needed to get over the fear and into my zone. Fortunately for me, he got careless and gave me the opening I needed. He dropped his right, and I hit him with a right cross, directly to the nose. I felt a crack under my knuckles as I made contact. His hands flew up to his face. In the next moment, I could see red. His nose was bleeding hard, and that dazed him enough for the ref to stop the fight and declare me the winner with a TKO. I was almost stunned that it had been that easy to win.

Boxing was not the only sport I enjoyed at Fairbridge, though.

For one, I really liked playing basketball and joined the school team at age 14. Mr. Grant, the day school principal, was our coach, like most of the lads on our team, I was too short to be seriously competitive against other teams. I was only five foot six.

The Canadian school teams in the league had a much taller average. With that natural advantage, they won most of the games.

I spent several games warming the bench, wondering why I was even on the team.

During one game against Duncan High, I watched as the clock counted down the time until we had less than five minutes left. The score was hopelessly out of our favor, something like Duncan 40, Fairbridge 20.

Right then, Coach turned to me and said, "Roddy, get out there and see what you can do."

Now?

I practically couldn't believe it. I took to the floor thinking, "Is he crazy? What the hell does he expect me to do with such a lopsided score and five minutes on the clock?"

I went straight for the guy with the ball, made a desperate grab for it, hit his arm, and earnt a foul.

The game ended 44 to 20.

No, basketball was not one of my better sports, but I still made the team and enjoyed the game.

The Fairbridge girls' basketball team was a much different story. They were a force to be reckoned with in our league. They did exceptionally well in 1945, winning the British Columbia provincial championship, which would be on par with winning the state championship in America.

The whole school celebrated when the girls and Coach Grant returned with the big trophy.

Much more than basketball, football (better known as soccer in America) was the game I loved. I dedicated myself every season to making the school team, training my hardest in the preseason.

My work paid off; I made the team around age 14 and played right half. I loved it because in this position, I got to play both offense and defense. It required all my speed and agility. And unlike basketball, I got to see a lot of actions and knew I was a valuable part for the team.

I treasured my first pair of boots that I got along with my uniform. Nowadays, they would be called cleats, but our football boots of the 40s were exceptionally hard, much like steel-toed work boots. Those boots could sure leave some nasty bruises.

Our coach was Mr. Chapel, better known to us as "Doc." He was an Englishman, tall and distinguished looking. He always had a pipe in his mouth. Over the years, I grew fond of the sweet aroma of the pipe tobacco that followed him everywhere.

Maybe it was because we were all Brits, but we played harder in football than in any other sport. We were upholding our national honour at every game.

It was not only the love of the game which drew us to the team, we also enjoyed the extra privilege of travelling to various towns on the island on away games. The school's rural, isolated location suited the Fairbridge mission of training farm hands, but that also meant we were lonely and could get very bored with all that damned farm work. The small town of Duncan didn't have that much to offer us either. We were looking for any and every opportunity to get away. So the away games were always a treat, regardless of whether we won or lost.

Of all the matches we played, one particular game has always stayed in my memory: an away match against Qualicum Boy's School, a prestigious public school. The boys there were sons of well-to-do families, as was the case in most public schools. The buildings and grounds looked as though they'd been plucked straight from Britain. What was more, Qualicum Beach was one of the most scenic towns on Vancouver Island, with gorgeous sandy shorelines and views of the mountains across the strait?

We were all rather wide-eyed when we arrived and entered the school's foyer. For most of us, if not all, it was our very first time setting foot inside such a grand, luxurious school building.

"Wow, geezers, is this a swanky place," we commented.

We were all eyes staring at the beautiful furniture, exquisitely patterned carpets; the rich and glossy wood paneling on the walls, and huge, varnished beams. The walls were decorated with various photographs and portraits of Canadian politicians or wealthy executives who had donated generously to fill the school's coffers. The largest and most prominent of the hanging portraits depicted King George VI and the Queen Elizabeth. That was the case in all British institutions of that era, even our lowly Fairbridge.

The Qualicum boys were dressed in short, grey flannel trousers and white wool V-neck jumpers, all looking very smart indeed. We wore a similar uniform, minus the rich wool jumpers, but we definitely did not look nearly as sharp.

That only made us grit our teeth and band together before hitting the playing field.

It was pouring outside when we did. The football pitch was close to the beach, and the wind coming from the sea gusted close to storm strength. The rain was coming at us in nearly horizontal sheets, making it hard to see. The conditions were truly terrible, but we played our game, and played it harder than any game we'd ever played before, fueled by a need to prove ourselves.

Even during an ordinary game, we played very physically. We built up a reputation for being tough as Bulldogs, so the other Canadian kids tended to be wary of us. However, that day at Qualicum, we put everything we had into the game, pushing ourselves harder, making it even tougher for them to score a single goal on us.

The Qualicum kids were no pushovers either. They also played hard in the torrential wind and rain, in the end we prevailed and won the match. Victory tasted so sweet.

We did not need Doc to warn us about acting sportsmanlike; we played a fair and honest game and shook hands with the other team at the end.

Afterward, we peeled off our muddy and rain-soaked uniforms and washed up quickly. We were glad to be back in dry clothes again.

Then the captain of the Qualicum team led us to a room that had a table with plates—real China plates—loaded with delicious sandwiches.

The food was finer than anything that had ever graced our tables at Fairbridge. The fifteen of us were starving following that match. We had to fight hard against the temptation to lick every last crumb off our plates. But we managed to remember our manners and conducted ourselves as gentlemen.

Honestly, though, we really enjoyed mixing with the rich kids. Some of us were putting on airs by saying such nonsense like, "Pip, pip old boy, and how are you today?"

This would be answered with, "Absolutely smashing, old chap."

Training to Become a Farmhand

Cheerio!
Here we are.
Working hard
On the land
On our Fairbridge Farm

Upon turning fourteen, I had reached the age when boys began formal training to do the work that Fairbridge intended us to do: farming.

However, by the time I reached that age, Fairbridge school policy had changed so that we stayed in school during the day and also did the farm work we were assigned twice a day. Farm work took up a large chunk of our days after that and school took on secondary importance. After all, we were only meant to spend the rest of our lives farming. It didn't matter if we were interested in other professions or in attending university.

I didn't like school much anyway. At the time, I had reached the upper grades; it became very difficult for me trying to learn facts and statistics by rote for tests. I could remember that General Wolfe of England defeated General Montcalm of France in the Battle of Quebec, but I could never recall exactly what date that happened. Tests always made me terribly nervous. I gripped my pencil too tightly as I stared at the paper before me. When I encountered a difficult question on minute details, my brain went into a panic mode. It was as though all my knowledge evaporated. My over thinking and second-guessing usually doomed me to failure.

My hearing problems also started in the later grades, and they made absorbing information from lectures difficult. One medical report indicated I had ruptured eardrums, likely the result of all those blows to my ears. However, it implied that hearing loss was not the thing that was holding me back in school. I was not sure if the report was suggesting I was mentally challenged, but it may have been doing just that. I will admit that a few of my actions and behaviors at Fairbridge may have deserved the label. I later learnt that this ear problem due to damaged eardrums cropped up quite often in Australian Fairbridge child migrants.

Mimi, the pretty, youthful teacher whom I'd wrote the love note to years ago, left the school before I reached the grade level that she taught. Her replacement was Mrs. H. We nicknamed her "Hawky" due to her large, beak-like nose.

By the time I reached her class, I quickly found out she was far different from Mimi. There was little joy in her personality; she was strict and impatient. Though in all fairness, my rebellious attitude was only growing in those years, which probably skewed my opinion of her.

One winter school day when the snow lay deep, three of us decided we wanted to start some mischief and throw some snowballs. Lo and behold, but who was the first person to pass?

Hawky.

As soon as she came into range, we launched three snowball missiles. One missed; one hit her shoulder, and the third found home hitting her square on her head. She let out a shriek, and before she could recover we were gone.

We heard later that she was in a foul mood the rest of the day. A notice also quickly appeared on the school bulletin reading, "Any students caught throwing snowballs at staff members will be severely punished!"

At the time, we thought it had been worth it, but reflecting on our misdeed now; we had also brought on more misery for our schoolmates in her class that day.

After turning 14, I went out with a group of other boys who had recently reached the same age for orientation to the farm with Mr. Brown, the farm manager. He had a number of other farm staffs working with him. He gave us new trainees a quick tour of the facilities.

The residential area and the surrounding buildings made up only a small portion of the whole Fairbridge property. Barns and hundreds of acres of fields, orchards, and pastures sprawling out far into the distance took up the rest of it. This was the farm site—the heart of Fairbridge. With all that acreage and a substantial animal stock, there was always plenty of work for the farm trainees to do.

I was already familiar with the fields because we had been assigned to work in them from a young age. Now I was introduced to the rest of the farm site. Fairbridge had separate barns for its horses, chickens, cows, and pigs, and one for the hay. On our tour, we also passed by the sheep barn that had once housed the Fairbridge herd. It now stood empty since they had all been sold off before we arrived.

I took to the horses and the cows immediately. They were

Clydesdale horses and Ayrshires cows—both Scottish breeds, maybe that influenced my impressions.

I didn't especially want to work with the chickens and the pigs; they both struck me as very smelly and dirty. The smell of horse and cow manure didn't bother me so much; it wasn't quite as pungent.

The poultry operation was huge. We had six hundred chickens in multiple coops laying several hundred eggs daily. Boys had to go collect the eggs daily and clean up all the manure the chickens left on the ground.

The yard where they roamed was all scratched-up dirt. Crusted droppings and fresh turds were everywhere, but especially thick on the bottoms of the wire mesh coops. The chickens milled about in the cramped space. They made quite a racket with their squawking. Some of them were missing bunches of feathers and looked a bit ratty.

The piggery had a stock of 54 pigs that wallowed around in the mud and grunted. When we looked out, we could usually spot the big 'un'—Sambo, the boar. He was a lot bigger than the sows. The pigs were fed scraps and taken care of until they were ready for slaughter.

Then there were my favourites: the Clydesdales. We had six of them, all purebred and I marveled at these beautiful creatures as they peered at us over their stall doors. Their dark manes fell along their long, stocky necks and hung over their gentle eyes. They breathed warm air onto my hands as I reached out to pet them. To this day I am still enamored with horses.

They were magnificent beasts—enormous and muscular

with chestnut coats and long, shaggy white tufts of hair growing around their hooves. I couldn't wait to work with them.

Bill Reid, a fellow Scot, and Jim Spence, an Englishman, were the teamsters responsible for the horse barn. Two boys were assigned with them daily, and the teamsters taught the boys in depth about working with the horses. Each day the boys had to groom, distribute feed, shovel manure, and change the bedding in the stalls. The teamsters were genuinely kind people. They took a sincere liking to one lad named E. Todd, who loved working with the horses. He eventually became a full-time fixture at the horse barn.

The horses worked hard, patient and never complaining. Most of the time, we also had a foal or two in the barn or romping around in the pastures. Two to four of the adult horses could be working on any given day. They went out pulling the plows in the fields and hauling in the hay as it was harvested. They were also called to pull carts or wagons full of vegetables wherever they were needed. This was still an age where horses were crucial for any farm.

Finally, we had the herd of cows, all of them purebred Ayrshires, a hardy breed distinguished by their mottled brown and white coats. They produce milk that is richer, creamier, and higher quality than the milk from the big black-and-white Holstein cows. These days, Holsteins are more popular because they produce more milk, and because many health-conscious people like the lower fat content.

Most of the herd came from Fintry Farm, a partner facility in the Okanagan Valley of British Columbia that had been donated to Fairbridge. It used to be that when Fairbridge boys turned fifteen, they would move to Fintry to continue their agricultural training there. However, the Fintry training program was discontinued in my time, so I never saw the place.

Despite how much I wanted to work with the horses; I was never assigned to the horse barn. However, I wasn't assigned to the chickens or pigs much either, thankfully. I seem to recall my mates Brian and Roy being assigned to the piggery, and they didn't mind it at all.

The dairy required much more attention than the horses did, and I frequently ended up working there. Of the 70 cows in the herd, 32 of them had to be milked daily. We also had to shovel manure out their stalls out and scrub them clean.

We went through several different herdsmen who were in charge of the dairy barn during my years. One of them, Neil, made a permanent impression on us for the one time he challenged Wallace, the bull in our herd.

It was the day Wallace was being stubborn and didn't want to go into his stall. He planted his feet in front of it and refused to budge no matter how much we pulled on the lead rope. Neil was a very muscular guy, and he appeared to relish this challenge. He had a wicked grin on his face. He didn't hesitate for a moment before grabbing Wallace by his horns and wrestling him into his stall. This took us all aback; we could only gawk at his bravado. Wallace must've been even more surprised because Neil won the fight, and Wallace had to settle into his stall for the night.

After Neil straightened his clothes, he told us sternly,

"Don't ever let me catch any of you attempting that."

I nodded and thought to myself, there was no chance I would even try. I had a healthy respect for that huge bull.

Still, there were days when a few of us would sit on the fence of Wallace's field and dare each other to jump inside the enclosure to see who could stay there the longest.

I really enjoyed working with the cows, though. They had very mellow temperaments. Most of them would stand calmly and eat their hay or chew their cud while we milked them.

The milking barn had two rows of stanchions facing the outside walls and a cement walkway down the middle. The stanchions were vertical metal bars that held a cow's head in place so it couldn't pull back or lie down while we milked them. Each cow had its own designated stanchion and in due time they knew where to go. We walked them to their spot and opened the stanchion. Once the cow's head was between the bars, we closed them back again and knew they were secure and reasonably comfortable.

A fresh layer of straw was laid on the bed of the cement floor under their hooves. When they dropped their poop, which often happened while we worked, we had to shovel it down into the wide gutter behind them and hose down their feet and the stall floor immediately afterward. We didn't exactly love shoveling and hosing down the stalls, but we were taught to keep things neat and spotless. The herdsman stressed cleanliness in the milking barn.

We used the Surge brand of milking machines. We attached one tube of the Surge to each of the cow's teats and drew much of the milk out mechanically. Then we took a pail and stripped the rest of it the old-fashioned way: by hand.

Sometimes, we practiced squirting the milk in other directions. The barnyard cat hung out nearby while we were milking. I made eye contact with her and aimed a squirt in her direction. She rose up on her haunches and caught the milk in her mouth. Then she came back down, licking her lips to get the last droplets off her whiskers.

Even more fun than that was hitting one of my pals across the aisle with a stream of milk. I aimed a teat at my target's head, which was focused on his work, and pumped. When I hit him squarely in the ear or the eye, I considered that a serious accomplishment, true marksmanship-level stuff.

Two boys were assigned to take the canisters full of fresh milk from the barn to the cooling shed while we milkers finished hosing down. They had to drive a good-sized wheeled cart downhill from the dairy to get there. It wasn't a terribly steep slope, but it was steep enough that if you weren't paying careful attention, you could easily lose control of the cart and it would drag you down that hill too fast.

One time one of the lads lost control and the two milk canisters went flying off the cart, spilling milk everywhere. I heard he got a severe tongue-lashing and a kick in the arse from the herdsman, and he never got assigned to work with the cows again for the rest of his trainee years. Poor bugger was likely assigned to the chickens.

As mentioned earlier, I didn't get to work with the horses, but I still liked to interact with them as much as I could. I loved to feed them carrot sticks or a lump of sugar from my outstretched palm. They would shake their heads in approval as their big eyes begged me for more.

I wanted nothing more than to climb up onto their backs and go riding around the grassy fields. Realistically, though, they were far too tall and large for a small lad like me to ride. I couldn't get one of my skinny little legs up high enough to mount them, even from the top of the fence.

In my teenage years, I still had a great and enduring passion for horses and the beautiful Elizabeth Taylor after seeing the film *National Velvet*, which had made such a big impact on me years before.

I had fallen in love with Liz and made a vow that when I grew up I would marry her and become a jockey. Mickey Rooney was far too short for her anyway. Of course, neither of those wishes materialized. Still, the dream of owning a horse had taken a firm root in my mind and it would stay with me for life. Years later I made sure that our son Iain took riding lessons when he was but a lad.

Of course, there was much more to the farm than caring of the animals, though they were my favorite. There was also a lot of mucking stalls and shoveling poop and carting it in the wheelbarrow to the manure pile.

We also had to spend many long, hot days in the fields with pitchforks, piling hay onto the wagons. Of all our assigned farm duties, the fieldwork was the hardest and most miserable. In the peak of summer days, the group of us would spend most of the day out in the fields with absolutely no shade, tempted by the sight of the tall shade-giving trees surrounding the fields. We could only quench our thirst with a sip from a big, old can full of warm barley water. Many times, we were stones throw away from a wonderful cool river, our swimming hole. That knowledge tormented us to no end.

We harvested the hay we grew throughout the summer and autumn months. We loaded large piles of it into the horse-drawn wagon. When we had piled as much hay as we could, we climbed onto the wagon ourselves. With all of us settled, one of the teamsters signaled the Clydesdales to go with a click with his tongue and a flick of the reins. The horses pulled us along the path and rode back to the large hay and feed barn.

When we arrived at the barn, the teamster reined the horses so the wagon came to a stop at the side of the barn underneath a large opening to the loft high above. Another team of boys was assigned to the loft above.

The lad that was manning the pulley rope lowered a big, four-pronged fork shaped like a grabbing claw down to us.

I scrambled over the top of the wagon and dug the four claws deep into the loose hay, so they could close around a large bunch of it. Then I signaled the rope lad to start pulling and lifting the hay.

Once the forkful of hay reached the top, it would connect to a steel rail with wheels. The rope lad would the let the rope go slack as the loaded fork travelled along the rail, until another boy called to him to release the load. With a solid tug on the release rope on the fork, the fork opened and the load of hay fell to the designated spot. The trick was timing the release so that the hay would fall exactly where we wanted it to fall. Then the loft crew would level the hay.

The first time I was assigned to the loft crew, I had no idea how the contraption worked, and the more experienced boys contrived to play a trick on me. They directed me to stand by the last stack and prepare for the next load to drop. Meanwhile, the rope lad lifted the load and pulled it across the rail. The other lad carefully watched its progress and then yelled, "And tug!"

The fork opened right on top of me. The next thing I knew, I was knocked off my feet and buried in hay. I got hay in my nose, my eyes, my mouth, and everywhere down my shirt. The other two laughed hysterically and then dug me out. I was mad but unhurt. The other two both laughed more as, I pulled hay off every inch of me in my hair, ears, etc.

Before too long, though, I was part on the team and became an old pro at directing the forks and dropping loads of hay exactly where I wanted them. And when another unsuspecting new trainee came along, I participated in the same prank with glee.

As I took so well to work with the cows, I decided to join the Calf Club later that year. It is similar to a modern-day Young Farmers' Club. We were given young calves as our own to raise and later show in the fair.

Neil, the herdsman, took us to a section of the barn where they had about six young heifers and told us to pick our calf. I spotted her immediately—a lovely calf that stood out from all the others. My hand shot up in the air, so I could secure her for myself before anyone else could. I told Neil that she was the one I wanted.

Neil gave me a calf-sized halter and told me to go ahead and get her. At first, she skittered around nervously a bit, but I gently stroked her head and throat and murmured soothingly to her. Her white and brown coat was as soft as a bunny's coat. She soon settled down and let me put the halter on.

I named her Bonnie. She was about three months old when I first met her and stood only a little taller than my waist. She was beautiful. She had a big white patch on her face between her big, lovely brown eyes and she had a soft black nose. It wasn't long before she would nuzzle my arm looking for attention.

We quickly developed a bond. I took extra time brushing her and feeding her. Sometimes she stretched out her head, nose pointing to the sky; I could stroke her soft, white throat.

As fair time approached, I couldn't wait to show everyone else how special Bonnie was, especially the judges. For me, she was the loveliest calf ever. Even her walk was graceful and elegant.

In the days leading up to the fair, I took extra time washing her with the garden hose, rubbing soap into her coat and then rinsing her down. She stood quietly for me while I groomed her. Once she was dry, I brushed her beautiful white and brown mottled coat until it was nice and lustrous. Finally, I took the long tuft of white hair at the end of her tail and combed it out and braided it and combed it out again until it was nice, soft, and wavy.

There were many other boys with calves during the fair day, but I knew they were no match for Bonnie. I led her into the judging ring with a confident smile. Bonnie walked beside me on the lead rope, turning a smooth and gentle circle with her head held up proudly and not setting a hoof out of place.

We got second place.

I couldn't believe it. Those 'frigging' judges had to be blind. The decision should have been obvious. I reassured Bonnie that she was the best calf out there, no matter what those judges thought. Next year, we would show them, I told her. I would enter her in more local contests, and soon we would see that coveted blue ribbon.

as fate would have it we never got the chance. Autumn passed, and winter closed in. The anticipated contests would start again in springtime. As the end of the year approached, Mr. Brown sold my beloved Bonnie, along with many other calves.

Though we had been warned in advance that it was coming, I was still devastated on the day when I came to the barn and she was gone. I must have bawled like a baby that day.

Bonnie was the first animal that I truly cared for, the first living thing that I had loved and then lost. It took me a long time to get over it. Having to go back to work in the cow barn, knowing Bonnie wasn't there anymore, and she would never nuzzle me again, was especially hard.

LATER YEARS
AND DUNCAN HIGH SCHOOL

In my later years in the school, life at Fairbridge began changing drastically. It was the beginning to be the end to the school. The shutdown had been coming in a while. New children stopped arriving from the U.K. in 1947. Some of the teachers, like Mimi, had observed signs of the school closure and left early for better prospects. In 1949, when I was around 15, the day school closed down completely. When that happened, they enrolled us in Duncan High School.

The rules loosened dramatically in Fairbridge by then. We could go to town on our own, and we could even wear long trousers, more commonly known as blue jeans, which we had never been allowed to do when I was young.

My living situation improved greatly by then. I was in Mrs. Bullcock's[9] cottage now, and she was a much kinder cottage mother than either Mrs. Green or Mrs. Bates. I really had no problem calling her "Mum" either, unlike the previous two women.

I think Mrs. Bullcock treated us much better because she was the mother of three boys. Two of the boys, Jeff and Fred, lived with us in the cottage. My feeling is that her being a mother made her more compassionate with children such as us.

I recall hanging out with John H. most of the time during

---

9   I use their family name, as Mr. and Mrs. Bullcock were kind and decent folks. In all my conversations with other Fairbridgians, I never came across one person who disagreed with that assessment.

that period. He arrived with one of the final groups of children in 1947 and was assigned to our cottage. We became fast friends.

As a late arrival, John was lucky enough to miss out on some of the school's worst years of management. However, the tradeoff was that his early years in Newcastle during the war had been much harder.

Most of the late arrivals had lived in Britain's large cities like London, Birmingham, and Newcastle, so they had lived through the worst of the WWII German air raids. Many of them lost family in the bombings and most, if not all, had grown up with the full terror of the nightly air raids. John was no exception. A few years back during a conversation, John reminisced about the details of the nightly bombings of Newcastle where he had lived. I was deeply moved. Whereas we, the party of 1941, had lived through three years of Nazi's bombings, John and his family had suffered five years.

On our first day of school in Duncan High, we must've been pretty excited to make the now-familiar trek out to town. We quickly made new friends in school with the area kids. A few times they even invited us to their homes. It was a natural gesture on their part, but for us it took a bit of adjustment. We had not really had much exposure to the typical warm environment of a family home and were unused to such invitations.

We also noticed how much more relaxed school discipline was at Duncan High than we were accustomed to in Fairbridge. After all those years of living under such a tight, restricted daily regimen at Fairbridge, my rebellious side had developed fully by the time I started at Duncan High. I don't believe I ever actually went so far as to cut class at Duncan High, but I did foolishly engage in far too many entertaining distractions during class. At the same time, I was careful not to 'Push the envelope,' too far. I knew full well that if I were suspended from school even once, it meant going straight to full-time farm work, and I had no desire to do that. Thankfully, it never came to that.

One really memorable teacher in the school remained in my good memories. That was Mr. Sprocchi, one of our English teachers. I enjoyed that subject more because of my love of books. He was physically short in stature and a bit rotund, with a dark complexion. He looked like his family came from one of the Mediterranean countries. Unlike so many of my teachers at Duncan, he had a cheerful and friendly disposition.

One morning in class we were discussing the subject of poetry. He asked students to read aloud a verse or two from a poem in our book. Being teenagers, none of us were too willing to volunteer except a couple of the girls. Most of the boys likely thought poetry were girly. I wasn't too keen on singling myself out for the task either. That was when, unexpectedly, Mr. Sprocchi turned to me and said, "Mr. Mackay, let's have you read a couple of verses from Robert Burns' poem, 'A Man's a Man for a' That.'"

I had to overcome my initial shock. For one thing, no adult had ever addressed me as "Mister." Secondly, there was no doubt on my mind that he picked me because of my Scottish accent. I was doubly honored because he was not only showing respect, but he was giving me recognition as a Scotsman. In Scotland, Burns is revered and recognized as the National Bard.

So, in spite of the slight embarrassment that came with having to stand up in front of my peers, with some trepidation I stood up and read two verses from the Burns poem. By the time I sat back down again, I felt a bit proud.

Maybe I read more into Mr. Sprocchi's request than he intended, but it made me feel really good at the time. After that moment, I was inspired to learn more about Robert Burns and his poetry. It was the beginning of my lifelong love for Burns' poetry, and it was all thanks to that moment in Mr. Sprocchi's class.

Over the years I have organized many Burns Suppers and I was also invited to be the "Master of Ceremonies" for private parties. In that role I would recite one of his many favourite poems, "The Address to the Haggis." This poem is challenging, best read with a genuine Scottish dialect, plus more interesting delivered with some theatrical skill. Whenever I recite works by my favourite poet, it still stirs feelings of passion. It is both strange yet wonderful how such a small incident created by a caring teacher can stay with a person throughout his life.

At Duncan High, I became good pals with two local teenagers, Dennis Campbell and Andy Barnes.

Dennis was one of the few guys at Duncan High who drove a car to school and his parents owned and also managed the original Cowichan Bay Inn. He was a bit on the wild side with his fast, cool car. He and I were both far more interested in flirting with the girls than doing schoolwork. With our similar personalities, we got along very well.

Later in life, I would compare hanging out and miss-adventures with Dennis very similar to the TV show *Happy Days* and hanging out with the 'Fonz.' In place of Arnold's Drive-In from the series, we frequented the Tzouhalem Café together.

My other pal from Duncan High, Andy, was a bit quieter than Dennis. Andy lived with his dad on a small farm out in the country, in the rural area near the neighboring town of Cobble Hill. His dad hauled milk from the local farms to a central distribution centre in his truck.

His dad was a fairly lenient man. On Saturday nights Andy would ask to borrow his truck, and he usually let him.

On a Saturday night, I would slip out of my cottage... yes, down the handy fire escape and he would come pick me up outside the Fairbridge gate. Other times I caught a Greyhound bus from Duncan that dropped me off at Cobble Hill and Andy picked me up there. We then proceeded to the Cobble Hill Community Hall Dance.

We were a couple of teenage kids, out to have fun and possibly 'raise a bit of hell. The dance hall crowd was a mix of loggers to farmhands with their girlfriends or wives. There was no alcohol allowed inside, so they left their beer or occasional liquor bottle in their trucks. They came back out for a drink while the band took a break. The couples were more interested in a necking session than their drinks; so one night, Andy and I decided we would swipe some beer while everyone was inside dancing.

We snuck into one of the pickups and grabbed a few bottles of beer and my hands closed around the brown glass. I had never touched a drop of alcohol before that night.

We took our loot and sat on the railroad tracks, well out of sight of anyone attending the dance. After a bit of drinking, I felt my cheeks going a bit numb. It was not very cold, so it seemed a bit weird to me.

By that point, Andy and I could not stop laughing. Everything was funny to us. I told him my cheeks felt numb and asked, "Is that what beer does to you?"

The next thing I knew we are both giggling and rolling down the side of the railroad bank. Thank God there were no trains running at that time of the night.

At some point, we heard the logger whose beer we'd swiped cursing, "Which son of a bitch stole my beer?"

Andy and I had to clap our hands over our noses and mouths to muffle our hoots of laughter.

The rest of the evening was a blur. I vaguely remember a long hike back to the school, because Andy was not in any shape to drive.

The next morning I had my first awful experience of the morning-after hangover. I was one very sick teenager. Mrs. Bullcock asked me why I was throwing up; I told her that it must have been something I ate.

I hate to venture how many times that whopper of an excuse has been used in my lifetime.

By the time I had reached the age of 15, I was past my phase of falling in puppy-love with a few girls at Fairbridge, namely

Mary and Evelyn. The first girl I fell really hard for with my whole heart was not a Fairbridge girl. She was a country-girl, her name was Carolyn, and she lived in Cobble Hill, the next town south beyond Duncan. She was the only child of a retired British Army Major. She and her widowed father lived out in the country in a very nice house perched on a few acres of land with a small barn that stabled a couple of riding horses.

Carolyn was a very attractive girl, particularly when she wore her riding jodhpurs. They made her look especially refined. In my eyes, she was every bit as beautiful as Elizabeth Taylor in *National Velvet*. I was completely smitten.

On the other hand, I felt that she was too far above my social level. She was the daughter of a decorated British army major; I was the lowly guttersnipe from the farm school. It did not stop me from trying to court her and spend as much time as I could with her.

Her father was polite to me when I interacted with the two of them, but acted very cool and reserved. I got the distinct impression that he didn't appreciate his daughter spending time with one of those Fairbridge outcasts.

The romance was brief, only lasting four months, and mostly one-sided. In retrospect, I think it was possible that Carolyn was spending time with me as a small act of defiance against her father during her rebellious years. Alternatively, maybe she was just curious about what a lad from the other side of the tracks was like.

I probably should've have seen the end coming, but still,

the day she broke up with me cut me to the core. I thought, "Here is the greatest girl I could ever find, and I've just lost her." I felt broken and hollow inside. On the way back to Fairbridge, I trudged down the old Koksilah Road singing Hank Williams' "Lovesick Blues."

That song became my nightly lament for many days to follow. But I would soon have something else to look forward to during the summers.

ARMY CADET CAMP VERNON

A few years before, my Scottish blood stirred when I saw a man in the full kilt uniform of the Canadian Scottish Regiment (CSR) arriving up the road to Fairbridge.

This had been my initial glimpse of Major Plows, the man who was replacing Mr. Garnet as our headmaster. Mr. Garnet had succeeded the kindly Prof. Logan, whom I had admired when I first came. Major Plows immediately impressed me in a big way.

He walked with a pronounced limp, but he was undeniably handsome and looked quite impressive in that uniform. He wore it like it was part of him.

In looks, he resembled the actor David Niven, who played the role of a Scottish officer in one of those war movies.

Later on, I learnt how he got that limp. He had taken over battlefield command of the Can Scots Regiment during the D-Day Normandy invasion, and he got wounded in the hip during the Normandy battle. When I read about his bravery, he immediately became my hero.

I made a promise to myself that if the opportunity ever came, I would join the Regiment and wear that kilt.

In the summer of 1948 when I was 14, the Army Cadet Camps gave me an opportunity to fulfil that oath. I took it excitedly.

Each summer the Fairbridge Cadet Corps attended a six-week Army Cadet Camp where we lived and trained much like real soldiers. Regular Canadian Army officers and noncommissioned officers (NCOs) organized and ran the camp. Around 1,000 to 1,500 teenage boys from Cadet Corps all over, British Columbia and Alberta attended these camps.

We were billeted in barracks, and our days began with breakfast in an army mess hall. We had to form straight lines in front of the mess hall and march inside in an orderly fashion, and then queue up with a tray to pick up our meal. After breakfast, our days consisted largely of various marching drills.

Many of the other boys thought life in the camps was too strict, but the Fairbridge boys were used to order and discipline. We didn't see much of a difference from how we normally lived. There was one major exception: the food was a hell of a lot better.

The first camp I attended was located in Chilliwack. It was a great adventure! Our first stop upon arrival was the quartermaster's store where we were issued our uniforms: khaki shorts, shirts, pith helmets, and so on. I learnt then that the military system tends to issue a soldier the wrong sized uniforms. It was no different in the regular army.

As we left the mess hall after a very satisfying breakfast to tackle the rest of the day, most of us still had improperly fitting uniforms. We were in for our first taste of the military manner of the NCOs running the camp. On parade, one former British Sergeant Major bellowed at us, "You are a miserable lot, I can't tell whether you are wearing long shorts or short longs!"

We were all a bit embarrassed, but nobody dared to speak out. He continued, "By tomorrow's muster parade, sort out your uniforms, or I will sort the bloody lot of you out!"

That night at our barracks we began trading. The tall kids exchanged their short shorts with the short guys for their long shorts. It worked out for those of us who had the wits to find someone to trade sizes to fit. The ones who failed to find their size did several laps around that old parade square, "At the double!"

We learnt quickly that this command meant you had to run your butt off.

With uniform sizes figured out, we had our next challenge: handling a rifle.

The leaders took us out on the rifle range for firing instruction. There they issued us the regular 202 British Enfield rifles.

I tested the weight and feel of the rifle into my hand for a moment. I wasn't sure how to grip it properly yet, but I settled down and pointed it at the target and took my first shot. The vicious kickback I got really shook me up. I was convinced my entire right shoulder had been shattered. I took my cap off my head and stuffed it between the rifle butt and my shoulder to make a cushion for my next shot.

That was a useless move; the recoil kicked me hard again. And it cost me 50 pushups when the range instructor saw me.

I could suffer the pushups but not his wisecrack: "Only pansies need a pad for their shoulder, soldier! Pull that rifle-butt into the shoulder next time!"

I learnt how to do it right eventually.

I enjoyed the marching drills on the parade square best. Fairbridge boys mastered most of the drills from our cadet training at Fairbridge.

Many of the NCOs instructing us were former British

Army types. They shouted colourful commands like, "You, you 'orrible little man, stand still! Stop picking your private parts! More of that and you will double around the parade square until your balls drop off. Then you will be left with nothing to scratch; do you 'ear me?"

Quite often they had us holding a rifle above our heads and shouting gems like, "This is my rifle, below is my gun; one is for fighting; the other is for fun."

One of the corporals Corky delivered nonstop commands laced with barrack room obscenities. He was hilarious but God help you if you so much as snickered at his humorous remarks. I caught on quickly, but I could not guess how many times I had to bite my damned tongue hard to prevent myself from cracking up.

Besides the drills, we also took classes in the various military trades like medical, driver, mechanical, electrical, sharpshooting, and signaling. We had to select our trade. Since I had been interested in first aid as a member of the Boy Scouts and later took courses to learn first aid from the humanitarian organization St. John's Ambulance, I naturally chose the medical corps classes.

Interestingly enough, I discovered years later that my father in WWII, and my grandfather in WWI had both served in both the Royal Army Medical Corps (Regular) and the Cameron Highlanders (Reserves). Perhaps it was something in the Mackay genes.

Each Cadet Corps attending camp had its own regimental title, such as the Irish Fusiliers, Calgary Highlanders, Winnipeg Rifles, Seaforth Highlanders, and the Canadian Scottish. We were simply known as the Fairbridge Cadet

Corps, but we were also part of the Canadian Scottish Regiment.

I was startled to find that the Canadian Scottish regiment from Victoria wore the full kilt uniform—the same one Major Plows wore. We had white shell mess jackets, regimental kilts with the Hunting Stewart Tartan pattern; leather pouches called sporrans hanging from their belts[10], and traditional diced wedge caps known as Glengarries[11]. Additionally, the band wore high feather bonnets, kilts, horse hair sporrans and scarlet doublet jackets.

They looked incredible. I was a man possessed. Their uniforms made our dull khaki ensembles appear worse than drab. It made me think, "Here I am in an army camp, surrounded by all these kids wearing "my uniform," and not a single native-born Scot among them." Ah well, we will sort that out or my name is not Mackay. That made me more determined than ever to lay my hands on one of those uniforms. I made myself a promise that before the summer was over, I would be wearing a "Canadian Scottish Regiment," (CSR) uniform as well.

I naturally gravitated toward those guys. It turned out that they were quite approachable. Around the second week of camp, I started hanging out with Alan Richardson, better known to us as "Sedge." He was a sergeant in the Victoria Canadian Scottish Regiment and had a great sense of humor. Like many of the Victoria guys, Sedge knew about

---

10   A sporran is sometimes decorated with fur or horse hair. It takes the place of pockets in regular trousers.
11   Often decorated with rosette cockade on the side, ribbons hanging down the back, and a checkered pattern around the rim.

the Fairbridge School. He had been on his Oak Bay School's football team and had played against our team, so he knew firsthand that we were tough players but good sports. He respected me for that. We started forging a friendship.

Around the same time, I had discovered something else that spoke to my heritage: the sound of bagpipes being played on the parade grounds. I had never heard the instruments played before, but as soon as I did, I was hooked. I immediately began hanging around the pipe band whenever possible, just like a lost puppy begging to be let in.

At the first chance I got, I signed up for the pipe band course and started learning to play the side drum hoping to eventually be promoted to drum major. Since I was already a drum major in the Fairbridge drums and bugle band, I had little trouble switching to the marching style of pipe bands. To earn that rank in the Scottish Regiments, you had to master the skills of playing the snare, tenor, and bass drums by taking the drumming classes and then earning a certificate. In those days, military-style drumming was basic, nowhere near as intricate as it has evolved in the pipe bands of today. I enjoyed the instrument, but my real intent was to become a pipe band member, so they would accept me in the regiment and issue me a kilt and the full uniform of a CSR cadet.

Despite my efforts, as brilliant as they may have been, they still did not earn me the coveted uniform of the Scots that year; but at least I had laid out the groundwork.

In addition to my work with the pipe bands, Sedge and I became great friends by the end of the summer. Since I was Scottish and still had my Scots accent, he and the other CSR guys nicknamed me "Scotty." It was one nickname I wore proudly.

During our off-duty hours, we hung out at the Chilliwack Roller Skating Arena where I learnt how to roller-skate. This paid off for me twofold, with the fun of skating and the opportunity to meet girls while doing so.

I found it very tough to say good-bye to Sedge and my new buddies when our six-week stay at Chilliwack ended, and we had to get on that train to begin the journey back to the misery school.

I didn't want to go back to Fairbridge at all. Every day at Chilliwack was an adventure. I had grown to respect the drill instructors, and I had made a wonderful group of friends.

I do not know how I made it through that winter and the spring of the following year, anxiously waiting for the summer and the beginning of the next Cadet Camp.

The next year, though, we did not go back to Chilliwack. The site moved to Camp Vernon, which proved to be a much better location. The army camp was situated in the sunny Okanagan Valley by the town of Vernon. The beautiful Lake Kalamalka[12] was close to the camp, and we spent many of our off-duty hours swimming there. I loved diving into the water there, just like I loved visiting the river back at Fairbridge.

The stark contrast between the Fairbridgians and the Canadian kids was once again revealed the very first day we set foot in the Camp Vernon mess hall for breakfast. We marched inside in typical army fashion and lined up to get our trays. The delicious aroma of bacon and eggs sizzling on

---

12   "Kalamalka" is a Native American name meaning "Lake of Many Colors."

the grill was almost overpowering. This was something I'd sorely missed.

The cooks were laying out fried eggs, scrambled eggs, hot cakes, and bacon in big serving pans down the line. There was also chilled orange juice, corn flakes, and buttered toast to grab. My mouth was watering and everyone else was just as eager as I was to get their hands on this feast. My mates were all pressing forward in line, some of them actually pushing the guys in front of them to get closer to the food.

We were behind the Canadian kids, who dragged their feet a little. As we were getting closer, one of the Canadians complained to one of the servers about his eggs being too soft, holding up the rest of the line. One of our Fairbridgian lads was standing two places behind him, close enough to smell the steaming food, and this were just too much for him. He barked at the guy, "Damn it, if you don't like what they are serving, get the hell out of the line and let us eat; we are starving!"

The poor guy had no idea that he was dealing with a group of kids who had not been served a breakfast of bacon, eggs, pancakes, buttered toast, and fresh orange juice in recent memory, nor much at all in their whole lives. At Fairbridge, we lived off a bowl of porridge (or as we called it, "mush"), bread, jam, and milk, for breakfast seven days a week. This guy took one look at the angry faces lined up behind him, dropped his tray, and double-timed out of the mess hall faster than a cat running from water.

I saw him later that day and apologized on our behalf, explaining the situation. We shook hands, and all was forgiven. A few days later, he was chumming around with one of our chaps.

My pal 'Sedge,' came to visit me in my barracks shortly after we arrived. He dropped a kit bag on my bunk bed and said, "Scotty, here is your new uniform."

I unfolded it and sure enough; it was my coveted kilt uniform.

I was practically speechless with awe. I had no idea how he managed to get hold of an extra kilt and complete CSR uniform kit. And one that was pretty much the right size for me, but I was so excited that I didn't question him. I just wanted to get into that uniform right at that very moment.

At that time, I had been promoted to Cadet Lieutenant in the Fairbridge Corps, but the CSR did not have officer ranks in their cadet corps. If I accepted the uniform and transferred to their ranks, I would have to give up my officer position. That didn't give me pause for even a second. I had no ego problem. Fulfilling this dream was far more meaningful than any rank.

Some of my schoolmates in the barracks ragged me a bit about it, but in the end, nobody made any big deal over it.

The next day, with some help from Sedge, I put my new uniform on. I wanted to make sure that I was wearing it correctly and would not embarrass myself on parade. I was practically buzzing with excitement to finally have my own CSR uniform. When I looked at myself in the mirror, my Scots blood stirred with pride. I was sure this would be the best summer ever.

After breakfast each day, we reported to the area in front

of our barracks and formed ranks.

I reported to my new regiment dutifully, uniform perfectly straightened. I fell in at the very back of the rear rank, hoping to appear less conspicuous and avoid confrontation with the NCO.

The NCO in command that day was CSR Company Sgt. Major Jim Colville, nicknamed "Digger." After commanding us to fall in, he began taking roll call. He was about half way through the roll call when his eye lit on me. He marched right up to within inches of me and snarled, "Who the hell are you? You are not Scottish."

I knew he had caught me red-handed, but I puffed up my chest and replied, "Sir; I am Scottish. I was born in Edinburgh, Scotland."

My cheeky answer certainly did not help my cause; it only pissed him off more. He ordered me to break off, return to barracks, and then remove and turn in the uniform immediately.

I had suffered many disappointments in my early life, but none of them were as painful as the experience of turning in my kilt that day.

Once again, I signed up to continue the military music courses for piping and drumming. We held our band practice later that day. One of the Seaforth regiment members in the band noticed my long, sad face and asked what the matter was. I told him that I had been stripped of my prized kilt and uniform by Sgt. Major Digger.

'As luck would have it,' he told me that one of their guys was going home, and I was about the same size. I could have his Seaforth kilt uniform if I wanted it.

I didn't hesitate. I told him yes, I would be happy and proud to wear it. It was not the same as the Can Scots kilt—it had a different tartan pattern on the kilt and different insignia—but it was a kilted uniform nonetheless.

The three of us got together for a meeting. The guy going home didn't mind loaning me his uniform for the summer, on the condition that his mate would bring it home to him when the camp was over.

That sounded more than reasonable to me. I thanked him and happy as a lark, I grabbed the uniform and returned to my barracks to change uniforms again.

I was whistling all the way over to Sedge's barracks. I shared the good news and showed off my new uniform. I assured him I would far sooner be wearing the CSR kit, but beggars can't be choosers. He laughed, saying, "Scotty; you are some character. The Scots should be proud of you."

Later that day I was walking across the empty parade square, still in my new Seaforth kilt, when out of nowhere I heard a voice screaming at me: "HALT!"

I recognized the voice immediately. Digger. I knew in that moment it was imperative to obey his order.

I braced myself mentally as he came over. Somehow, I had just known I was going to have another run-in with him before long. However, I resolved to be better prepared—both mentally and verbally—this time.

He was in my face in an instant. "Mackay, what the hell are you doing wearing that fucking kilt?"

I planted my feet firmly and responded to C.S. Major

Colville, "Excuse me, but you are aware that it is customary for other ranks and NCOs to salute officers?"

This had him practically purple in the face. Before he could open his mouth, I pointed to the lieutenant pips on my shirt, freshly reinstated. Furthermore, I told him, since he had not seen fit to allow me to wear the kilt of the CSR, the Seaforth Regiment had invited me to be an honorary member.

So there I was, standing my ground, face-to-face with a guy, who was a senior ranker in the regiment? I didn't think pulling rank of an officer in mu Fairbridge Corp. was really going to save my skin. Surely he would call my bluff.

Then the unexpected happened: he broke out in laughter and said, "You are one hell of an imposter. Look, if you really must wear a kilt, return that rag of a Seaforth kilt and meet me at my barracks. I will reissue the CSR kilt. However, only on the condition you remove those bloody lieutenant pips!"

"My pleasure, Sgt. Major," I said.

Fifty years later, Digger and I met again at a CSR reunion in Victoria. After all those years it was surprising that we still recognized each other, he knew who I was.

"Hell, if it isn't Scotty Mackay, the great imposter," he said as he approached me.

He won my eternal gratitude and friendship that evening when he made a motion to have me installed as an official member of the "Old Guard of the 263rd Canadian Scottish Cadet Corps.

I could not be prouder wearing my kilt every day at camp and be part of the Can Scots regiment. The guys accepted me as one of their own.

The Canadian kids had gotten used to us Fairbridge kids, too. By now, word had gotten out that we didn't have much in the way of pocket money, so they quite willingly shared their candies and pop with us. They were also a bit amused by our variety of British accents.

When our day's training was over, I would get together with Sedge and some other guys like Tommy Ward or Joe Pullen and we would leave camp to pursue the young beauties of Vernon. We had to get a special pass to leave camp each day. It allowed us to stay out no later than 2000 hours (10:00 pm) on weekdays or 2100 hours (11:00 pm) on weekends. I had never experienced such freedom as this, and I was only sixteen years old.

When we went out, we always wore our CSR uniform kilts because the girls were really attracted to them. Quite often, we took the girls to the lake for an afternoon swim. The ladies were always curious to know what we wore under our kilts. We had a good laugh at the surprised looks on girls faces on the beach when we responded by unbuckling our belts and dropping our kilts on the sand and revealing we wearing swim trunks, ready to go.

The old tradition of the Scottish Regiments was that *nothing* is to be worn under the kilt. It was taken seriously by all ranks. We only made an exception for that one swim trunk joke on the beach. A standard answer we gave to those rudely inquiring as to what we wear under the kilt was: "Nothing, everything is in fine working order, thank you very much."

I picked up another stock answer for pretty girls: "Are your hands warm, darlin'?"

They all had a good giggle at that one.

It did not take more than a few days before Sedge, Joe, and I had regular dates with three of the Vernon girls. I first saw the girl I fell for at the roller skating rink. She was so graceful gliding across the wood floor, and very cute too. I knew I had to meet her.

Her name was Doreen, and she became my very first "steady" girlfriend. I entered a new world, one filled with the thrills of romantic evenings and weekend dates with a real, genuine girlfriend.

My pal Sedge's girl had parents who owned one of the local motels. Both she and Doreen worked at a soda fountain, so we got free sodas when the boss was out.

That summer of 1950 was truly one of the best summers in my young life. The girls' parents were really nice to us and invited us into their homes. The girls arranged house parties, and we arranged swimming trips to the lake.

One day after being out with the girls on the Kalamalka, we all ended up having a meal of hot dogs at Doreen's house. Then we sat around the dining room table playing cards. I got up from the table to get a soda pop. When I came back, one of my jokester pals pulled my chair out as I was just about to sit down.

I fell over backwards and ended up on the floor flat on my back with my kilt in my face. Yes my "manhood," for what it was at that age, was totally exposed to everyone seated around the table. I quickly pulled myself up, extremely embarrassed, and strode out of the house burning in anger.

It took some time for the others to talk me into returning inside. One of the girls, in an attempt to soften my bruised feelings, quite innocently assured me, "Scotty, we didn't see a thing."

I put on a look of humiliation, and I replied, "Pat, then you are in bad need of spectacles." This of course cracked everybody up. The tension eased, and the night was saved.

Like most of our evenings, it ended with soft music, dimmed lights, and couples necking as if the evening would never end. Nat King Cole frequently provided the soundtrack, as he did for many young lovers in the 50s.

On one weekend when I had a date with Doreen, her parents let her borrow the family car. Doreen asked me if it was OK if one of her girlfriends came along and I told her one of my mates was also coming sot hat would not be a problem. I invited my friend Glen, who was also a member of the CSR and a fun kind of chap. Doreen picked us up at the main gate and introduced her friend Patsy to Glen. I could tell that they both took an instant liking to each other. This was going to be a good evening.

We went into a drive-in movie and saw *Little Women*, starring Peter Lawford, June Allyson, and my heartthrob, Elizabeth Taylor. It was one of those romantic films, so it did not take long before both of us couples were necking amorously in the car. Glancing around at the steamed up car windows surrounding us, it seemed most everybody else in the drive-in had the same idea.

After the movie, we went back to Doreen's house. Her parents had gone to bed so we played cards in the living room and enjoyed some of the slow, romantic music of that era. Then some wise individual turned off the main lights, and we were soon back to 'necking and nuzzling.'

As it often happens with young lovers, we completely lost track of time. Suddenly, Glen and I realized that we had less than 20 minutes to make it back to camp. If you violated the official posted time on your pass, you would be confined to barracks, possibly for the duration of the camp. There was no way we could stand to spend the rest of the summer stuck there or much worst be sent home..

Glen and I blew kisses to our girls, grabbed our Glengarries, and 'hit the road" back to camp racing like Olympic runners.

At some point, we realized we would arrive too late if we continued along the main road. Then we would be facing a very unpleasant visit with the camp commandant.

However, we knew a shortcut: a path going through a cabbage field that extended right up to the perimeter of the camp. We made a strategic decision and took the path through the cabbage patch even though it entailed scaling the seven-foot barbed-wire fence surrounding the camp.

Once we altered our route, we figured we didn't need to continue racing. All of sudden Glen was overcome by the need to relieve himself. He called out, "Hey, Scotty, do you have any paper?" In the darkness in the night, all I could see was a shadow of him squatting.

"Negative," I replied, "but here, try this out." I pulled a head of cabbage out of the soil and threw it at him. Glen clearly did not appreciate my sense of humor when he ducked my missile and fell over among the cabbage heads.

As he got up, I saw that he was most aggravated and ready to get even with me, so I took off toward that fence.

Somehow I scaled the fence and skirted the barbed wire, but then my sporran belt got hooked on to the top strand. Luckily, I could shake it loose or Glen would definitely have caught me, or much worse; the military police would have hauled both of us to the guardhouse.

We both made it back to our barracks safely with Glen's cursing, "Scotty I will deal with you in the morning." Being good friends, we managed to laugh it off the next day. Of course, I told him the episode would remain confidential with us.

While most of our activities at the camp were a mixture of hard but satisfying work and fun, I learnt there was also some viciousness that went around.

One of the nastiest tricks pulled by some kids with a morbid sense of humor was known as the "black ball" prank. A group of boys—usually the older, bigger, bully types—ganged up on a victim from a different regiment, so he wouldn't be able to identify his attackers. As most of these cowardly deeds go, they would spring an attack on their victim when it was dark, and he was alone and most vulnerable. Once they had him down, they would pull the terrified kid's trousers down and smear his testicles with shoe polish.

This sort of prank rarely happened, but when it did, details of the ugly episode spread all over camp. One time at Camp Vernon, one of our own CSR cadets was attacked like this.

Because he was one of the younger and smaller boys in our regiment, it struck us as especially dastardly. He barely saw his attackers and didn't recognise them. He only knew that they were members of the Irish Fusiliers. His testimony motivated a group of the Can Scots to concoct a plan and take revenge against the Irish.

Our scheme would not inflict any physical pain on them, but it would definitely send a clear message to our Irish cousins to lay off our cadets. A couple of hours after the "lights out" by bugle call, we gathered a small contingent of senior cadets who volunteered for this mission. From our barracks they surreptitiously made their way to the barrack that we knew housed several of the sleeping Irish cadets. In the semi-darkness, outlined by the distant light of outside lamps, they prowled to their target, carrying two sets of scissors.

See, our quarry was not the cadet themselves but their hats: the army berets. The Irish Fusiliers had a green-feathered cockade attached to their berets and always wore them proudly.

The Can Scots carried out their mission successfully and made it back to their barracks undetected. The next morning, several of the Irish lads donned their berets and, much to their horror, discovered someone had cut their beautiful green cockades right off.

When the truth came out as to why this happened, the Irish took matters into their own hands and beat the shit out of the guilty cadets who performed the lowly black ball prank in the first place.

When I found out, I grinned to myself and repeated one of my favourite proverbs: "What goes around comes around."

Those crazy, mostly funny episodes that happened over three summers at the Camp Vernon army summer camps remain amongst my fondest memories. I remember being truly happy there.

I was writing letters to my father from time-to-time, still trying to earn his acknowledgement, possible some small praise, by writing him about my achievements. During those later years at Fairbridge when I was attending Duncan High School, I would have really been stretching the truth if I had listed any decent reports of school grades, so I didn't mention school at all. Instead, I wrote in detail about all my accomplishments in the Boy Scouts and army cadets and boxing. I really did feel quite proud of them, more proud than I had felt about any of my few previous accomplishments.

In more recent years, a former Vernon Army Cadet wrote a book titled *Stand by Your Bunks*. It was a bestseller among those of us who attended the camps, which was several thousand boys. It is still running and quite a strong programme. The book was a work of fiction with fictitious characters, but the events were based on the author's experiences of attending the cadet camps.

He had attended the camps in the 1970s, some 20 years after I did. I read the book avidly and discovered that he was writing about many of the same-old traditions that had been part of camp in my time. Many of our traditions very likely stretched as far back as WWI.

What surprised me most, though, was reading about how they still performed our infamous Sporran Parade. We organized the very first one in 1949, reading about that all these years later brought me back to those wonderful years of my youth. All the Scottish regiments got together for the Sporran Parade. Any participants daring and crazy enough to participate had to wear a very specific uniform: basically a Glengarry, a sporran, socks, boots, and absolutely nothing else. No kilt indeed, and no jock short either.

We had plenty of volunteers to march in the parade and a small contingent of pipers and drummers willing to lead it. A specific date and time were selected in advance, and that information did not leave the group. Secrecy was essential. If any of our regular army staff instructors caught us, we would be on the next train out of Vernon homeward bound.

When the appointed day came, we lined up in ranks following our regular drill procedures in our 'Sporran Parade,' uniform.

We picked an isolated area around the camp for the parade route, so we would not run into staff members. A handful of our guys who knew about the parade but were too chicken to participate came to watch.

Our pipers and drummers led the parade playing "Scotland the Brave." When they took a break from their pipes and drums, the marchers filled in with a rendition of our stirring regimental marching song, "Glenwhorple."

Thus the first March was named "The Glenwhorple

Sporran Parade."

To this day, over seventy years later, I can still sing most of that song from memory. I have sung it many times over the years when the pipes were playing and the whiskey was flowing.

In my last Sporran Parade, a carload of American tourists spotted us from the road running alongside the border of the army camp. They must've been quite surprised indeed to see a bunch of nearly naked teenage Canadian Scottish cadets marching quite proudly to the tunes of "Bonnie Dundee." It's possible that somewhere in America there still exists a photo or two of us marching proudly in the Sporran Parade.

During a recent visit in the early 2000 to the Can Scots Regiment Armouries in Victoria, I was talking with a young soldier at the Men's Canteen who wanted to know what it was like in the regiment 60 years ago. He also asked about my service during the Korean War. I told him, war stories were not my bag, but I did dig out tales of Army Cadet Camp Vernon, our Sporran Parade and our regimental marching songs. Of course, he begged me to sing a few lines.

Within a matter of minutes, we had the whole canteen of young soldiers gathered around listening to my rendition of our infamous "Glenwhorple." They genuinely enjoyed listening to those old regimental songs, so I bought them all a round of beer.

It saddened me to realise that the marching songs that we sang back in the 50s hadn't been passed down to the new generation. At the request of several CSR Reservists who were present, I did send them the words of "Glenwhorple," so hopefully it will see a revival.

At the end of those magic summer days at army camp 1951, it was tough to leave and say good-bye to my CSR pals, particularly Sedge. The hardest emotional part was leaving Doreen, absolutely heart wrenching. We were two teenagers madly in love we had dated daily during the two summers, then written love letters with great regularity during the winter months. We vowed to write to each other and stay in touch. And we did her letters would be filled with words of romantic passion and fond endearment, and I responded in like fashion. As I opened them, I could catch a faint whiff of her perfume on the paper. Thoughts of her and memories our dates on the beach of Lake Kalamaka kept me warm even during the coldest months in Korea.

Those of us that had been in the Vernon army cadet group promised we would keep in touch, but we drifted apart and followed our separate, branching paths through life.

I wrote Doreen faithfully for a couple of years, but when I signed up to the regular army, both time and distance diminished our beautiful teenage relationship. Our flow of letters was reduced to a slow trickle, and then they ceased entirely. We both moved on. I heard years later that Doreen married a member of the RCMP.

For years, I was unable to reconnect with my pal Sedge until a Can Scot Reunion in 1997, and thank God, our youthful friendship passed the test of time. We were able to reconnect immediately as though we'd only been apart a year or two, not close to five decades. We remain good friends to this day. He married a wonderful lady named Lorna and I visit with them on practically every trip I take to Canada. He is still just as funny as he used to be. He often did a spot-on impersonation of Prince Charles and Sedge happens to be a look-alike for the Prince too.

I can quite honestly tell you the summers of 1950 and 1951 were two of the happiest summers of my life. For the first time ever, I took orders from those in command without resentment. New relationships, particularly with girls, helped bring me out of my low self-esteem. With my improved sense of confidence, I was ready to new take strides into an uncertain future.

FINAL DAYS AT FAIRBRIDGE

Sometime during my final months of Fairbridge in 1951, a few of us signed and joined up with the Canadian Reserve Army. We trained one night a week regularly and on several weekends they trucked us up to a Reserve army base in Parksville to do intensive drills and mock battle schemes. On one of those weekends, we had been training in the field for hours and I lucked out and got to ride back to camp in a Jeep with one of our officers. The rest of the platoon got stuck riding in the cramped bed of a truck, enduring every bump and pothole along the way. Meanwhile, the officer and I struck up a conversation about my time at Camp Vernon. When we arrived back at the barracks, he invited me to join him the Officers' Mess.

It was practically unheard of for one of us "other ranks" to be allowed into the Officers' Mess. I don't think anybody else was in there. I couldn't believe he had invited me and was a bit taken aback, but mostly I was honored. Naturally, I accepted.

I was a bit nervous as I walked in and past the tables packed with ranking officers.

The officer led me to his table, and as we began dinner he invited me to sing some of the Canadian Scots Regimental marching songs I'd learned at Camp Vernon and that I'd told him about.

I wish I could've prepared better for this. But if this had earned me a privileged spot in Officers' Mess, I'd better start singing.

I went right into the old "Glenwhorple" from our infamous parade.

The officers nodded their heads and tapped the toes of their boots along as I sang. They were in a good mood. When I finished they encouraged me to do more. One of them passed me the Scotch whiskey, a type of liquor that I'd heard much about but had never tasted before. On the first sip, the fiery liquid burned my throat on the way down, and it was all I could do to swallow it. However, as many a young idiot has done before and will do again, I clenched my throat to keep it down and struggled to keep a manly expression.

The rest of the evening was a blur. I sang a number of other songs. As I went on, they probably got increasingly bawdy.

The next day, I was one hell of a sick 17-year-old soldier.

By September 1951, the school was in the process of shutting down completely. Most of the staff members were already gone. The last remaining kids were in the process of being placed in area foster homes or in jobs in the farming community. Major Plows was still in charge of Fairbridge, although he was now the aftercare agent rather than the headmaster. He had the task of overseeing the whole process. I have trouble trying to recollect where and when the girls were sent. I am now convinced that our Fairbridge girls faced a far more difficult future than the boys did upon leaving Fairbridge. They had fewer options than the boys. Fairbridge left most of the girls under-educated without any marketable skills save for domestic work. However, this was not unusual given the time; in the 40s, women were still treated as second-class citizens and had very few career options.

I learned much later the few girls who remained at the school were placed into positions as domestic maids for the upper-class in Victoria or Vancouver, just as most of the girls who came before them had. It struck me as a terribly dead-end occupation. The lucky ones became housewives in decent, stable marriages; the unlucky ones found themselves in poor or abusive partnerships, which only brought them misery.

I cannot help but wonder how many Fairbridge girls became pregnant out of wedlock and were forced to give up their babies. The ones who kept their babies faced severe social stigma.

Later, I discovered an unbelievable example of the callous and cruel way Fairbridge dealt with our defenseless young girls.

The following story, "Betty's Bible" by Pat Skidmore, is from the Spring 2006 edition of the *Fairbridge Gazette*.

In early September 1938, Betty P was sent out to Fairbridge with a party of 16 children in the ship Duchess of Atholl. *As was the custom, Betty, like all the child migrants sent to Fairbridge, was given a small bible.*

Betty's time at Fairbridge was not an easy one, still in her teens she was placed for employment as a housemaid in a home in Victoria. In 1946, she became pregnant; her family in England heard of her plight and offered to have her and the baby sent home. However, this was not to be, and Betty's baby girl was born in Victoria and given up for adoption. Betty, quite distraught with losing her baby, was sent to Essondale, an institution for people suffering from mental illness. On her release Fairbridge had her deported back to England. Sometime after her return she became pregnant again; this baby girl was also taken away and put up for adoption.

Betty's two daughters grew up in homes halfway around the world from each other, unaware of each other's existence until they were well into their adult years. Neither sister ever met their birth mother. Typical of so many children born under such circumstances, as they got older began to question who their birth mother was and why they were given up for adoption. Their search led them to each other, and together they began to unravel the pieces in the puzzle.

They discovered their mother Betty had eventually married, had two other children but sadly had died sometime in the 1960s. Their search also uncovered the facts of their mother being sent to Fairbridge at an early age as a child migrant. One of the sisters, Patricia P, contacted the editor of our Fairbridge Alumni News Letter, Pat Skidmore, who did some research with hopes of providing the sisters with whatever information she could find in our archives—photos, etc.—of their mother, Betty. 'As luck would have it,' Pat discovered Betty P's small bible among many in the display in the foyer of our Fairbridge chapel. Pat notified Patricia of finding the bible, and the response was: "I cannot believe you have something of mum's that she held in her hands, no words can say how I feel."

Of course, we have no idea how many other single teen-aged Fairbridge girls who became pregnant were treated in a similar manner. According to a report made by the BC child welfare department in 1944, teenaged pregnancies happened to a disproportionate number of Fairbridge girls who were placed to work in the upper-class homes of Victoria.

John and I were among the last kids to leave the school. John had been my closest friend in the final years; even though he was had not been part of the original *Bayano* crew.

A really nice family took my mate John H in and enrolled him in the local high school to finish his studies. John did very well in school at Fairbridge, unlike me. He later went on to study at the University of British Columbia and remained quite close to his adoptive family. Even today they are still remarkably —a true family in every sense to the word.

The *Bayano* crew was also broken up as we left school going in different directions. My friend and fellow accent-impersonator Brian, who provided me many a good laugh over the years, got a job in a British Columbian logging camp washing dishes in the workers' bunkhouse. While he was there, he helped Roy get hired for the same job. Roy eventually graduated from dishwasher to a full-time logger. As I write this, I find myself asking why Brian's godfather, the owner of the largest lumber company in Canada, did not take Brian and Roy in for entry-level employment in his firm. A position there might have offered better advancement opportunities in that industry.

Since Roy was a hard worker and a very independent and private person who preferred to keep to himself; the solitary life of a logger suited him well. He later built a log cabin for himself away from the town which has been his home ever since.

While Roy stuck it out in forestry, Brian eventually left. His life became a very turbulent one. He first became a postal carrier in Vancouver. Then in his mid-twenties, he ventured to South Africa to pursue other prospects and later returned to Vancouver flat broke. He called on his millionaire former godfather Mr. Bloedel and asked for a loan of $25. For a man of his resources, $25 should've have been a handful of change. Yes, he said he was willing to give Brian the money, but he told him in an intimidating tone, "You had better to be sure to pay it back!"

Brian had every intention of doing so, and he didn't rest easy until he paid his wealthy godfather the full amount. After that, he never called on Mr. Bloedel again.

Other guys I knew at Fairbridge went on to various fates, some good and some bad. Eric L., the sharp-minded boy I'd met in the hospital, became a success story. I honestly believe that during his long convalescent hospital stays, he was developing a great degree of mental acuity, and the skills he developed there led him to become a very successful entrepreneur and millionaire.

Daggy had a very difficult life after Fairbridge. He left the school poorly educated and emotionally unstable. He had a very hard time adjusting to living on his own. At some point, he became so disgusted with the political system that he became a Communist. He ran afoul of the law several times and was brought face-to-face with the Vancouver criminal court system. Pat Hood, a former Fairbridgian schoolmate who had become a lawyer, did his best to defend Daggy in court. Daggy still ended up serving multiple prison sentences.

Ultimately, Daggy was unable to cope with his chaotic life and committed suicide in a Vancouver jail cell.

I honestly believe the terrible abuse he received during his childhood at Fairbridge contributed directly to his struggles in life and his untimely death.

When I think about him, I remember the awkward, quiet kid with glasses who tended lovingly to his pumpkins. Fairbridge broke him. And that kind of sad story really cuts my soul when I think about it.

Many avoid mentioning Daggy's story and the others like it when they tell the account of Fairbridge, but these stories belong in the assessment this organization, and I think it's important to honour their memories by telling the whole truth.

When it came time to discuss my future with Major Plows, he sat down with me in his office and went over my options. He counseled me about continuing my education. As for how I was supposed to do that or where, I had no idea. Major Plows never mentioned a potential foster home placement for me. Maybe there weren't any more foster parents willing to take us. The only other option was to remain at Fairbridge until I was sent out to one of the local farmers to be his farm hand. For me that was not a choice at all. I definitely was not keen on spending the rest of my life as a farmer, not even for one more year.

I had great respect for Major Plows and still admired his military record. So instead, I asked him to sign the necessary papers to let me join the army. I told him that if he placed me on another farm, I would simply quit and take off for places unknown. I was restless. I wanted to see new places beyond the Island and its mundane towns. I felt that

I could do well in the army, and I hoped it would give me the opportunity to travel and see the world. I also hoped the army following my basic and corps training would assign me to allied occupational forces in Germany. From there, I figured I would be close enough to make my way to Scotland and find my family.

After a brief discussion, Major Plows gave his consent for me to sign up for the army, and with that I was ready to leave Fairbridge and my past behind and take the first step toward a rather unknown future.

EARLY YEARS

MY FAMILY IN SCOTLAND

BECOMING A CHILD MIGRANT

FAIRBRIDGE FARM SCHOOL

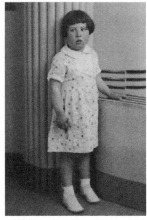

My sister Minnie, age 8

My Family in Scotland and Becoming a Child Migrant

My passport photo, age 6, 1940

My older brother Rob, age 10

My two younger brothers (in white), Alexander and Billy

HMS Bayano, the ship we sailed on from Liverpool, England to Quebec, Canada, in 1941. During the early 40s the North Atlantic was heavily infested with Nazi submarines. The convoy our ship sailed with was attacked by Nazi subs. They sunk one ship and badly damaged another; miraculously, The *Bayano* made it to port safely.

FRONT ROW: R.MYHILL, B.TIBBLES, E.FOSTER, LOUIS FIELD, P.MEIN, R.MARKAY, H.TAYLOR, LEON FIELD
BACK ROW: C.BRAY, M.BEAN, J.DEAN, C. SMITH, T.RICHARDS   M.REDSHAW, A.TRAIN

LEFT: Our party of migrant children waving "Cheerio" as we left the port of Liverpool, Nov. 1941.

BELOW: Children and adult escorts aboard the *Bayano*.

WELCOME

PRINCE OF WALES
FAIRBRIDGE FARM SCHOOL

LEFT: FAIRBRIDGE FARM SCHOOL—A partial layout of the cottages

RIGHT: On arrival at the Fairbridge Farm School the Bayano party of children were immediately taken to the school hospital. Each child was given a thorough medical inspection by a physician.

Fairbridge Farm School

LEFT: At Fairbridge all the boys were trained to be farmers (regardless what talents in other occupation one may have had.) Yes, that's me pouring the milk from my first cow of the day.

RIGHT: Cliff Cooper and Leon Field pushing the milk cart down to the dairy. I guess the herd- manager wasn't around, or those boys, including me, wouldn't have been sitting on the fence and enjoying watching their mates at work.

Our favorite place in the summertime, the Fairbridge River. During my annual visits to the school I would always make my way down to the river for a dip (right up to age 70).

Youngest lads lead the race off for the school annual cross country run. I am the lad in the front row wearing the dark shirt.

LEFT: Boys' Basketball team.
Front L-R, Roddy M., Roy H., Leon F., George G., Middle L-R, John H., Eric F., Cypriot G., Back L-R, Raymond C., Louis F., Hugh T., Peter M.

BELOW: The famous Fairbridge Annual Cross Country Run; making their way past the School Chapel. Some praying they would win; many of us praying we would just make the finish line.

ABOVE: Line up of runners for sports day.

BELOW: Choir exiting at the end of the service at the Fairbridge Chapel.

ABOVE: The school boxing team. These were the winners of their weight division "House Fight Offs." They would represent Fairbridge by boxing in the local area "Kinsmen Boxing Championship."

Boxers Louis F., Eric F., Roddy M., Roy.

Doreen, a Vernon girl, in her ice skating costume. Doreen was my first 'steady' girlfriend. I still hold many fond memories of those days in Vernon.

ABOVE: Fairbridge School Cadet corps led by Captain John C, Drum and Bugle Band led by Drum Major Roddy M. At age 84 I am still a Drum Major with Scottish Pipe Bands in California.

Vernon Army Camp Commanding Officer's parade on Saturday mornings. There were approximately 1,000 cadets (teenagers) in these six-week training camps. It was extremely hot and a medical jeep ambulance was parked close by as many a cadet collapsed.

Army Cadet Camp Vernon. Author back row far right in his kilt-uniform.

ADULT YEARS

THE CANADIAN ARMY

THE VANCOUVER YEARS

FAMILY REUNIONS IN SCOTLAND AND ENGLAND

MY FAMILY IN THE U.S.A.

OFFICIAL APOLOGY FROM THE UK GOVERNMENT

MEETING THE PRIME MINISTER

Life in the Canadian Army

THE MINIATURES OF THE LATE MAJOR A N PLOWS
PRESENTED TO THE OFFICERS' MESS
CANADIAN SCOTTISH REGIMENT (PRINCESS MARY'S)

LEFT: Major Plows, A "Teacher, Soldier, Hero." Before WWII broke out, Major Plows was Principal of the Fairbridge day school. In 1939 he volunteered to serve as an army officer in the "Canadian Scottish Regiment." He fought with his regiment during the Allied invasion of Normandy. During the battle, according to an eye witness, a fellow officer stated, "Major Plows led his troops with cool calm direction under heavy fire on the Normandy Beach, and should have been awarded a Victoria Cross. He was seriously wounded during the Normandy Battle. Following his discharge from the CSR, he returned to Fairbridge as the new headmaster. Major Plows signed the papers allowing me to sign up in the Canadian Army.

The three barrack roommates: Darcy, Ron, and Roddy.

Ron and RDM, and it looks like Ron was serenading the girl who took the photo.

Basic Training Company graduation 1951. Yours truly, back row, fourth from right.

RIGHT: Yes, Corporal Mackay was as happy as this photo indicates; he had completed the Surgical Technician Grade 4 exams, and shortly after was promoted to Corporal. He was sailing to war-torn Korea!

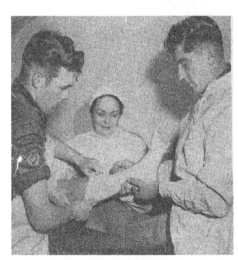

ABOVE RIGHT: Looks like Corporal Mackay was taking a vacation cruise … uh, uh, this was the U.S. Troop transport ship the *USS General Gaffey*, transporting mainly U.S. Troops and our small 100 detachment of Canadian Special forces troops.

LEFT: News copy of photo in *Armed Forces News* (Korea). The shattered leg of a Canadian soldier in Korea received prompt attention at the 25th Canadian Surgical Field Hospital; Cpl Roddy Mackay directed the procedure, observing surgical nurse, Lt. Margret Hill, assisting Pte. Larry Hill.

Cpl Mackay takes a break from his duties and enjoys some sun.

Our surgical team loading up a wounded soldier to U.S. Helicopter for evacuation to Brit Com Hospital, Japan.

The Vancouver Years 1955 -1960

Enjoying a family dinner: L-R, Lily Hope, Peter Topolnisky, RM, John Hardy, Mary Hardy, Young Peter Hope.

ABOVE: A trio of our "Vancouver Rat Pack." The tall guy with the shades, Peter T.; our resident scholar, John H.; and RM. It was a nice sunny Saturday, so we were strolling down Granville Street checking out the lovely Vancouver "Dollies."

"Rat Pack" duo all tuxed-up for the New Year: Roddy, ala Dean Martin and Phil Peers, "Old Blue Eyes," Frank Sinatra, with dates.

RIGHT: Looks like another New Year's Eve party. Front L-R, Sarah, RM; in back, Johnny Fulford, Lily Hope, Anne Peers, Phil Peers, Eddie Peers and friend.

Family Reunions in Scotland and England

On my return to Scotland in the 50s, Aunt Kate took me into her family home at the time when my cousin Cathy married a U.S. airman, Karl, who was stationed in Edinburgh. Attending the wedding were the Gray and Mackay families plus many friends. I was charged with the care of my Granddad Sandy (I took a wee flask in my book for him). It was a beautiful wedding and I felt badly that I hadn't packed a kilt.

LEFT: The Gray family. On the left side: nephew Gary, his mum Joan, and Betty. Right side: Heather, RM, Ross, and Lewis. RIGHT: L-R: Cousins Cathy and Robert, Aunt Kate, Roddy, little cousin Dorothy, and Uncle Robert. The Gray family were special to me and I will never forget their kindness.

The Mackay brothers finally reunited L/R; Rob, Roddy, Sandy and Billy.

The four Mackay brothers finally reunited in 2001, following my locating younger brothers Sandy and Billy. L-R: Rob, Roddy, Sandy, and Billy. Pictured 1st row L-R: Roddy, Robbie. 2nd row: Sandy; our sister, Minnie; Billy. 3rd row: Karen, wife of nephew, Alec Ward; Ruth, daughter of Sandy; Robbie Ward; Alec Ward Jr.; Betty, my darling wife, holding young Luke; Gillian, Sandy's wife; Edna, Billy's wife; sweet Sylvia; my brother Rob of 70 years. Sylvie passed away this year; she was an angel in life. Back row L-R: Kevin, son of Billy; our son, Iain; and Robert.

My Family in the U.S.A.

On January 15th 1983, I married, not only a beautiful, intelligent woman, but one who brought the happiness I had sought most of my life—sweet Betty Sue. Our wedding party L-R: John Dalton, Harvey Hillbun, Jim Anderson, Roy Thiebeu, Bill Merriman, the Groom and Bride, Jeanie Merriman (Bill's wife) my beautiful daughters, Christine and Tara who is holding hands with Briana, and Paddy Dalton.

Betty and me at one of the many Scottish Tartan Balls we've attended.

January 12, 2008, our 25th wedding anniversary L-R: Briana, Tara, Roddy, Betty, Iain and Christine.

The Monterey Pipe Band led by Drum Major Mackay and Pipe Major Michel d'Avenas. This was a traditional annual "Parade of the Caber," on Ocean Avenue in Carmel By the Sea.

Father and son Iain. We had great times participating and travelling with the pipe band.

Official Apology From the UK Government

A visit with Dr. Margaret Humphreys, C.B.E., O.A.M., at the Child Migrant Trust office in Nottingham. She brought public recognition to the scheme that took thousands of British children and shipped them to Canada and Australia, New Zealand and South Africa. Through her efforts, the UK Prime Minister Gordon Brown in 2010 made a Public Apology at the UK Parliament. Which also set up a family restoration fund to help those who wished to be reunited with their families in the UK.

The Former Guttersnipe Meets the Prime Minister

PM Gordon Brown met with all the former child migrants in the Westminster Parliament and made what most, if not all of us, felt was a very sincere and heartfelt apology.

My wife and I enjoying lunch with the only surviving teacher, "Mimi," well into her 90s, yet still quite active and fun to visit.

PART II

1951-1955

You're in the Army Now!

Within a week of receiving the OK from Major Plows, I was on my way to join the army. I packed my old cadet kit bag with the very barest of necessities—some clothes, a wash kit, and not much else. With all the proper documents in hand, I caught a bus to Nanaimo to take the CPR Ferry for Vancouver. I stood in the stern of the vessel watching Vancouver Island slowly disappearing from view. I swore I would never return to "that stinking island" again. Little did I know it would be one of the dumbest vows of my life, and later I would be taking every opportunity I could find to visit the island of my childhood.

I slung my Kitbag over my shoulder, disembarked the ferry, and was off with only $10 left in my pocket, determined to make the best of my new life and erase all the bad memories of Fairbridge from my mind.

I was keen on signing up for the Canadian Scottish Regiment, but they informed me the Regiment was no longer part of the active forces. The officer who interviewed me knew Major Plows. He was impressed with my application and noted I had held an officer's rank in the cadets. As we were discussing other options for me, he mentioned that I might be a candidate for Officer's Training School. I perked up at that notion. However, upon closer scrutiny, the officer observed what I already knew... my weak academic history, killed that glorious option. As the officer further combed through my Cadet and Reserve Army history, he noted that I had taken medical corps training and told me I would do well to consider the Royal Canadian Army Medical Corps (RCAMC). He emphasized that I would have a much better opportunity for advancement in the Medical Corps. This sounded good to me, so I took him at his word and signed up for the Medical Corps. Later, that week they issued me a train ticket for Army Camp Borden in Barrie, Ontario, and dropped me off at the railroad station in downtown Vancouver.

Ten years earlier in this same station, I had arrived on a train bringing my Bayano shipmates and me to Fairbridge. Now, ten years older, I was boarding an eastbound train going as far away from that school as I could get.

Army recruiting staff picked me up at the rail station in Barrie and delivered me to Camp Borden. The next day I underwent all the routine intake procedures for new recruits. First, I and several other recruits had a complete medical exam. Following that, a corporal marched us off to the quartermaster's stores where they issued us our uniforms, bedding, and so on. In the afternoon, we attended an orientation class presented by a sergeant major, which introduced us to a captain who would be our company commander. If I closed my eyes and mentally substituted corporals for cottage mothers, sergeants for duty masters, and the captain for a headmaster, it felt much like the same environment I had left behind at Fairbridge.

Basic Training, which is often referred to as "Boot Camp" in the U.S. Army, really posed no difficulty for me. The Cadets and Reserve Army had prepared me well for the training, and Fairbridge had certainly prepared me for whatever discipline the army dished out. At least, discipline within the army was in my experience fair and evenhanded, unlike at Fairbridge.

I was already used to eating my meals off metal plates, drinking out of metal cups, and sharing a long table with 10 other guys or more jostling next to me. Sleeping in bunk beds in barracks with 20 to 30 other men was much the same as it had been in the cottages, except the army cot was actually a hell of a lot more comfortable than our cottage beds. It was a much softer mattress and pillows for the head. The best part of it all was that I no longer had to contend with a nagging cottage mother, It did not bother me at all, having drill sergeants screaming obscenities at us from dawn to dusk. Just like in cadet camp, I found the instructors had a wild sense of humour.

I quickly discovered that most of the guys in my barracks had never needed to launder or press their own clothes. Their good-hearted mums had performed all these chores for them, and now that they needed to do it themselves; they were at a loss.

Here I spotted an opportunity to put the domestic skills Fairbridge had imparted on me to good use and make a bit of pocket money. Soon I was washing and pressing shirts and uniforms and shining boots and brass. The guys were happy to pay the moderate fees I charged if it saved them the effort of doing it themselves. Before long, I built a small personal cash base. It felt good to have folding money in my wallet for a change when most of my barracks-mates were broke.

I got on quite well with most of the lads in my platoon. We had a couple of older guys who had served in WWII in our ranks as well. All of us young 'bucks,' showed them due respect. My best friend was Ron Stapleton, whom I met in the first few days of basic training. We had the same build, and our facial features looked so uncannily similar that we could have passed for brothers. The NCOs quite often confused the two of us in fact.

We had quite a few laughs over the mistaken identity situation during our time at Camp Borden. One time, though, it was less than funny.

Ron and I had been flirting with a couple of secretaries who worked in the HQ offices. Towards the end of training, the Commanding Officer (CO) rewarded the company with a pass allowing us to go off base on a Saturday night. We made a date to meet the two girls at a dance hall in the town near the camp.

Unlike my cadet days, when our kilted uniforms drew interest and respect from the townspeople, soldiers were no longer very popular with the local civilians. Our army uniforms landed us many a cold shoulder. So for our big date night, Ron and I went shopping for some civilian clothes. The store had casual windbreaker jackets that we both liked. They were black with wide angled red stripes down the sleeves. For laughs, we bought identical jackets.

Then on Saturday night we met the girls in the dance, both us wearing the newly purchased jackets. The first few hours went great and we were dancing and having a great time. When the band took a break, I took my date outside. We sat in her car and necked for a while. Then we went back inside and my date went to the ladies' room. The dance hall had a balcony, and as I waited for the girl I spotted Ron running down the balcony stairs towards me. He grabbed me by the arm and said, "We've got to get the hell out of here before we get killed!"

I was startled by the sudden change of tone, but I could tell by the look on his face that he was deadly serious. Then I spotted a group of surly soldiers looking like they were in search of some big trouble and heading towards us. They looked positively boiling mad and worse still they were glaring at me. As they started pushing their way over, I knew that my boxing skills would not be of much use with this scenario. We were outnumbered five against two.

There is a military axiom: "There are times it is best to retreat to survive and fight another day." This was certainly one of those times.

We jumped over chairs in a mad dash to the nearest exit. When we hit the street I shouted to Ron, "What about the girls?"

"Forget them, keep running," he said.

I did exactly that. I sprinted at a fast clip on Ron's heels until we were safely on the outskirts of the town. We finally slowed down, our lungs burning. Only then did we look back to see if there was anybody on our tail.... nobody. We breathed a sigh of relief and collapsed on a lawn in front of a house that was shrouded in darkness. Still trying to catch my breath, I panted to Ron, " "Hell with that kind of speed I could have placed first or second in my school's cross-country race."

 It wasn't too long before we spotted a taxi and flagged it down to make our retreat back to the safety of our barracks. Sitting in the cab, still winded and trying to catch my breath, I sputtered out, "Ron, 'what the hell is going on'?

Ron admitted he didn't know the whole story, but he told me what took place in the dance hall. He said a livid sergeant had confronted him. His nostrils were flaring like a bull as he pointed to Ron's jacket draped over a chair and accused him of stealing his steady girlfriend. But his girlfriend was my date, not Ron's. With our matching jackets, the sergeant had mixed us up.

He was a drill instructor of the Royal Canadian Regiment, and he and his cronies were infantrymen, trained for one thing: killing the enemy. Ron managed to convince him it was a mix-up. He said the jacket wasn't his and he certainly wasn't with his girl.

The sergeant bought it, but he was still incensed. "When I find that son-of-a-bitch that is with my girl, I will take his nuts off!" he swore.

Luckily, Ron found me before the sergeant, and his cronies did, he definitely saved my skin. As for those snazzy black jackets with the red-striped sleeves, Ron never went back for his and mine went into an incinerator the next day.

Quite coincidentally, while having a beer in the canteen a week later, Ron and I found ourselves sitting around a table next to another table with four soldiers from the Royal

Canadian Regiment. One of them was telling his buddies a story of what happened in the dance hall last weekend. Our ears instantly perked up. We got a bit tense. Our first instinct was to get up very quietly and leave without drawing attention, but I had always been the curious type, so I signaled Ron to stay seated. I needed to know the whole story. So we stayed where we were and discreetly leaned in to hear their side of this hair-raising tale.

The fellow was describing it as the thriller of the night. He said the sergeant had been gone on a temporary posting to the west coast. He had just returned that very evening. Upon arriving back at Camp Borden he called his girlfriend, only to discover she wasn't home.

The dance hall was the most popular hangout in town so it did not take long for him to track her down. One of his mates spotted her dancing with a guy wearing a black jacket with red stripes on the sleeves.

Now the sergeant knew she was not only out; she was out on a date. Of course, he was livid. He was determined to teach this guy a lesson.

A little later he spotted the jacket hanging on the back of this guy's (Ron) chair. The girl was nowhere in sight. He confronted the guy, who claimed he wasn't the one on the date with her. By the time Ron explained the apparent case of mistaken identity, the sergeant and four of his regiment buddies were hell-bent on finding the other guy and skinning him. They spotted him for a moment in the crowd across the dance hall wearing the jacket.

At this point, in the story, the fellow shook his head,

expressing his disappointment at the outcome, because the real culprit escaped. I could only surmise that this guy felt that the removal of my testicles would have been a far more fitting end to this thrilling episode. I was grateful that I had a staunch friend like Ronnie, who had stuck with me that night.

After that, Ron and I agreed we'd best steer clear of this 'Nutter,' drill sergeant and that girl. We actually managed to avoid the sergeant and his girl for our entire training at the camp.

It was during this time of my life at age 17; that the final step young men eventually take: I lost my virginity.

I was not the instigator of that first sexual encounter. We met at the dance hall, and she was quite attractive, and we danced well together. The whole time we were on the dance floor she was pressing her body very close to mine. When time came for the last dance, she invited me to come to her flat for a nightcap. With no hesitation at all, I readily accepted her invitation. I think it best I don't go into further intimate details, other than to say she was quite skilled at the art of making love. Being a novice, I simply accepted the role of a complete innocent student; I was there to learn. We kissed goodnight, and I walked (actually skipping like a kid) back to camp positively bursting with joy. I was giddy at the thought that I was no longer a virgin. I felt I had passed over the threshold into some sort of manhood club. Maybe I was equating this imaginary club with King Arthurs', 'Knights of the Round Table', Wow! What a night that was.

Of course as many a young man will do I had to share this news with my best friend right away. I could not wait until morning; I was bursting at the seams. There are certain life experiences that one just cannot hold in, and this was one of them.

I expected Ron, would congratulate me and welcome me into the brotherhood of man.

It took quite a few shakes to wake Ron up. He grumbled and muttered something about leaving him alone. I had to turn the bunk light on to wake him and get his attention. He grumbled and snarled some more.

I blurted in his ear, "Ron buddy I've finally won the spurs of manhood!"

I thought I was whispering, but apparently I was being much louder than that. My announcement woke up a few other guys. They stirred grumpily in their bunks, edging up onto their elbows to see what the ruckus was all about.

All I wanted to do was share how I had lost my virginity and what a wonderful experience, but nobody, including my best friend seemed interested. Somehow I was under the impression that I had just gone through one of the most important stages of a man's maturity.

A guy two bunks down threatened to throw his boot at me if I didn't shut up. That was my big unwelcome into the "brotherhood of what"? The next morning I woke and the euphoria of the night before quickly dissipated as my barrack roommates lit into me in no uncertain terms. One guy cursing me with, "Mackay… that fucking midnight in the barracks is not really the best time to share the joys of losing one's virginity."

In the years of the Korean War, there was little difference between the basic training we received in the Medical Corps and what was given to the infantry and other regular units. By Geneva Convention rules, Medical Corps personnel do not engage in armed conflict, but we still received the same training as infantry did on the use and maintenance of weapons. However, we knew our mission was to save lives, not kill.

At the time, we were still using the old British Enfield rifles, which featured a ten-round box magazine loaded with the .303 British cartridge manually from the top, either one round at a time or five-round chargers. The Enfield was standard-issue weapon to rifle companies of the British Army and other Commonwealth nations in both the First and Second World Wars and was still being issued during the Korean War. Our Basic Corp training also included mastering weapons such as the Sten and Bren guns and learning how to loft grenades without blowing ourselves up.

Ron and I had both received training with the Army Cadets and Reserve Army, and so we quickly rose to leading positions in our platoon, and then later did the same at company levels. We graduated as the top two soldiers in our basic training class. After that, we were assigned to the next training phase, titled "Medical Assistant Group 1," which would focus specifically on the medical curriculum.

It took over four months of daily classes to complete. We spent six days a week doing a combination of classroom sessions and a considerable portion of intensive hands-on training at the camp hospital under the supervision of Army doctors, nurses and medical techs. Much of the class material was not too difficult for me, as I had learnt most of the basics in my Cadet Army Medical Corps training. However, topics of anatomy, blood circulation, and organ function were all new and fascinating to me.

In the camp hospital wards, I was not too keen on doing the menial tasks like making beds and emptying bedpans. Some of the other service personnel mockingly even called us "Bedpan Jockeys." There was no greater insult to a medic than that particular nickname. However, I was satisfied to think then, that a few of those smart asses would feel differently when they came under our care in the battlefields or hospitals.

Besides these ward duties, we also learnt a lot of practical skills and got to work with an actual patient under doctor's supervision. We learnt how to dress wounds in emergency situations, administer blood transfusions, treat burns, and wrap casts on fractured bones. Our training covered many of the same procedures that a civilian medical institution would teach their ward orderlies, but our army medic course was shorter yet far more intensive. Plus, on top of the basics, we had to cover the typical trauma wounds of war. Historically speaking, wars have always led the way in developing treatments for trauma patients.

Back then, our duties, as surgical techs in the army required a finer skill set than our civilian counterparts had, and we took on many more serious responsibilities. The battlefield medics would be part of a team, working directly with the surgeons on the front lines and dealing with immediate, life-threatening situations. Today that has changed considerably and an army medic and a civilian paramedic are likely to be on par with one another in their skill levels.

Upon the completion of our medical assistant training, we received a 30-day leave warrant before our next training posting. I really had no place to go for my thirty days. I had no home to return to, and I certainly wasn't going back to the island, so Ron invited me to join him and visit his family in Edmonton, Alberta. I took his offer gladly.

In order to make the best use of our finances, we decided to hitchhike south across the U.S. border, thumb our way west across six states, turn north again when we hit Montana, cross into Alberta, and make it to Edmonton. Going through the States was a much longer route—nearly 2500 miles all told—but we figured with how much Canadians disliked soldiers at the time, the chances of us getting rides in our own country were slim to none. We were much more likely to end up frozen on the side of the highway, like two ice sculptures with arms out and thumbs upright. In 1951, there was no trans-Canada highway, either.

Neither Ron nor I ever visited the U.S. I knew nothing about Americans other than the little I had read or gleaned from the movies. Ron, like many Canadians back in those days, did not care much for Americans initially. He thought Yanks were ill-mannered loudmouths that bragged too much, as the stereotype went. It was the same story that is still told today, where a few poor examples come to typecast an entire nation. I admit I had a similar preconception but not as intense as Ron initially, but that was soon dispelled. Our venture hitchhiking across the U.S. convinced me that the majority of Americans are decent people. We found them to be far more generous in their hospitality than Canadians were at that time. To be fair, though, I must point out that Canadians and Americans had markedly different attitudes toward military personnel at the time. While Canadians back then thought anyone in the service was a "loser," incapable of keeping a job as a civilian, American held their men and women in uniform in high regard. However, Canadian attitudes have changed with the times as they now also hold their men and women in uniform in high regard.

On our great adventurous trip through America, we had absolutely no problems hitching rides. Many times people not only gave us a ride but also offered us the hospitality of their homes overnight.

One man who picked us up was a WWII U.S. Army veteran, so he liked us young soldiers instantly. Our Canadian Army uniforms were quite similar to the British uniforms, and this brought back good memories for American veterans like him who spent wartime service days in Britain.

He talked us into taking a break from the road and spending the night at his family home. Ron took a bit of convincing. He was in a big hurry to see his girlfriend in Edmonton. However, by the time we were eating dinner at the family table, Ron was much more relaxed and showing signs of welcoming the break. He found their daughter quite attractive too.

After dinner, the Yank took us out to a nightclub, where we danced until the wee hours of the morning. Though Ron and I had very little money, we offered to buy a round of drinks, but our host would not hear of it. While we drank together, our host insisted we sing all the old British war songs he had learnt in London, and we obliged. "I've Got Sixpence" was his favourite. He was quite delighted when we merrily struck up the tune, bobbing his head and leading the chorus.

We made friends with the other locals at the club, and several other people sent drinks to our table. Ron was openly flirting with the daughter and certainly showing no signs of any distaste for Americans that night. Our host embarrassed me a little by trying to fix me up with any pretty girls without dates who came to our table.

I spent much of the night dancing. I danced with three different girls and had a wonderful time. One of them even invited me to stay over at her place. Of course, I had to politely turn her offer down. It was one of those nights that will always hold a special place in my memories.

The next day, our host took a day, off so he could drive us a good two-hour further west on our journey. Suddenly, Ron, who had been very eager to continue on our long journey, was reluctant to leave. He seemed to have changed his mind about rushing home to his Edmonton girl. I knew his eye was still on the pretty daughter. Like any good mate would do, I teased him about it. And so we moved on.

Further down the road, we found ourselves on the outskirts of one town standing on the pavement with our arms outstretched and thumb up looking for the next ride.

As we were waiting, we glanced up at an office building across the street and spotted a couple of girls looking out the window at us. Ronny and I exchanged grins, and I immediately began smiling flirtatiously at them and tilting my chin rakishly. One of the girls opened the window, so they could wave at us.

The hormones were going in high gear again, and we were about to lower our outstretched arms and put our westward journey on hold when, as Murphy's Law would have it, a car stopped to pick us up, right when we least needed or wanted the lift.

We certainly did consider telling the driver that we made a mistake and really needed a ride in the opposite direction, so he'd go on without us, but the long miles ahead and common sense convinced us to carry on.

Eventually, we did make it to Edmonton and spent what was left of our furlough staying with an uncle and aunt who had brought up Ronny. Ron's Uncle Mac, short for MacDonald, was retired from the RCMP. As a young man, Mac had served with the former North-West Mounted Police, the forerunner of today's Mounties. He was a big man, and even in his late sixties, he retained the physique of much younger man. When I first saw him, I thought he looked far better than most Hollywood actors whom I'd seen in the role of a Mountie.

He shared a few stories of his early adventures with the Mounties. He told us about the time he went searching for a criminal in subzero temperatures and the unpredictable weather of the Northwest. I was struck by his fearlessness. Of course, as the legend of the Mounties goes, "he captured his man." I was always captivated listening to him.

Our visit was short and I never was to see uncle Mac again, but he is one of those interesting characters who made a lasting impression on me. Ron's Aunt Vi didn't make such an impression. She was nice enough and I liked her, but she was also overweight and spent most of her days sitting and nibbling away at unhealthy snacks, listening to the radio soap operas or reading romance novels. She was an excellent cook, though, and at her table, I enjoyed some of the best family-style meals that I'd ever eaten in my young life. I relished every dish she put in front of me and savored it gratefully. Food had become tasty and appetizing, exactly what we had been missing out on all those years at Fairbridge.

Ron belonged to a roller skating club in Edmonton, so we went skating practically every night. Ron knew the managers well, and we had an arrangement where they let us skate free, and we in turn helped out by volunteering as skating rink attendants. We would go around, cautioning the rowdy guys and controlling the speedsters on the floor. Of course, we also spent most of our floor time chatting up the girls, or at least, I certainly did.

I had learnt to skate at the Army Cadet Camps, so I was a fairly proficient skater. Ron had also taken lessons, and he taught me a few moves I didn't know. His girlfriend also loved to skate and came out with us to the rink. Soon I paired up with one of her friends.

That entire trip was very special for me. It was the first time I'd ever spend a holiday with a family. I felt welcomed to their home. For the first time, I felt a sense of belonging. It was almost like taking a peek into what it was like to live with a loving family.

Upon our return to Camp Borden, Ron and I were

posted to different army sections. We were both eligible to take advanced classes in the medical technician courses. I had selected and qualified for Surgical Tech Training and requested to go through it, but I had to wait for the class to be offered. Ron left Camp Borden, and I'm not sure where he was posted.

Initially, the HQ assigned me to a holding company where I would await for an opening in the next available Surgical Tech class. In the meantime, I was assigned to be a batman for a visiting general. In our military, batmen were personal servants to high-ranking officers. My duties were to tend to all the general's needs, like pressing his uniform, shining his brass, polishing his Sam Browne belt and boots, and so on. I hated it after a week. I felt like I was his valet or manservant. It was belittling and reminded me of caste system that I had experienced as a child.. All I could think about was how much I wanted to say, *"To hell with this uniform along with the rank and special privileges!"*

My frustration made me consider applying for the OTC— Officer's Training Camp. One of my training officers had prompted me to apply so he must have felt I had the potential to become an officer. Unfortunately my limited education and lingering inferiority complex once again put a damper on those ambitions. I never applied.

So I stuck it out as a batman, and when that stint was over, an opening in the Surgical Technician course was available. I was transferred to the Toronto Military Hospital where the ST classes were held. Whereas I had spent my last years of high school doing minimal work, I applied myself dutifully and studied hard throughout that course. In Fairbridge, I lacked any real motivation, but now I was eager to learn and set goals to succeed in my chosen field. I was fired up and determined. Although I make no excuses for my earlier shortcomings, the fact that I had chosen my field of study made a huge difference to my attitude toward schooling.

After I successfully completed my classes, I graduated as a Surgical Technician Grade 4, which was a highest technical grade at the time. Having done fairly well in my classes, the army promoted me to the dizzying heights of lance corporal. I'm not sure how much respect that rank receives today, but back then it was the first necessary promotion to move up in the ranks. At age eighteen, earning that rank was regarded as quite an achievement. I became a member of the surgical staff at the Toronto Military Hospital and remained there for about six months. My work was incredibly stimulating. Each new operative procedure challenged me and helped me hone my skills. I gained experience, and I enjoyed working in the operating theatre. The working relationships between the doctors, nurses, and us "other ranks" were more relaxed and friendlier than I'd known before, and I enjoyed that a lot. Of course, we still followed the military custom of addressing the doctors and nurses by rank. The nurses were commissioned officers, and we addressed them as "sister," a title taken from the British military.

To this day, I still have good memories of the nurses. They looked very professional in their crisp, starched blue uniforms and white aprons in the WWII British style. To my mind, the uniforms didn't detract from their femininity. Many of them were quite pretty, but as commissioned officers, they were automatically off-limits for us, the "other ranks." There was one very pretty nurse, in particular, on our surgical ward that I would have dated in a minute, if given the opportunity to cross the threshold of fraternizing with an officer.

That same attractive young nurse unknowingly caused considerable discomfort to one of our recovering post-surgery patients. He underwent surgery on a certain private sex part of his anatomy. He suffered considerable pain every time our attractive (yes, she was quite sexy looking) nurse gave him bedside care, i.e. simply taking his pulse. The young stud kept begging me to see if I could arrange to have one of the older, and not so appealing nurses take his daily temperature. I finally could relay his problem to the surgeon who took care of the problem.

The next day the nurse came up to me and said, "Corporal Mackay, thank you, but you really should have told me directly. Please tell the patient, I am sorry to have caused him any pain."

I assured her that I would do that even though I was also suffering slightly. This gorgeous nurse had no idea how painful it was for me to be unable to ask her out on a date. However, as they say in Quebec, "C'est la vie, soldier."

I often wish I pursued the medical field all the way. Of all the vocations I had over the years, that short two-and-a-half year period when I worked, as a surgical -tech in the army was the best, most challenging, most interesting, and the most rewarding time I'd ever had in a career. I truly enjoyed the medical classes and the opportunity to observe surgical procedures as they were being performed, and later applying what I had learnt to the surgical ward and operating theatre where I worked. I think under different circumstances; I could have earned a higher medical degree. Even as I write this, the self-doubt, a lifetime complex from my youth, casts serious doubts about that lofty aspiration. I think Marlon Brando said it best for the film *on the Waterfront*: "Charlie, I could'a bin something."

THE KOREAN EPISODE

When I joined the army, I had great hopes that following my training, I would be deployed to Germany, and from there I could locate and visit my family in Scotland. I really knew nothing about my family and had no clue where I would start looking, but I was determined to try. I felt that they must be out there somewhere, and I longed to be reunited with them.

While still in Canada, I requested the special European Forces posting in Germany and fully expected to be deployed there. I would soon learn the hard way that armies are known to change the rules when it suits their purposes.

In 1953, rumours circulated through the hospital that some of us were going be shipped out to Korea. The Korean War had been in full swing for some time, but it seemed to be winding down. From what I had heard and read of it, I had no desire to be part of it.

Like most teenage soldiers, I was clueless about the cause of the Korean War. The media told us it was a war between the people of the North and the South in this small Asian country. Then the "Big Boys"—Russia, China, and the U.S.—got involved. After that the United Nations stepped in and brought Canada, the U.K., all the British Commonwealth countries, and other European and Asian countries into the conflict. The army informed us that, in its simplest form, this was a war to save democracy from the Communists.

Now, I was still a teenager, only 19 years old. I had little interest and scant knowledge about global political affairs, and I didn't think or worry about Korea much.

I had settled in and was enjoying my work as a surgical tech at the Toronto Military Hospital. I was keen on learning all I could, and once I had gained the knowledge and skills of the operating theatre procedures; I qualified as Grade 4 Surgical Tech Specialist. Around that time, they promoted me to the rank of a full corporal, making me the youngest soldier on staff to earn that rank.

In addition, my social life in Toronto was quite pleasant. I met a pretty blonde-haired girl named Barbara at one of the popular dance halls. We clicked almost immediately. We both enjoyed dancing and being together, and soon we were dating steadily. As we grew closer, her mother invited me to her home. She was impressed with my good manners and said, "Roddy; your parents really brought you up well."

I just accepted her compliment with a "thank you" and offered no further explanation. I didn't want to bring up the reality of my childhood or talk about Fairbridge.

I spent most of my off-duty hours with Barbara. We had a great relationship. She was good fun and we both enjoyed skating; dancing, swimming, and taking walks together in a nearby park. Many evenings we had supper at her house and stayed in order to watch the latest shows on her new TV set, which was quickly becoming a household staple in the early 1950s.

I was enjoying life in Toronto and my work at the hospital. I fully believed I would get posted to Germany eventually. However, I was about to learn that when you enlist in military service, you would go where they want, when they want.

One day during my work shift, I received word to report

to the adjutant's office. Upon my arrival there, what had been an unpleasant rumour became a hard fact? Some of us were going to be posted to Korea, and I was one of them.

When I got the news, I protested, saying, "Excuse me, sir, but I signed up for Germany!"

I received the standard military reply: "Go see the chaplain." This, of course, in its bluntest form translates to, "Tough shit, buddy!" I was one of three soldiers who got reassigned to the Far East that day, and that was that.

As I write this, I recall how in 2006 U.S. Senator John Kerry received a lot of backlash for a speech he gave before a group of students during a campaign rally at Pasadena City College. As part of his opening remarks, he said, "You know education—if you make the most of it, you study hard, you do your homework, and you make an effort to be smart, you can do well. If you don't, you get stuck at war zone like Iraq."

That comment touched off a political firestorm of criticism. From my experience, though, I believe he spoke the unpleasant but truth. Not much has changed since the Korean episode. The fact remains that it is mostly the young men fresh out of high school that didn't go to college who are the first to be sent off to fight and die in these wars. It was that way back in 1914 with World War one.

The Korean posting was not the destination I had hoped for, but as they say in the army, "Orders are orders." I was scheduled to proceed via CPR train to Vancouver the following week.

With a heavy heart, I made a date to see Barbara for our last evening together. Her mother insisted on taking us out to dinner at a nightclub. They were both sorry to see me go.

Over sixty years later, the memory of that night is still vivid. Barbara and I dined and danced, savouring each precious moment together. At the end of the night, someone heard that I was being shipped to Korea and requested that the band play, "Now is the Hour When We Must Say Good-bye." I pulled Barbara close as the melody began. She buried her face in my shoulder. She was in tears, and I was having a hell of time choking down my own emotions. I didn't want to let her go.

As the song finished, some guy on the dance floor grabbed my arm and squeezed it tightly to wish me luck. That arm was still very tender from all the immunizations they had given me the day before, and his gesture certainly didn't help. I knew he meant well, so I just clenched my teeth through the pain until he released his grip. I squeezed out tears of both pain and sadness as I then gave Barbara a final kiss good-bye.

Next day, with my travel orders in hand, I climbed aboard a train bound for Vancouver. On arrival, I reported to the Vancouver Military HQ where I had originally enlisted. I spent a couple of weeks going through orientation procedures for the Korean assignment. During my stay, I had my first celebrity encounter. Robert Goulet, the Canadian singer and actor, was hanging around the area.

He was on his way to entertain the Canadian troops serving in Korea. These were years before he became a major celebrity in the U.S., so he didn't cause a huge fanfare, but we were still very excited to see him. Some of us hoped he would travel on our ship. An older, more seasoned sergeant said,

"Forget that. They don't put celebrities on troop ships. They fly first class where beautiful stewardesses serve cocktails all the way."

We were bussed to Seattle for our departure. Our contingent consisted of approximately 150 men from the Royal Canadian Regiment (RCR) and several special service types: medics, service mechanics, and so on. In Seattle, we boarded a troop ship named the *USNS General Hugh J. Gaffey*, bound for Yokohama, Japan.

As I walked on board I reflected on how this was the second time in my life that I was boarding a big ship to sail thousands of miles to a strange land. The first crossing had been far more dangerous, traversing the submarine-infested waters of the Atlantic during WWII, but in spite of this fact, this voyage to Korea had me feeling more nervous. I had an unpleasant sense of foreboding sitting heavy in my gut. However, judging from the photos taken aboard, no one would have guessed it. In the pictures, I am smiling as though I were on a pleasure cruise.

Upon boarding the ship, we, the Canadian personnel, were informed that we had been assigned with ship security. We were issued arm badges and white helmets, both emblazoned. with "MP" for Military Police. An officer briefed us as to our duties, and then assigned us to various areas of the ship. My first duty was to take a detachment of four soldiers on a special assignment to go to dockside and meet a busload of approximately 36 U.S. Army personnel and bring them aboard. The 'GIs,' on the bus were in prison garb and shackles. Most of them were serving time for desertion or going AWOL.

When the U.S. officer in charge of the prisoners saw my small detail of four soldiers, he nearly had a fit. He refused to relinquish the prisoners to the care of one NCO and four unarmed RCR infantrymen, and he demanded I call one of our officers to the dockside. I turned around and brought one of our officers back with me. He was slightly irritated with the American. He did not see how in hell the prisoners could escape when they were so well shackled, and he told the officer that. He further added, "What are they going to do, jump in the ocean?"

Our officer outranked the U.S. officer, so that resolved the dispute. My detail would escort the prisoners as we were assigned.

That encounter gave me my first look at the differences between the training and styles in the two armies. During our voyage, I could talk to and observe many of the U.S. soldiers. It quickly became apparent that they were very young and most had little or no training. Most of them were infantry or artillerymen, both groups very likely to end up on front lines. At 19 years old, I was just as young as they were, but I felt our training was thorough and had prepared me well for the duties that lay ahead. I thought that it bordered on criminality to be sending these untrained, young soldiers into a war zone. Many years later, I learnt the Canadian military was equally as guilty as the U.S. in this regard. My contingent may have been an exception, but Canada sent its share of untrained young men to the front lines as well.

Nowadays, with all the ongoing conflicts in our world, most countries make great improvements in preparing and training young soldiers before sending them off to war. For example, the U.S. Marines and other special units are superbly trained and are as professional the best military units worldwide.

On the ship, it did not take long for word to get around that the Canadian troops were an all-volunteer army. After that, hardly a day went by that the Americans didn't ask us, "Did you guys really volunteer for Korea?"

I grew tired of explaining, "Yes; I signed up voluntarily as did all the Canadian troops on board this ship. And in this army that means you go wherever the brass or politicians decide to send you." After a while, I just shrugged off their questions. The Americans thought the Canadians must be absolutely nuts to be volunteering to serve, period. For the most part, though, we got along well.

Many of the U.S. troops aboard the ship with us were black guys. Growing up in a small, isolated farming community in Canada, I did not meet any black people. As a matter of fact, the few I had seen worked as porters on the Canadian trains. They were always polite and much friendlier than the white train conductors. Personally, I liked them. Now I was interacting with black troops daily, and I found them to be good company.

I was intrigued by the different accents of the Americans on board, particularly those of the black 'GIs.' I found their accents and speech patterns very colourful and fascinating. It was to be first of so many times during my army years that I would hear soldiers calling each other "you mother-fucker."

A black guy's response to that address really cracked me

up. When one guy called him a motherfucker, the other guy responded with, "I wouldn't be any motherfucker if you'd kept your mother off the street." He was certainly a quick-witted guy.

When our ship hit some rough waters early in the voyage, the decks were full of soldiers hanging over the rails' puking their guts up. Some had to learn the hard way not to stand downwind of another soldier upchucking. While I was on deck with them, I heard the ships PA system crackling to life for the first time and craned my head up curiously. I'd never experienced anything like this firsthand. A rough voice belted out instructions: "Now hear this, there will be bingo tonight for compartment B." Then the line went quiet again.

I thought, "Hell; this is just like those WWII war movies." As this went on, I noticed the voice always seemed to have a distinctly Southern drawl.

One day, one of our RCR staff sergeants got into the PA system unauthorized and announced, "The 'RCR's refuse to fight unless their brass is shining bright. Uniform inspection will be held at 0600 sharp, now get your 'arse,' out of those bunks, over and out!"

The Yanks got a big laugh out of that. Some thought the guy would be disciplined for his prank, but none of the 'brass' (officers) was offended by his lark, so he got away with it.

I cannot recall how many days we were at sea, but finally we arrived and docked at Yokohama, Japan, and were bussed to our various bases. All the British Commonwealth (Brit Com) Forces were housed at base camp Ebisu. There were Brits, Canadians, Aussies, and New Zealanders all together in one place, so this environment of troops from several countries was every kind of excitement to me.

We underwent more physical exams, and received more shots for diseases native to the Far East. We also had to attend orientation classes that covered topics such as the customs of Japanese and Korean people, the climate, and so on. The lectures put especial emphasis on how to avoid sexually transmitted diseases like syphilis, which they referred to as "social diseases." Finally, on our last evening, they gave us a special pass to leave the base. All of us were anxious to enjoy the strange new delights of Japanese nightlife. Before we were allowed out, we had to watch a special training film titled "Protection against Social Diseases." This film was gruesome and graphic, showing men in the terrible stages of certain venereal diseases. We sat through it uncomfortably, and then with that out of the way we grabbed our wallets and headed for the gates. It is strange how many somewhat normal young men of average intelligence can quickly forget such dire warnings after a few beers.

With consideration for my family, I will leave the details of that evening's activities to the reader's imagination. However, I will recount one small incident that happened during the next day's "short -arm's inspection," which in our military was the euphemism for the medical inspection of one's private parts. As a medic, I never understood why they subjected soldiers to such a humiliatingly embarrassing examination right before sending them into a war zone. The procedure dates back to WWII, possibly even the Great War.

So there we found ourselves all lined up, bare-arsed, and

waiting for the doctor to inspect our "pride and joy." The guys with big dicks stood tall and proud with their chests puffed out like Charles Atlas. Those with a somewhat bantam-sized appendage hunched over as if to conceal poor, wee "John Thomas."

I waited for my turn in line, ready to have it over with. Then the doc paused at the chap ahead of me and said, "Skin it back again, son."

The poor soldier's face turned crimson red. He stuttered, "Doc; I don't know what those little bumps are on my dick."

The doc took a closer look and then gave a small chuckle. He asked the soldier if he had ever gotten blisters on his feet after a 10 or 20-mile route -march. The soldier replied "Yes, sir."

The doc said, "Well, son looks to me that over the last couple nights, your "sex weapon," has been on one hell of an extraordinarily long sexual route-march."

With our training and orientation classes complete, we were loaded onto trucks and taken to the docks again to ship out to Korea. The voyage escapes my memory, but I vividly recall arriving in the Pusan Harbor. You could smell the foul stench of excrement well over a mile out from the docks. I learnt later that human waste was the primary fertilizer they used on the rice fields at the time. That was quite a welcome to this strange land where we were going to be stuck for a year or so. The stench was overwhelming and had us all gagging. One of the guys said, "Why the hell are we fighting a war over this 'shithole' of a country?"

From the docks, a detail of officers and senior NCOs

sorted us out and directed us to our assigned base camps. I was to be posted as a Surgical Tech at the 25th Canadian Field Dressing Station (FDS). It was located close to the village of Took Chong, 20 miles north of the capital of Korea, Seoul and 15 miles south of the front lines.

The FDS hospital consisted of a bunch of tents and several elongated, semicircular Quonset huts built of lightweight steel sitting on concrete. The hospital had beds to accommodate approximately 100 patients. Our surgical unit was housed in one of the Quonset buildings. Separate sections were designated for major and minor surgeries and another for the medical ward. We had a fully equipped operating room, X-ray unit, pharmacy, and electrical generator. We slept in field tents that held approximately 10 men each. There were separate tents for officers, nurses, and other ranks, and a guard tent at the main entrance.

I reported the next day to the officer in charge of the surgical team and, after a brief orientation of the layout; I proceeded with my duties as assigned. At first, my duties were to set up the operating theatre (O.R.) for the daily scheduled surgeries, most of them for bone fractures, moderate to severe burn cases, amputations, appendectomies, and chest and head wounds. I had to make sure the required surgical instruments were packed, sterilized, and ready for the surgeon.

As I settled in and began doing my work, the surgeons felt that I was fully competent so, occasionally called me in to scrub up and assist in many of the daily surgical procedures, that included many late-night emergencies. I often acted as a "scrub nurse," the nurse who passes the right instruments to the surgeon and acts as a second pair of hands as directed. In addition, surgical techs like me would apply casts for seriously fractured limbs. The surgeon set the limb and instructed us on how he wanted the cast wrapped, and we would take care of the rest.

During the fighting, the FDS hospital took care of most battle wounds and other injuries. Severe chest, abdominal, limb, and head wounds were flown out by helicopter to major trauma units in Japan. We took in not only Canadian but also U.S. and all UN personnel and Korean civilians, any casualties who occurred within our area of operations.

When we arrived, negotiations for a cease-fire were ongoing. We assumed that with a cease-fire, there would be no more war wounds to treat. In reality, that was not the case. Soldiers and civilians were still injured by mines or other explosive booby traps. We also dealt with accidental and intentional shootings. Many people were injured or burned in traffic accidents on the poorly built and war-damaged roads. While it was certainly not as hectic as it would be during wartime, our unit still received a constant influx of injured and sick soldiers daily.

An eight-foot tall barbed-wire fence surrounded the site. Army personnel of the Republic of Korea guarded the entire perimeter of the camp. From our perspective, the South Korean army soldiers had some very unusual forms of discipline. Almost every day we would see one of their NCOs slap or punch a soldier for the slightest misdemeanor. In our army, it was considered a major offence for an officer or NCO to strike someone of a lesser rank. Any such incident would lead to charges and possible court-martial for the offender. Apparently in the Korean army, this kind of physical discipline was a common practice. From books, I read later in life much of this harsh discipline was passed on to the Koreans by the Japanese forces in WWII. In spite of the well-guarded fence, we quite often had civilian Koreans infiltrating our camp. Mostly they came to steal whatever was unguarded, whether that was food, equipment, or just about anything else. It could be a real problem when we had valuables lying around.

In addition to the soldiers, we also had several civilian Koreans working for us. Some of them picked up our terrible slang of calling them "Gooks" and began using the term themselves. They'd say things like, "Hey Corporal-san, me number one Gook; I shine your boots, polish brass eh?"

They were hardworking fellows, and most of them were honest and wanted to please us. All of us, except for the few typical soldier idiots in our ranks, treated them with respect. Personally, I felt quite sorry for them. They survived in dirt-poor conditions and had all suffered from the war.

One night, a helicopter touched down at our station carrying a severely wounded New Zealand soldier, one of the Maori natives of the island. He had stepped on a landmine that exploded on him. His lower body was a bloody mess. Both of his legs were really torn up. One of them was dangling from his knee in a very unnatural angle. He was in intense pain and whatever drug they had given him was wearing when off as we took him in. In spite of the pain, he was determined not to let it get the best of him. He kept his face controlled as we rushed him into the OR.

I scrubbed up with the team, and as soon as the anesthetic had him sedated, we went to work. It was a long, nerve-wracking procedure. The surgeon managed to save one leg but the other was too badly damaged, and we had to amputate it.

This was my first amputation case. Frankly, I was a bit overwhelmed, and I had to fight back my feelings of pity toward the patient. It did shake me up emotionally, but I managed to overcome it and continue. I will never forget having to carry the remains of his amputated leg out of the OR. It was almost surreal.

During the entire treatment and recovery period, the Maori soldier never once complained. In fact, he was one of the most helpful and cheerful patients in the ward. He truly was an inspiration to all the other patients and the staff. I was humbled by how he could maintain such a positive spirit in spite of losing one leg and being in so much pain. He did recover eventually. Now that Maori soldier stands out in my mind as one of the bravest men I ever encountered.

Work in the OR kept me busy. Many a night I never even bothered returning to my tent. I just wrapped myself in a blanket and slept on a stretcher in the OR. In the winter when the temperatures dropped below freezing at night, staying in the OR was a hell of a lot better than walking outside to get to the tents, especially knowing you might be called back at midnight for an emergency. The cold cut even more deeply into your bones if you had to go outside right after crawling out of a cozy sleeping bag.

The winter months brought us many severe burn cases. This was because many soldiers did not heed strict orders that the oil fuel stoves in their tents must be turned off at lights out. They left them burning all night for warmth, and when a soldier got too sleepy or had one beer too many, he could accidentally knock the stove over. It only took one small spark, and the sleeping bags caught on fire.

After several months of working diligently with the Field Surgical Team, I was promoted to the NCO in charge of the OR. I welcomed the assignment as I felt it would lead to more promotions down the line. However, like most promotions, the new assignment also entailed more work and longer hours. Many days I worked double shifts. That didn't really bother me at first, but over time, the strain would take its toll and help turn a bad situation into a serious problem for me. However, that was still waiting 'down the road.' For now, I was taking my duties in stride, having some fun when I could, and getting involved in some mischief.

Every Saturday morning we had a fall-in parade and inspection by our Commanding Officer, Major Garside[13], to keep us in shape. Major Garside was very typically English in his speech and manners. As he inspected us, he would make many comments like, "I say, Private Jones, your boots are rather a mess. Sergeant, take this man's name down for extra duties."

We would refer to that kind of discipline as "chicken-

---

13   His name has been changed.

shit." Unlike regular parade squares, which were paved with concrete, ours were only compressed dirt and sand so most of the time it was dusty as hell. You left your tent with shiny boots and within two minutes on the parade -area, they were covered in dust. Of course, our boots were a mess during the weekly inspection. As I had grown up around all kinds of British people, I could do a fairly decent upper-class English accent. One Saturday after we were dismissed from inspection, I did an imitation of Major Garside to amuse the other lads. It was really unusual for an NCO like me to be mocking an officer, but I figured, to hell with it, this was Korea. I took one of the guys and called him to attention. Imitating the major's speech pattern and Oxford accent, I said, "I say, Private Jones, are you awake yet? What would you do if a bomb burst here?" Of course, Jones was tongue-tied, so I answered for him. "Jones you are an absolute chaar.... don't you realise that if a bomb burst here, you would be here, there, everywhere, you foolish man?" The lads got a good laugh out of it, and I made it a bit of a routine. Believe me, a little humor was sorely needed in a place like Korea.

We certainly found ways to entertain ourselves and decompress during off-duty hours as well. We frequented the station's canteen to take our minds off the stress of camp life. They served beer there and showed old movies sometimes. Some of them were duller than dull, though. The film projector also broke down frequently or went haywire in the middle of a showing. When that happened, we razzed the poor guy running it in true army style. We stomped our heavy boots on the wooden floor like a bunch of kids until the frazzled projectionist had the film running again.

One night a week, the canteen ran a bingo night with some highly coveted prizes like short wave radios, watches, cartons of cigs, and so on. They were hidden inside a large prize box, and no one knew what was inside until the winner opened it. Bingo night was very popular, and all those not pulling duty showed up. The winner went back to his tent happy, and the losers moaned and groaned and blamed the guy calling the numbers. Soldiers have a pattern of seeming to derive great relief from pissing and moaning when things are not to their liking.

In my lifetime, games of chance have not been very profitable at all, and bingo was no exception. After several months of disappointment, there came a night when I finally won, shouting "Bingo!" out so loud it rang through the canteen. I was very excited as I ran up to the table to pick up my mystery prize. I was sure it would be something very expensive like a radio or expensive watch. I deserved something valuable after suffering through all those winless nights, right? My fingers twitched with anticipation as I removed the lid from the box.

Well, the prize was special, all right. It was a pair of Japanese lady's silk pyjamas. Useless. To top off my complete disgust, all my so-called buddies let out a roar of laughter as soon as they saw. One guy shouted, "Hey, Mackay, save them for a Geisha girl when you get your R&R in Tokyo."

When I had simmered down later, I decided to send the pyjamas to Barbara with a note saying that if they did not fit maybe her mum would enjoy them.

Just across the road from our station was a U.S. Army radar station. After seeing the nice setup and the very comfortable canteen the Yanks had, some of us decided to become friendly neighbors. A few of them soon started inviting us over whenever we could get a temporary pass to leave camp. One of the older guys hailed from the Deep South, and his strong Southern accent and great sense of humor really cracked me up. He was quite a character, saying things like, "Hell boys, let me tell y'all, you ain't seen nothin'. I was here on the radar hill when the Russkies[14] were still flyin'."

We liked to visit their small Post Exchange (PX) and buy some sodas, snacks, candy bars, cigs and other such as things they stocked. The smaller PXs were much like today's 7-11 convenience stores for soldiers. For us, the PX goods were on par with the luxuries of home. They certainly were not available at our Brit Com Forces NAAFI shops.

The larger PX stores also carried some finer goods. One time I purchased a nice, expensive piece of luggage at the PX in Seoul. Thieving by the locals was still a problem at the station, and I really didn't want such a good bag disappearing. Because the technicians' tents were the least guarded, I asked one of our surgeons to keep it in his tent. All these years later, when I open a box of my old army memorabilia, I come across a note handwritten by that surgeon stating, "Cpl. Mac, if my tent burns down I am not responsible for your suitcase." Happily enough, that never happened and that piece of luggage served me well for many years.

---

14   Slang for Russian aircrews that had flown the Russian built MIG planes during the Korean War.

Some things, however, simply couldn't be found at the station or across the road, namely, a night out with the girls.

The small village of Tokchong was within walking distance, but it was officially off-limits to us. We were restless soldiers bereft of female companionship, and we knew there must be some women in that village. That sort of temptation can really screw with a young soldier's decision-making process.

So, one rare night when I was not 'pulling,' OR duty, a few of my buddies talked me into an unauthorized visit to the village. This was absolutely dumb on my part because I could have lost my rank and the position that I had worked so hard for.

One of our guys had given one of the Korean guards a carton of cigs with the understanding that we would be leaving, and he would let us come back through a break in the fence that we would have set up. However, our accomplice was unexpectedly relieved of the guard duty that night, and we had no idea until much later.

Our escape went without a hitch. In the dark of the night we went over the fence as planned. We did not see any guards on our way out, so chortling away; we proceeded towards the village.

Much to our disappointment, the girls were not too pretty. Though I hate to use such harsh judgment, I found some of them downright ugly. Their breath reeked of kimchi, the fermented cabbage dish they ate. We were very disappointed. Most of us agreed that this was not going to be any sort of enjoyable evening, and we should just head back to camp. One guy was desperately hard up for any kind of sexual encounter that night and wanted to stay. When we told him, we were not that eager and didn't want to take any more risk by staying out later; he grudgingly agreed to come back with us.

Keeping low, we skulked back to our camp, stepping very carefully through the stinking, shit-filled rice paddies. We made our way to the prearranged spot along the fence line with the break in it and went through. We had barely crossed into the perimeter of the camp when we heard the guards screaming something in Korean and the crack of rifle shots. The three of us scattered as fast as we could and bolted to our tents. We all made it back inside without injury. Then we lay back in our sleeping bags and listened nervously to the commotion of the guards with their flashlights combing the grounds for intruders.

So, where other brave souls can tell you their war stories of being under fire, the only time I was in personal danger of being shot in Korea was that incident of going over the fence. It scared the crap out of us. Believe me, friendly fire is just as deadly as what is fired by the enemy. I saw enough patients in the OR to know that.

On a few occasions, I escorted sick or injured soldiers to Seoul by Jeep or ambulance. From there they would be med-evaced to the large Brit Com Hospital in Japan. These trips provided a nice, short break from the routine of my OR duties. However, on one of those trips, I learnt how professional and slick a Korean street- thief could be. I had just received a very expensive Parker pen and pencil set from Barbara. Perhaps it was her way of giving me a hint to write more often. I decided to take it with me on one of those trips to Seoul. It was the dead of winter, so I was wearing a heavy army-issued parka jacket, and I placed the pen set in one of the small upper sleeve pockets.

Two of us were walking down a fairly busy street in Seoul. It was the middle of the day, and we had not gone more than four or five blocks when we stopped to let a Jeep cross. My mate looked at me and said, "Hey, Mac, what happened to your right sleeve?"

I quickly looked down and, much to my disbelief, saw that somebody took a razor and cut the pocket with the pen set clean from my sleeve. Hell, the job was extremely neat excision on my sleeve. The thief had the ability of a surgeon. I had no idea when it could've happened. I had not felt anyone bump into me, nor felt the slightest tug on my sleeve. Neither one of us had noticed any suspicious characters passing us, nor the street was not so busy that we were brushing past people. Maybe we had been momentarily distracted by some of the battle-damaged buildings, and that was enough for the thief to do his work and vanish unnoticed. Whoever did it was truly an expert. I was so impressed by his professionalism that I wasn't even that angry about losing my new pen set.

The jacket was easily replaced at the quartermaster's store. I wrote Barbra that night and told her that despite losing the pen set, I would do my best to write more often.

The truth was I had stopped writing her so often because, bluntly put, there was little substance in the letters she wrote to me. I was learning from the letters that we really didn't have that much in common. There was little to talk about in our correspondences. She wrote about the weather at home and what she was going to wear. She read fashion magazines but no books. She was pretty and all, but our only shared interest that I enjoyed was dancing. Despite this, I tried to make good on my promise, at least for a while.

An Unexpected and Unpleasant Turn in My Life

I didn't know it, but trouble was waiting around the proverbial corner around six or seven months of my time at the FDS station. As I mentioned before, I was taking on a lot of work in the OR. One night after one of my double shift sessions, I got a night off and three of us took the opportunity to go over to the Yank radar station. Our good humor mate, the Southerner, greeted us at the gate and we all went into the canteen. After several beers, he invited us to his tent to share a bottle of 150-proof rum. At that stage in my life, it did not take a lot of liquor for me to get well inebriated, and that rum had a stronger proof alcohol than I was used to handling. It definitely got me a way out in the twilight zone. One of the older guys, a WWII vet that could really handle his booze, led us back to camp. I had no recollection of leaving the radar station and returning to the OR. Apparently, I fell asleep upon the floor, and one of the guys threw some blankets on me and left me to sleep it off.

I woke up during the night to a very strange feeling down below. I thought I was having a wet dream. As I slowly came out of my drunken stupor, I realized it was not a dream of a sexual encounter at all. Actually, a guy was lying beside me, kissing my belly and fondling my penis. When I realized what he was doing, I pushed him off me, cursing him and calling him a 'fucking faggot.'

The guy was in my section, and while not a close buddy, I thought he was a decent guy. He was quiet and well liked by most everyone in our section. I was shocked that he'd do this to me.

I could hardly think I was so shaken. He began telling me repeatedly how sorry he was and begging me not to turn him in. I only remember yelling at him to get the hell out of the OR and stay away from me.

The following days, thoughts of what happened kept swirling through my mind. I could not dispel them even though I tried. I was really rattled and felt so many conflicting emotions. I did not know who I should be more disgusted with: him or myself. I kept trying to rationalize why this had happened to me. Why had he picked me? I couldn't find an answer. I even began to question my own sexual orientation, which only made my mental state worse.

By that age, I had encountered some guys who had more feminine ways and mannerisms, but that had been in Toronto, and they were civilians. Among us, we had ridiculed and mocked them, calling them "fairies" and queers and other such insults. I was immature and stupid like many guys my age. As army medics we often had to deal with some idiotic macho infantry types calling us queer, but they quickly changed their attitude when they needed medical attention from us. Their taunts never affected me too much before, but now the very thought of them fueled my growing fears.

Had the incident happened back in Canada, an evening with Barbara or another girl would have curbed much of the mental anguish and self-doubt I was putting myself through. Unfortunately, though, I was in an army camp in this God-forsaken country of Korea. There were a dozen or so nurses around, and I considered talking to one of them, but I dismissed the idea as soon as it came, knowing it would be far too embarrassing. So I kept it locked inside me, not daring to discuss it with anyone, and suffering in silence.

I had flashbacks to my days at Fairbridge when I felt guilty about things I never did but was accused of doing. However, this was a far worse feeling. Back then; I had always been able to work my way through unpleasant situations by talking to mates, reading books… not this time, though. I could not keep my mind focused long enough to read a single paragraph.

I was unable to take my mind off the ugliness of the incident and nagging questions of "how" and "why." It became an obsession. The nights were the worst of all. Something about the quiet and the dark thoughts seemed to make everything going on in my head even worse and I could barely sleep.

I took on even more shifts in the OR trying to keep my mind completely focused on my work. Work only gave temporary relief, as I couldn't keep it up nonstop. During my off-duty hours, I would find an isolated spot in the camp and sit for hours just staring at the hills, brooding. It did not take too long for my mates to become concerned and start asking what was going on. The very thought of telling anyone was still too unbearable, so I simply clammed up and pushed them away. I never spoke to the guy who committed the despicable act; somehow he managed to stay out of my sight. My depression led to severe anxiety and an awful fear that I was losing my mind. I felt there was no one I could trust enough to talk to about what had happened. How could I possibly discuss how screwed-up I felt inside? As time passed I became obsessed with my fears. I remained aware of my actions, others, and my surroundings, but at times I felt as if I were not real. It was as if my mind had somehow floated away and there was nothing, no feeling throughout the body I had left. I once had a vision of myself as a corpse.

After several weeks of this, I broke down during my shift. I was standing in the OR and bawling like a child. One of the surgeons whom I highly respected took me aside and talked to me. I did not tell him what happened, but I did admit I was having thoughts of suicide. He was extremely supportive and told me he would take care of the situation.

There was no mental health specialist stationed with the 25th FDS to handle psychological cases, so I was evacuated to the Brit Com Hospital in Japan. I went through normal admission procedures at the mental ward, and a nurse took me to a private room. I changed into a hospital gown and climbed into to bed. In a short time, the nurse came in and gave me some medication to help me sleep. The trip to Japan had been a long and tiresome journey, so the medication did its job in no time.

I was awakened in the middle of the night by a loud voice coming from the room next to mine. I could hear a man talking to himself, and every now and then he would get very agitated and start screaming. I learnt later that he was an Australian fighter pilot who had suffered a nervous breakdown. On top of the usual stress he had to deal with as a fighter pilot, the poor guy received a letter informing him that his wife had run off with another man, and that pushed him over the edge.

Somehow, with help of the medication, I got through that first night. Knowing that they had placed me in a mental ward caused me even more anxiety. I feared this meant I was really losing my mind, completely.

The next morning, they took me for an examination by a psychiatrist. Even though I had been completely reluctant to open up before, something changed when I met with him. I felt an overwhelming urge to unload what had happened.

During the first session he did not say much. He just listened and let me talk. I filled the time voicing all the strange, warped thoughts that had consumed me for so long. Finally, I could unload all the crap in my head. It was like excising a nasty boil that had been painfully festering far too long. I felt so much relief when my thoughts were out in the open, and I had the psychiatrist's reassurance. Of course, this session did not totally solve my problem, but it was an important first step.

That week, we had daily sessions. When the psychiatrist asked me to tell him about my life, I held nothing back. He actually spent as much time inquiring into my childhood as he did into Korea. He asked if there had been any homosexuality at Fairbridge. I told him that we were isolated from the girls and the only sexual activity I really had any part of was masturbation. I added that most of us had known about the perverted duty master who had molested the boys when he was supposed to be disciplining them with the strap.

The psychiatrist said it was possible that the depressions I had suffered as a child and the lingering feelings of inferiority from my Fairbridge days had left me vulnerable to mental-health problems. He also told me that had the incident happened in Canada and not Korea, I probably would never have driven myself to such a bad state. It was a combination of many factors, including my past and the strain I was experiencing in Korea that contributed to this.

After a spending a few unsettling days in the room next to the Aussie pilot, I requested a new room. I didn't know it then, but it was one of the best moves I could've made. Not only was my new ward-neighbor a lot quieter and less unsettling, he also contributed unintentionally to my recovery.

His name was Roger, and he was a sergeant in the Royal Canadian Regiment that had been in Korea for almost a year. He was admitted to the mental ward under false pretenses. One night, he had gotten into a terrific physical fight with one of his own men. Normally, this would easily warrant a court martial. However, his commanding officer had a lot of respect for the sergeant, and to avoid putting him up for trial; he had the Medical Officer sign him out as suffering from duty fatigue.

Roger was a career soldier, a "spit-and-polish" type, but not one of those we described as chicken-shit. Once he figured out that I was not completely deranged, he took me into his confidence. By then, I was into my second week of treatment, and while I felt considerably calmer, I found myself still suffering from bouts of anxiety. The sergeant asked me what

I was in the psych ward for, and I lied by telling him it was fatigue from working long hours in the OR. He responded by saying that what both of us really needed was a night out on the town. I replied, "How in the hell can we do that? They won't give us a gate pass from the hospital."

I was soon to learn he was one hell of a resourceful soldier. One morning, Roger knocked on my door and asked if I would be interested in getting an afternoon pass to leave the hospital. I looked at him disbelievingly. Before I could react, he said, "Hey, don't ask; it's a yes or no question!"

I responded with a none-too-enthusiastic, "Well, OK, as long as we don't end up in the guardhouse."

He said, "Trust me; it will be strictly according to regulations."

Somehow he managed to get on the good side of the senior NCO in charge of the ward. With that connection, he requested and received two official passes for us to leave the hospital from 1200 to 1800 hours that day.

I was nervous as hell when we stepped out of that hospital door. Roger flagged a taxi, and I got in before my anxiety had a chance to make me turn around. Roger was so easygoing and full of humor that I found myself deciding to relax and simply go with the flow. I thought to myself, " What the hell; we hell, we are just two crazy young soldiers out for a little R and R."

I had not had a drink since the night of the incident, so I quickly made a resolution to go easy on the alcohol. However, I had no cause to worry about that because Roger had something far better than booze on his agenda.

The cab stopped at a fine hotel in the city. A man who led us to an elegant, carpeted lobby, where we each booked a room, greeted us at the door. Then the man introduced us to a couple of very nice-looking, young Japanese women. They were both friendly, yet seemed quite bashful in their approach. They led us to the cocktail lounge with a dance area. A band was playing nice, soft, romantic music followed by a Japanese singer who performed an excellent impersonation of Frank Sinatra. In this intimate atmosphere surrounded by soft melodies, familiar love songs, and beautiful women, all the old passionate feelings came back. The attraction I was feeling for the young women was unmistakable.

Roger and I conversed for a little while with the two girls sitting with us, but there were several other girls in the lounge as well. Within minutes, I spotted one girl that I definitely wanted to dance with. She was very pretty and her facial features looked Eurasian. Her skin was fair and her almond-shaped brown eyes were beautiful. I was stealing admiring glances at her, but I was still feeling too hesitant to go over and talk to her. That's when Roger also spotted her. He nudged me. "Look at that beauty over there," he said.

Clearly, I wasn't the only one with an eye for her. With that, I knew I had to make the first move right then before Roger beat me to her table. It was all I could do to restrain myself from jumping over our table to get to her. Instead, I kept my composure and stood up and told Roger I'd be right back. Then, as calmly as possible, I made my way to her table. My nerves were slightly on edge as I approached, worrying that she'd turn me down. I didn't have to fear. As soon as she saw me, she smiled warmly and that removed any lingering doubts. She let me lead her to the dance floor.

She was an excellent dancer, and when the first song finished, we stayed for the next one. We exchanged names between songs. Her name was Yoshi, and in accordance with the Japanese custom, mine became "Roddy-san."

The two of us barely left the dance floor for a long time. My strategy was to give Roger as much time as possible to find another girl to woo. Sometime later, I looked around and was greatly relieved to see that he had found another girl, and the two of them were cuddling close on the dance floor.

After a while, I took Yoshi up to my hotel room. Without the music to distract us, we had the chance to talk. She spoke some English and told me about her life. She worked as a shop girl in town. After what seemed like an eternity, I took her in my arms and kissed her. Holding her soft body erased all those insecurities about my masculinity and sexuality. It felt so natural.

She was a bit shy and timid in my arms, and I could tell she was not one of the sex girls working for the hotel. I decided not to rush the situation and make her feel uncomfortable. We did not make love that day, but for me, it was paradise holding her close to my body and kissing her. I was in seventh heaven experiencing all the sweet, sensual feelings from just being alone with this beautiful girl.

Considering the deep depression and anxiety attacks I had gone through, I cannot describe the relief that flowed through my mind that day. As I reflected on it much later, I found it hard to believe I put myself through so much agony and self-doubt. Hard to believe how irrational my thought process had been, but then, it had been a deeply unsettling experience. Yoshi and I eventually returned to the cocktail lounge and found Roger sitting at the table with the two girls. As soon as he saw me, Roger laughed and said, "Mac, you look like a new man." He had no idea how true that statement was.

I told him he was the best shrink in Japan and had missed his true calling. We laughed like a couple of overgrown kids. Roger had to drag me out when our curfew neared. Both of us took the girls' addresses before we left. I was determined to see Yoshi again and soon somehow. We parted with a final kiss.

We had only 10 minutes for the taxi to get us back to the hospital. I was singing love songs for several days after that memorable afternoon, especially Sinatra's "Let's Fall in Love." At times hearing that song, it will bring back memories of Yoshi and Japan.

During my next session with the psychologist, I told him that I finally felt OK and was ready to return to duty. He may have wondered how this miraculous cure came on so quickly, but he could see the change. After a few final follow-up sessions, they discharged Roger and me from the hospital on the same day, and we went on our separate ways. He returned to his unit in Korea, and I was reassigned to the Brit Com Hospital. I was never to meet Roger again and often wish I had been able to tell him how he had unwittingly given me the exact thing I needed to regain my sense of happiness and normality.

The Brit Com Hospital was part of a former WWII

Nipponese naval base in Kure, which had been the main base of the Nipponese fleet. I did not know it at the time, but it was quite a historical place. The battleship *Yamato* was the largest and last battleship of WWII. It sailed out of the Kure harbour to her sinking. The kamikaze suicide pilots who took to the air to die trying to sink American ships were also based in Kure.

Once I had settled into my assignment at the hospital, my first priority was to find Yoshi. The shop where she worked was not far, so at the first opportunity I dropped by to see her. In no time at all we fell into a steady relationship. I became very attached to Yoshi, but I felt our blossoming love affair could not be a lasting one. In those days, the army protocol made it difficult for a soldier to marry a local girl and bring her home.

I also stopped writing to Barbara by then. As I said before, I was losing the motivation to keep writing as I realized how little we had in common. It was unkind on my part to just cut her off, but I found it difficult writing that type of letter. Yoshi and I were far better matched in our personalities and our interests. I always had something to talk about with her. I hope Barbara eventually met a man who was better suited for her.

My duties in the Brit Com hospital were far less intensive and demanding than what I had experienced in Korea. Frankly, after Korea it was a "soft touch." In addition to working on the surgical ward, I frequently escorted patients to Tokyo where they would be evacuated home. On one particular run, I accompanied a medical transport to Tokyo for an injured British soldier who was being sent home. They issued me a three-day pass to stay in Tokyo. I knew that in the city, the U.S. forces had special hotels, clubs, and PXs for their service personnel to enjoy while getting some much-needed rest and relaxation from their assignments in Korea. To get the misery of Korea off soldiers' minds, that relaxation consisted mainly of women and booze, though I doubt very much you would've ever found that written in any military handbooks. None of the Brit Com military forces had any facilities that could compare with what the Americans offered in Tokyo. The PXs were as big as department stores and the R&R hotels were like luxury hotels back home. Fortunately for us Canadians, the Yanks extended special permits to allow us to use their facilities.

I decided to take advantage of my permit after delivering my patient to the airport in Tokyo. I bummed a Jeep lift into the city and checked into one of the U.S. forces R&R hotels. I dropped my uniform off to have it pressed, and my boots shined. I took a long, hot shower, enjoying the spacious facilities and amenities in my room. I was really impressed. This was my first experience seeing how well America treated its military, and it was definitely first class.

When I was all spiffed up, I proceeded to the lounge. Most of the tables were full, so couple U.S. aviators invited me to sit with them. We had a few beers and told some stories. I found them to be good company. Then one of them suggested moving on to a nightclub and invited me to join. He claimed it was great and there were loads of girls.

Just then a Japanese civilian driver came to our table.

He addressed me, saying, "Corporal, your Jeep is out front waiting."

Before I could explain that I hadn't called for a ride, and he probably wanted the two Aussie NCOs at another table nearby, he turned around and walked briskly out of the lounge. The three of us followed him, intending to explain the mix-up and hire a taxi instead. Then we saw there were no taxis around, and we had a better idea. We could have the driver drop us off at the nearby nightclub and send him back for the Aussies.

We laughed like a bunch young lads pulling a prank as we slid into the Jeep. We nearly got away with it, but before the Jeep had left the driveway, the Aussie corporal came running and knocked angrily on my side of the vehicle. The driver hit the brakes, halting our getaway.

"Where the hell are you going with my Jeep!" the corporal shouted.

I got out and tried to pacify the Aussie, explaining we only wanted to use it for a quick five-minute drive and fully intended to send it back right away. He was so pissed that he was not going to accept that, and he began making physical threats. His friend was also threatening to do serious damage to my person, so the odds of me escaping unharmed looked slim indeed.

The two of them didn't realize that I wasn't alone. My partners in crime were pretty hefty, and as soon as they got out of the Jeep to back me up, the odds changed dramatically. Word has always been that the Aussies loved nothing better than a good brawl, but that day reason prevailed with the lads from Down Under. At my suggestion we all trooped back into the lounge and I bought them a beer for the trouble. They then generously gave orders to the driver to deliver us to the nightclub.

We were ready to spend a fun and boisterous evening in the club, but our adventure came to a close shortly after we arrived. We had barely lifted our first cocktail to our lips when the U.S. Military Police (MPs) raided the club, and we were busted. This club was off-limits for U.S. military personnel. The MPs hauled my newfound friends off, and I barely managed to talk to them out of them arresting me. I questioned whether they had any real jurisdiction over Brit Com personnel, and they backed off. I decided I'd best get the hell out of there before they notified the Brit Com command MPs, better referred to by the troops as "Meat Heads." As I turned to leave the place, they requested I be kind enough to give them a call if any U.S. personnel offered to accompany them to any off-limits nightclubs. Then, as I walked out, I laughed to myself, thinking, "Ha, ha! Are you kidding? Turn a fellow soldier in? Fuck no, siree!"

The rest of my time in Japan, which was about four months, was fairly quiet and uneventful, but Yoshi's company considerably sweetened it. I looked forward to spending time with her and enjoying our romance while it lasted. After I returned to Canada, I missed her terribly. It took several months to stop thinking about her. However, pleasant memories of her and Japan still cross my mind occasionally.

TIME TO GO HOME TO CANADA

It was the middle of 1954, and as the time was rapidly running out on my overseas posting, I found myself reluctant to leave. My posting to Japan was a very pleasurable experience. Japan was my once-in-a-lifetime Shangri La. I had been shipped there in a sorry state and left a cured and happy man, fully recovered from the mental health issues that had brought me there from Korea.

Like many Canuck soldiers in Japan, I was actually quite depressed at the thought of having to return home. I would have been perfectly willing to serve another year in Japan, particularly with Yoshi as my girlfriend. Believe me, during that period of my life, Japan was a hell of a lot more appealing than Vancouver.

I was rather sullen as I boarded the aircraft headed home with a bunch of my fellow soldiers. But then, I had a stroke of good luck. It turned out the flight home was overloaded, and six men were bumped off, and I was one of them.

My mood rose at an instant. I drew myself up and smirked gleefully. I could have six more days in Tokyo with Yoshi before the next flight left.

As the six of us made our way to the aircraft door, a few guys stuck on the plane grabbed for their wallets and waved at us with bills in hand, begging to let us switch places. One guy shouted he would give a hundred dollars for one of us to take his seat. Half of the selected men took the money, but I could not be tempted to accept. I would not give up my precious six days in Tokyo with Yoshi for anything. I was going to take advantage of them.

I had Yoshi take the train from her hometown Kure to Tokyo. She was just as thrilled to see me as I was to see her. We spent all six of those precious days together touring the city, eating at restaurants, dancing at the clubs, and enjoying every moment of each other's company. When my borrowed time was up I realized staying might not have been the wisest choice. I couldn't keep Yoshi and the sweetness of our time together only made the final parting that much more painful and heartbreaking. For the entire flight I was crestfallen, feeling the pangs of lost love.

After arriving back home in Canada, I was posted to the staff of the Western Canadian Army HQ at Jericho Beach, Vancouver. I didn't realize it at the time, but that posting would be the final one in my military career.

For the one-year service in the Far East, I had a 30-day leave coming my way, which I could request at my convenience. I decided to save it and combine it with my regular annual leave for an extended visit to reunite with my family in Scotland, which had been my ambition for a long time.

The first few months in the Jericho camp kept me busy. I had to familiarize myself with my assignment and barrack's life. When I was not preoccupied with my duties, I was lonely and thinking about Yoshi, and how much I missed her. I had to come to terms with the fact that the love affair was truly over.

I took to heart the old adage that the best way to mend

a broken heart is to find a new love. When a little time had passed and the heartache was no longer so fresh, I ventured out to do exactly that. I poured all my energies into finding a new girlfriend.

However, when it came to courting the Canadian girls, I was once again lacking in self-confidence. With Yoshi, I had felt secure and self-assured, but that was because with her, I felt no need to pretend to be anything other than myself. I didn't feel the need to project a more appealing persona for her. I knew she liked me for who I was. With Canadian girls, that was an entirely different situation. The army uniform only complicated matters because soldiers were still unpopular in Canada in the 50s, and most respectable girls would not entertain the thought of dating us. When I went out to socialize with the girls, I got the impression that the ones, I liked had higher expectations of what they wanted in a man. I didn't measure up in their eyes and one can take that quite literally as I stood at a height of 5' 7" with my shoes on.

Those past feelings of self-doubt came rushing back, and the old inferiority complex hit me like a ton of bricks. I wondered whether it was my looks that disappointed them, or my height, or my personality. The pay for a soldier didn't help my prospects, as I couldn't afford a car to take a girl out on a date. A few times, I would offer to see a girl home from a dance, and as soon as she found out I meant I would walk with her, not drive her; she lost interest. "No thanks, maybe next time," she'd say, and that would be the end of it.

Many a night I walked home alone feeling disgusted and lonely. All of this did nothing to help rebuild my shaken self-confidence. Whenever a girl declined a dance or a date with me, I was extremely hurt. In retrospect, I think I was far too sensitive, my spirit still bruised from the end of my relationship with Yoshi.

I remembered how in Japan we soldiers had been really spoilt when it came to dating. The girls there were happy to be invited to dance. Just to be clear, they were just ordinary girls who worked in shops or cafés, not street girls or geishas. A lot of misconceptions surround geishas even today. They are not high-class prostitutes. They are Japanese women specially trained in the traditional art of entertaining Japanese men by singing, dancing, playing music, and making conversation. They are highly respected. Your average soldier, me included, would not have a clue what it was like to experience an evening with a Geisha. They are part of an entirely different culture. From books that I have read on Japanese culture the Geishas are highly respected.

I felt that I needed to find a woman to date on a fairly steady basis. That conviction was so strong that I endured a lot of disappointments and came back every night to try again rather than let the issue go. Having at least one girl to date didn't seem like an option. Finally, there came a break to this lonely existence. I met a civilian nurse named Pat who showed some interest in me. She was pretty, personable and intelligent, and—thankfully for me—not in a military uniform.

Pat and I dated off and on for about four months, and I was once again feeling the pangs of love might be in the air. I was quite smitten with her, and our causal relationship was helping my self-confidence with the fairer sex. I realise later my feeling that I *had* to have someone was actually detrimental to forming a good relationship. One can't rush the process; it needs to happen mutually and naturally.

Later, it became evident that my relationship with Pat was one-sided. I was on the rebound from one love affair and tiptoeing through a minefield. While I was beginning feel strongly in my relationship with Pat, deep down, my intuition was saying she did not share the same feelings. I knew Pat enjoyed going out on dates with me, but a serious, long-term relationship was not on her agenda.

We were still dating when my annual leave was approaching. Around that time, Pat told me she was leaving Vancouver. She and two other nurses had made plans to take a short holiday in Scotland before starting work at Hammersmith Hospital in London.

When I heard this, I was thrilled. I told her I was making plans to visit my family in Scotland, and I thought we could meet up in Edinburgh. I fantasized about sweeping her off her feet in the countryside surrounded by the beautiful Scottish Highlands. I was swept up by my wild romantic imagination into the world of the musical, *"Brigadoon,"* where two American tourists find a mysterious, magical Scottish village and fall in love. I imagined serenading Pat with the song "Almost Like Being in Love" from the musical. I didn't consider it then, but that song was ironically appropriate considering how this was a one-sided fantasy affair. It was *almost* like love, but not quite.

I wrote my father to tell him that I had put in the

request for my extended leave and would be booking travel arrangements to Scotland as soon as it was granted. I was restless to return to my native land and be reunited with my family. I was brimming with excitement when I posted the letter, and I expected he would be just as glad to receive the news. I was shocked when his response came back, and he wrote that this would not be a good time to visit. He vaguely mentioned financial reasons, but that didn't make sense. Sure, I wasn't rich, but I could well afford to take care of my own expenses. I later came to the conclusion it was his financial situation.

After all the years of separation, I was not going to be put off making this visit any longer. So even though I had not completed all the travel arrangements, I wrote back stating the plans were all set, and it was too late to cancel.

His next letter offered the first hint of why he actually didn't want me to come. He told me that he had remarried, and I now had a stepmother and three new sisters. This was information that he had never shared with me before; I had previously assumed he was single and a widower. After reading his letter, I began to suspect he had been concealing the existence of my mother, my siblings, and me from his new wife and family all along. Now my visit was forcing him to tell the truth, or part of it.

The news I learnt from that letter shook me up a bit at the time, but it hit me much harder decades later when I learnt the whole story of my family's break up.

The truth was that he had remarried in 1940, about year after his divorce with my mother. Then, in November of 1941, only a year after he remarried, he requested that the Middlemore Homes Institution send me to Fairbridge Canada, effectively shipping me as far away from his new life as possible.

His past correspondences rarely mentioned anything about my brother Robert or sister Minnie. I did suspect that he and Rob were on bad terms because once, after I mentioned Rob had written to me, my father responded at length about how he disapproved of my brother and warned me to stay away from him. As for Minnie, he had written that she was also trouble, though he never explained why. Now that I'm older I feel like he had intentionally kept all of us at arm's length because he simply did not want any of us to be involved with his new family.

Though the news of my stepfamily had come with a shock, I did not feel any real reason to be upset with him at the time. I just felt pleased that I finally had a family to visit, period, the more the merrier.

However, I had another surprise coming. Pat told me her travel dates and mine would not overlap. Her short holiday would be over before mine began, and we could not meet in Scotland. That news jolted me out of my idle dreams of wooing her in the Highlands.

Attempting to make the best of the situation, I asked her if she could stop in and visit my family ahead of me during her time in Edinburgh. She agreed. Then later, she wrote me a letter telling me how she enjoyed her visit with my family. She described how nice my new step mother and intelligent and polite my father was, and how my young stepsisters were excited at the thought of my upcoming visit. In closing, she gave me the address and a phone number for the London hospital where she would be working so I could contact and meet her when I visited London during my trip.

With my leave approved, I booked a flight with British Overseas Airways. From the moment, I started packing my suitcase; I felt extremely excited about the thought of finally meeting my family.

That fight with British Overseas Airways stands out in my memory as the classiest flight I've ever taken. It was my first time flying on a commercial airline, and I was very impressed. The plane had a full cocktail lounge above the passenger cabin. Back in the 50s, passengers dressed up in their finest clothes for the flight. The seats were spacious and very comfortable, unlike the ones in today's airplanes. I felt like I was travelling in luxury.

I knew my father didn't own a car, so I didn't expect him to meet me at the airport. Like the average wage earner in the 1950s U.K., he could not afford one. I took a taxi to my stepfamily's home. They lived in a two-bedroom flat in Edinburgh a couple of miles outside the city centre in a nice neighbourhood.

I hesitated for a moment before I knocked, taking everything in. This was the big moment I had waited for. I was sure that as soon as the door opened my life was about to change to the better. I would find a way to once again be part of the family I had lost. I reached out and knocked eagerly.

Mary, my new stepmother, opened the door and greeted

me warmly with a welcoming embrace. When she let me go, I saw a few tears of happiness glistening in her eyes. I could tell instantly that she was a very nice, caring, and accepting woman, and we would have a good relationship. She was also very beautiful.

In contrast to Mary's show of delight and affection, my father was stiffer and more formal, hanging back in the main room and keeping his emotions on a tight rein. He seemed happy though, restrained on the occasion, we exchanged cordial handshakes.

Next, I was introduced to my new sisters. Annie was the eldest at around age nine. She seemed a bit reserved but friendly when she greeted me. Rosemary, about age seven, was all smiles, gushing with excitement. Finally, there was little Christine, the youngest at about age five, her head wreathed in angelic blonde curls. She hid nervously behind her mother's legs. She was obviously very shy and wary of me.

Annie appeared to be the serious and responsible one, and I thought to myself that I would need to earn her approval. Rosemary, on the other hand, was so enthusiastic about my arrival that I knew getting along with her wouldn't be a problem. I had a feeling shy little Christine would definitely be a challenge, though. Her mother tried to cajole her out to meet her new big brother, but she was a bit fearful. She seemed to be wondering whom this stranger standing quite proudly in his army uniform and big, shiny boots was doing in her home.

I felt very welcomed into this home and looked forward to taking the time to bond with my new family and getting to know them. I felt pretty optimistic. Their flat was a bit small but nicely furnished and cozy. Everything was really comfortable. Mary laid out a spot for me on the large couch in the front room. I was pretty exhausted from the journey, so I went to sleep early.

The next morning Mary woke me gently. She was holding a tray with a cup of tea that she placed beside my makeshift bed. She asked me what I would like for breakfast. I told her I would appreciate whatever she served anything would be good. She brought in another tray loaded with a full Scottish breakfast complete with toast, sausage, mushrooms, baked beans, a fried egg, a potato scone, and black pudding. I was speechless; nobody had treated me with such overwhelming hospitality before. This was the first time in my life that anyone had ever served me breakfast in bed. If this was any indication of what the rest of my visit would hold, I was ecstatic.

I spent my first few days there getting to know my father and my new mother and sisters. We went sightseeing around Edinburgh and I fell in love with the city almost immediately. The next thing on my agenda was meeting some of my extended family.

Back then, family gatherings were nearly impossible to arrange. The average family residence in Scotland was very small, and nobody owned a telephone. To make contact with someone, I had to wait in line for the red phone booth with 20 other people or more ahead of me.

Since calling was impractical and cars were a luxury few could afford, we were used to jumping on the bus and dropping in for a visit unannounced, hoping someone was home. It became a lifelong habit for me to make surprise visits to friends and family even as phones became a common fixture in households. I ended up making a lot of these surprise visits to family members during my visit. I wanted to maximize my time there.

My Grandad Sandy had a flat within walking distance, so I could spend a lot of time with him. In the span of very short few days, I became very fond of my grandfather. He was an entertaining and lively character with lots of stories to tell.

I met my father's sister Kate, her husband Robert Gray, and their children Cathy, Jean, Dorothy, Robert, and wee Norman, who later grew up to be the tallest of the family. I became very close with Aunt Kate, Uncle Robert, and my cousins during that time. We interacted a lot during my stay, and that cemented our strong familial bond. I would remain close to them for the rest of my life.

I also met a few other family members, including Aunt Jean and her family. Unfortunately, I only spent one afternoon with her, and that wasn't enough time to get to know each other. We never got in touch afterward. I learned some time later that she and the family moved to South Africa and one of her daughters became a top fashion model there, but I was unable to find her again.

Between sightseeing and meeting all my relatives, the days just flew by, leaving me dazed. I somehow found the time to take my father, Mary, and the girls for a day trip to Loch Lomond, which was incredible. And of course, I carved out a couple of days from my busy timetable to take a trip to London, so I could spend some time with Pat. We had arranged a couple of nights before to meet at a set time at Trafalgar Square in the heart within the city.

After arriving in London with plenty of time to get from the station to the square, I made my way directly there and looked around. She was nowhere to be found. I decided I would try calling her to let her know I'd arrived. Unluckily for me, there was only one phone box that I could find, and it had a line a mile long in front of it. Even worse, I realized that, in my haste to get to London; I had forgotten to bring the piece of paper where I had scribbled Pat's phone number. I was undeterred. I felt sure that if I could just get to the phone, the operator would give me the hospital's main number, and I could reach her from there.

It took ages of restless waiting to finally reach the phone. When I finally got connected with the hospital, the line was continuously busy. I waited and waited for someone to pick up, but no luck. After several minutes having people glaring at me for holding up the line, I gave up.

I paced up and down the square in frustration, still waiting for her to come. I was one exasperated, love-smitten soldier, doing my best to dodge the pigeon crap that missed the head of the statue of Lord Nelson. I made one more attempt at the red phone box, but the Hammersmith Hospital line was still busy.

All told, I spent about three long, anguished hours in the square before I accepted that she wasn't coming. I hung my head in defeat and mumbled a soft curse or two at myself as I headed towards King's Cross rail station and caught the next train back to Edinburgh. The train ride was long and miserable, and I was feeling very dejected and angry at myself for the whole journey. I felt it was somehow my own fault.

When I arrived back, my father greeted me with a very cool reception. Though I had told him far in advance of my intention to visit Pat, he apparently thought it was rude of me to make that trip to London. He was angry and barely spoke to me for several days, even though I felt I had done nothing wrong.

By now, I had learnt that father was an unpredictable character prone to mood swings. He might seem fine one day and be in a foul mood the next, and I might find myself on the receiving end of his nasty moods.

Later, it crossed my mind that he may have thought I was going to London to try to find my brother Robert, though the notion was absurd. It was ludicrous to think how I could possibly have located Rob in a city the size of London with no directions and no clue where to start looking.

The rest of my trip was very pleasant, and I enjoyed every day I was there. When it came time to leave, I was reluctant to go. We said our long good-byes and Mary wrapped me in a warm embrace, telling me to come again. I promised her I would, and I headed to the airport. On the plane back to Vancouver, I knew I would find a way to return to my homeland again. Even after only one visit, I felt like I belonged there. The feeling of being with Scots, "my ain folk," was strong in my blood. I felt more complete now that I knew where I had come from. Whether it would take a little while or a long time, I would be back.

Soon after my return, I received a letter from Pat apologizing and explaining why she never made it to our meeting at Trafalgar Square. She had been called in to cover for another nurse who had fallen ill, and she had no way of contacting me. Pat closed the letter by saying that she planned to stay in the U.K. for several months. I could recognize this as what we called a "Dear John," letter back in those years. The one-sided love affair was fini.

When I returned to Jericho Beach HQ, they informed me that my posting there would be permanent, if that is even possible in any army. I was to be the NCO in charge of the Medical Inspection Room (MIR). I was responsible for conducting preliminary medical checkups of all HQ service personnel reporting for the "daily sick parade." Put simply, I would check over all the soldiers reporting in with illness or injury complaints.

Thanks to all my experience feigning illness at Fairbridge, I could usually distinguish men who were really sick from those who were faking symptoms. If I considered that their case was a minor ailment i.e. Band-Aid situation, or fixed with an aspirin or such, I would take care of their problems. For the more serious cases, I scheduled appointments for them with the medical officer. I also prepared the necessary reports for the medical officer. It was an easy job that put very little pressure on me. My hours were great, I had the evenings off, and most weekends I got a pass to be off base. The regulations for the permanent staff were a bit on the lax side.

The military personnel at the Jericho Beach HQ were

a mixed bunch, with both permanent staff members and many transients awaiting orders for new postings. Most of the long-term staff was service personnel like mechanics or caterers. Among them, I met a few 'unusual' characters; some of would become my close mates. Dougie Flett was one of them. He was a part Native Canadian fellow medic who had a well-kempt, scholarly look about him until he had downed several beers. Joe Wilkes was another. For the first six months I mistook Joe for a civilian employee as he was rarely seen in regulation uniform. He was in fact an army mechanic, and his "uniform" seemed to consist of a pair of dirty, well-greased coveralls with no insignia showing his unit or rank. When he finally showed up in a regulation uniform for one of our periodic weekend inspections, I was amazed. Of course, he looked just as sloppy in the uniform as he did in the greasy coveralls. Joe was definitely not your spit-and-polish type of soldier, but he was a master mechanic.

Finally, there was Pete Topolnisky, soon to become my best pal at that time in my life. Pete was one of those tall, dark-haired, handsome guys whom short, average-looking guys like me envied. With his looks and physique, he could turn many a woman's head without even trying. When we were out on the town I tried to stay in his vicinity so just possibly the girls could notice me too by extension. Much like Joe, Pete's uniforms rarely saw an iron; his belt brass existed in constant need of Brasso polish, and he never looked or acted like a military man. He had an independent streak and an air of defiance about him. How the two of us became pals I have no idea.

When we met I was still pretty much a classic spit-and-polish, regimental type soldier, but that began to change as I spent more time in Vancouver.

I think it was the easy lifestyle at Jericho Beach and the lax regulations that lulled me into a slightly more independent way of thinking. There were other factors, too. The longer I stayed, the more I started to get frustrated with my assigned duties. My duties as an NCO in charge of a surgical team were far more interesting and challenging than that of an NCO running a sick room. I still held vague hopes that with some additional education, I could qualify for officer's training school and move on. I sure as hell didn't envision a military career stuck as a two-striper. However, my mental health episode in Korea would've been on my profile records, and back then something like that could have precluded any chance of further advancement.

Still, even as I got more restless and bold, I didn't start all-out rebelling against regimentation. In all fairness, I still feel strongly that regimentation is a necessity for any worthwhile army, and unrestricted, loose behavior is not acceptable in the life of a soldier. In my experience, that is the quickest way to put you at serious odds with the military system. As I found myself going down that road, getting more out of step with the organization, it became the beginning of the end of my military career. Pete, Dougie, Joe, and I lived in the same barracks. As the NCO in charge of the unit, I had a private room. On weekends, we would shower, grab a meal at the mess hall, and then head to downtown Vancouver together. Of course, we swapped our uniforms for "civvies" whenever we went out, but there wasn't much we could do about our military haircuts.

My old mate John Hardy from Fairbridge days was actually enrolled at the University of British Columbia and didn't live too far away. He also became incorporated into our little group, for better or worse. The poor guy would be submerged deep in his studies when we dropped in to coax him out for a night with us in the Vancouver beer parlors. Between the distractions that we caused him, John is lucky he graduated. It is testimony to his intelligence and perseverance that he did graduate, and went on to have a very successful career as a teacher and later editor of the BC Teachers' Federation newspaper.

We had an established set of favourite pubs—or beer parlors as they were commonly known then—on upper Granville Street that we frequented. The Cecil Hotel was probably our most common haunt.

The liquor laws in those days required beer parlors to have to separate sections and entrances, one for men and another for ladies and their escorts. A bouncer always guarded the door to the ladies' side. Pete and I worked out a crafty system to either sneak or outright burst into the women's side. From the street, we took note of the single girls entering the pub and as soon as we spotted some pretty ones we wanted to talk to, we'd create some kind of diversion to distract the bouncer. The minute he took his eye off the door we dashed inside the women's side door entrance.

Once inside, speed was of the essence to locate the table that the girls had taken before we raised suspicion. We slipped in beside them uninvited and turned on the charm. Be it sheer luck or Pete's good looks, I honestly cannot recall even one time that any girls turned us in for crashing their table.

On Fridays and Saturdays, after a couple of hours with the lads in the beer parlors, I would take off for the dance hall. I did not like drinking beer all night and much preferred dancing and flirting with the girls.

We had some very memorable and fun-filled nights in those beer parlors. One particular evening Dougie was playing up the fact that he was part-Native American as he tried to get a date. One of the girls asked him what tribe he belonged to and Dougie said, "Me Blackfoot Indian." She didn't seem convinced by his fake accent, so Dougie proceeded to take off his shoe and show her his black foot. He had stained it with boot polish before heading out that night. Needless to say, she was pretty stunned.

Another night was very memorable, but for a much different reason.

It was still early in the evening. The clock hadn't struck 6:00 yet. The four of us were making our rounds, leaving one beer parlour to visit another across the street. It was a Friday night and a payday, so there were tons of loggers around town spending extra off the top of their earnings. The cops knew this, and they were out patrolling the streets in full force.

In front of the beer parlour, one of the drunken loggers stumbled into Dougie. Doug pushed him off to get through the door. Then another logger jumped in and shoved Pete, and that was a big mistake. Pete was a lady's man, but he would not hesitate to start throwing punches at the slightest provocation. In a moment, all hell broke loose between the loggers, Pete, and Dougie.

Joe and I were smart enough to stand back and let them have at it. It was not long before a cop car rolled up curbside and immediately called for backup. The cops pulled the brawl apart and were going to put Pete, Dougie, and the loggers all in the paddy wagon for a trip to jail. I approached the officers to plead the case for the innocence of my mates. They ignored my appeal and swiftly tossed me into the wagon with them. Joe, observing my dumb mistake, wisely melted into the crowd. The rest of us were taken away.

From my second-floor jail cell, I watched people strolling the streets below without a care, laughing boisterously and making their way to the diners, clubs, and bars. After an hour of taking in the Friday nightlife crowd going where I couldn't go, I was really pissed off. All I could think about was all the girls I could've been dancing with if I wasn't stuck up here. I soundly cursed Pete and Dougie for screwing up my Friday night out on the town. That elicited a hearty laugh from both, and that only ticked me off more.

One Saturday each month, the HQ adjutant would order all HQ personnel to report for a morning command parade inspection. After the inspection, we had to attend a three-hour-long mandatory classroom training session. It was boring as hell, but misses it, and you would end up confined in the barracks for a spell. After a few of these long, tedious Saturday classroom sessions, Pete and I devised a scheme to get out of them.

We had duly noted that they took the roll call on the

parade square only at the beginning of the inspection, well before we marched in and entered the classroom building. We also had noted there was an unlocked loo in the hall leading to the classrooms. So one Saturday we craftily placed ourselves at the end of the two rear ranks of the file when the platoon reformed to march into the classroom building. We trooped inside with the rest of the unit, and as soon as we were passing the loo door, we broke off and slipped quietly inside the washroom.

We hunkered down until we heard the last of the steel-heeled boots come to a resounding halt on the wooden classroom floor. We waited another five minutes, listening for the start of the lecture, and then we hastily tiptoed out of the building and marched boldly across the square to our barracks. We changed into our civvies, and the next bus had us downtown looking for girls and excitement in no time.

We had this routine down so well that on one occasion we even had a couple girls pick us up in their car outside the barracks as the lecture was starting. But, as my favorite poet Robbie Burns once wrote, "The best-laid plans of mice and men aft gang agley." Our scheme was discovered when one of the officers finally noticed that there seemed to be fewer men in the classroom than during the parade inspection, and he implemented separate roll calls for the parade and the classroom sessions. That of course put an immediate halt to our escaping from the Saturday morning lectures. We were none too happy about that.

Between all our boldness in bending regulations and my growing restlessness, my military career surely was heading for an abrupt ending. However, there was one final fiasco that really put the icing on the cake. I am not very proud of it, but it illustrates my trajectory well.

It happened on a Friday, another payday night. Pete and I had downed a few beers in the Cecil Hotel, and since we had folding money in our pockets, I suggested that we moved on to one of the classier nightclubs. Pete agreed.

As we often did when we frequented the nightclub scene, we packed a flask of whisky and poured shots of it into our glasses when the bartenders weren't looking. I was more inclined to go into nightclubs. They were a more favorable venue for meeting up with a couple of girls. However, either we were out of luck that night or we picked the wrong club because as the evening progressed, we noticed all the girls in the club already had male escorts. The jukebox was killing me by playing a hot dance numbers like "Mack the Knife" by Bobby Darin and not a single girl was available to dance with. I enviously eyed the next table over, where two soldiers in uniform huddled close to their pretty dates. The soldiers were wearing the trademark red boots and insignia of paratroopers on their jackets. They were real hotshots. Early in my military career, I was desperate to sign up with the para section of the medics. Why? I was young, stupid and willing to jump out of a plane for the privilege of wearing the classy red boots and beret of a paratrooper.

So there I sat, stewing with one whisky too many in my system, glaring at two unknown soldiers wearing the coveted red jump boots and escorting two good-looking dollies. I was keenly aware of my lack of both those things. Pete sensed from my sour look that I was close to becoming belligerent. He grabbed my arm, indicating it was time to go.

That particular club was located upstairs, and you had to descend a steep flight of approximately 20 stairs to leave. My vision was becoming fuzzy. The last thing I recalled was Pete leading me toward those stairs.

The next day, when I woke up with a very sore, bruised body and a sizeable plaster stuck to my lower jaw. Pete gave me a sorry account of the evening. Apparently, at the top of the stairs, I slipped out from his hold and raised my voice to drunkenly announce for all to hear, "What the hell... Who needs guts to jump? I could a' been a paratrooper! Don't think so? Well, watch this!"

I jumped.

From what step Pete picked up my crumpled and unconscious body, I never asked. My jaw was so sore that I felt it would be weeks before I could open my mouth again. In any case, it would take several days of serious thinking before I was ready to open my mouth on any account.

I was at a crossroad in my career, a career that consisted of one vocation an army medic? I had to consider whether I would stay or leave, as my current tour of duty was coming to an end. On more than one occasion, I came awfully close to being on the report for disciplinary action. Fortunately for me, none of my off-duty escapades drew the attention of my senior officer. Only my clean on-duty records over the past four years kept me in his good graces. Meanwhile, Doug, Pete, and Joe were all reaching the end of their terms of service, and they had all decided to take their discharge papers. I began seriously considering taking the same course of action.

As I wrestled with this choice, something else developed, which, frankly, took the decision process out of my control. About a year into my Vancouver posting, an infection in my ears began to trouble me. It had flared up a bit in Korea, but since I was working so closely with the FDS surgeons, I had one of the medical officers write me a prescription for an antibiotic, which cleared it up, and I forgot about it. Now in Vancouver, the infection returned. Both my ears were itchy and irritated, and I spotted fresh draining on my pillowcase every night. I put myself on sick parade, and the medical officer decided to have me admitted to the hospital for treatment. They put me on another antibiotic treatment, and that seemed to help temporarily. The ear specialist examined the ear canals thoroughly and noted that both my eardrums had been ruptured. In the report, he recommended that I be given medical discharge from the army due to the condition of my ears.

In all likelihood, the ruptured eardrums had happened during my years at Fairbridge when I received all those blows to the ears, and it had simply gone unnoticed until now. There is abundant evidence of Fairbridge kids in Australia suffering the same condition as well. With that being the case, they probably should never have passed me as being fit for enlistment in the army in the first place. The Canadian veterans affairs office more or less admitted as much in recent years and adjusted my veteran medical entitlement accordingly to cover expenses associated with my condition.

The decision whether to sign up for another term became a moot point. The medical board reviewed the case and decided to give me an honorable discharge for my ear condition. So with that, another chapter in my life had closed and another would begin.

You may have concluded that for a soldier who never spent time on the front lines, I did manage to encounter my fair share of action in my army years. However, I can assure you none of that action would merit any mention in dispatches to HQ.

PART III

1956-1959

RETURNING TO SCOTLAND AND FAMILY

On my release from the army, I began to think seriously of returning to Scotland to live over there for a while and make a serious attempt at establishing my family roots. I was still entitled to a 30-day leave prior to my official discharge date. I made the decision and booked a third class passage on the United States liner leaving New York destined for Southampton, England. To this day, I retain wonderful memories of that voyage across the Atlantic on that ship. While at the time I could not afford to travel first class, I did manage to spend a few magical evenings dancing with pretty women in the first class ballroom. On formal evenings, I wore my dress blue uniform minus my NCO stripes on the sleeve. Several people mistook me for a commissioned officer of the Canadian Army, and who was I to correct their mistaken assumptions? Remember, I once had lofty aspirations of being an officer in her Majesty's service. More importantly, my small subterfuge seemed to work, as none of the ship's personnel challenged my presence in first class.

One evening, I was dancing with a woman who so enjoyed our dance; she introduced me to a chap who was a dance instructor for the Arthur Murray Studio in Los Angeles. During our conversation, he asked me if I was interested in taking up dancing as a career. He gave me his card, but I never followed it up, as I had a feeling, he was gay. That made me dubious as to what his real motive was in making the offer.

The entire voyage was a wonderful adventure, and I arrived in Southampton ready for new adventures in the U.K. From Southampton, I booked my train passage up to Edinburgh.

I arrived at my father's flat and asked him if it was OK to stay with him until I found a job and could afford my own flat. This was a big mistake because whatever remained of the father-son relationship from my first visit soon turned completely sour. I had arrived with enough money that I did not need to look for work immediately. I decided to spend a couple of weeks or so relaxing, visiting relatives and touring the countryside close to Edinburgh.

My cousin Robert and I had hit it off during my earlier visit, so we started hanging out together. He showed me around the city, and we would go 'girl-chasing,' at the two most popular dance halls of Edinburgh, the Cavendish and the Palaise. The dance halls in the U.K. were so much better than the dance halls of Canada. The big difference was the girls in the U.K. went to a public dance with full intention to dance. From experience, my impression was that most of the Canadian girls went to a dance hall seeking serious relationships. I once told a girl in Toronto who refused my offer to a dance, "Look, this is not a proposal for a permanent relationship. It is simply an offer to dance with a guy who loves to dance." In that particular situation, it not only worked, I ended up taking her home on the bus. However, so many girls would stand there most of the night waiting for Mr. Right to show up.

One night at the Palaise, I met and danced with a girl, Margaret McKellar; she was pretty, had a nice personality, and we began to date. I asked my father if it was OK to invite her up to the flat for a visit. He responded that he did not approve of "dance hall girls." Had I heard the story that Uncle Robert told me a number of years later of him meeting our mother in a dance hall, I would have had an appropriate response to his rude remark. As it was, I responded by telling him that just because we met in a dance hall, it did not make her a "dance hall girl." Actually, she had a position as a secretary for a law firm in the city. In any event, I did not take his remarks lightly and walked out of the room in anger.

The very next day I could tell he was in a foul mood, so I did my best to avoid him as much as possible. The following day he made some remarks about my leaving water rings in the bathtub. I apologized and went to clean the tub. Mary jumped up and said not to bother, that she would take care of it, but I put her off and insisted that I would do it.

Following this episode, I attempted to have a talk with him, hoping to resolve whatever issues were causing his foul mood. My efforts only resulted in further angry comments, and soon we were both shouting at each other. I ended the tirade by telling him, "Apparently; I am not welcome here so I will move out tomorrow morning."

Mary, who waited on him hand and foot and from my observations always suffered his angry moods in complete silence, came across the room in tears. She begged him not to let me leave like this. She also said, "Robert, this is the one son who has come home. Please don't do this."

I never forgot her statement and the courage she had in challenging him. I was feeling terrible on her account and realized how difficult it was for her to stand up to him. Though our time together was short, I have retained loving memories and much respect for Mary. She was a beautiful lady and the kind of mother I spent so many years' longing for. I packed up and left the next morning. I caught a bus to my aunt Kate's house. I explained what had happened. She simply shook her head and said, "Well, son; you better come on in; we can put up an extra bed in Robert's room."

While Aunt Kate and Uncle Robert had never taken sides over what had happened; they understood why I had moved out. They took me in like one of their own. Of course, at the time, I had no knowledge that this would be the second time that Aunt Kate and Uncle Robert had taken in her brother's offspring.

The Gray family during that time consisted of my Aunt Kate, Uncle Robert and their children, my cousins: Cathy, Robert, Jean, Dorothy and Norman. Cathy was the eldest (about 20), Robert and Jean a year or two younger, Dorothy about 11, and then wee Norman, a toddler of three. Cathy, Robert, Jean and I were only a few years apart in age. Robert and I already hit it off well during my first visit; over the years we became more like brothers than cousins.

At the time, Cathy was seriously dating an American Air Force lad, Carl, who was stationed at a U.S. airbase close to Edinburgh. They were to get married while I lived with the

Grays. Carl was a very likable guy and had an American Southern accent, which at times presented him with a problem in verbal communications. Mostly, for Carl it was his not understanding the Scottish dialect, so I used to interpret for him on occasion.

One of my memories of living with the Gray family was that of the constant verbal battles of my cousins Cathy and Jean. Cathy always had nice clothing, and younger sister Jean had a terrible habit of borrowing (without asking) Cathy's clothes and make-up. Jean apparently was not very careful with the Cathy's clothes. Consequently, this led to some very noisy, bruising outbursts between the sisters.

Odd as it may seem, I relived this same scenario with my daughters Christine and Tara during their teen years. I recall one early bout between my daughters and thinking to myself that this scene seemed so familiar. Where had I witnessed this before in my life? I swear at times both sets of sisters seemed to be on the verge of killing each other. Fortunately, they never did and as life normally works out, the sisters matured and arrived at a loving relationship that is solid for a lifetime.

During this reunion of my family, I learnt more about my mother and father. Uncle Robert told me our parents had first met in an Edinburgh dance hall. They were ballroom dancers, and my father also played drums in the band. He was a man determined to improve his lot in life. He could be quite witty and sociable, yet could become very taciturn, isolating himself for long periods of time. When I briefly visited him in 1955, I found myself on the receiving end of his mood swings. He was angry and barely spoke to me for several days. I'm sure he suffered from serious bouts of depression that seem to run in our family.

According to Uncle Robert, our mother was young, pretty, and restless. Her permissive lifestyle and fiery temperament clashed with his, and that was probably a major reason behind their split.

After my two weeks of fun and relaxation, I decided if I were to remain in Edinburgh, I had best find some form of employment. This was to be my first taste of looking for a job as a civilian. Compounding that fact was that I was also in a different country and lacked basic employable skills. My previous work experience really consisted of labouring on the farm as a kid, followed by my military training. Obviously, neither of those experiences would help much in seeking civilian employment available in Edinburgh.

Cousin Robert was working as an apprentice at a steel plant, but there were no openings there. On his advice, I went down to the labour office and discovered an opening as a labourer with a construction crew. The construction company was building a post office in the outskirts of the city. When Aunt Kate heard it was labouring, she said, "Roddy, that is hard work. I dinn'a think you will last a day."

Her remark stung and I replied, "Aunt Kate, it can't be any harder than the work I had to do as a kid labouring on a farm at Fairbridge." Her feeling was understandable as the little she observed of me in Edinburgh was that I was a "party lad." I willingly admitted that yes, hard labour was not my first choice, but Fairbridge had certainly prepared me for that eventuality should it be necessary.

Next morning, I reported for the work site after meeting the supervisor "gaffer." He instructed me to dig a foundation trench. Being Canadian, I was a bit of a novelty for the crew. My work clothes consisted of regular jeans and sport shirts, in a style that was not common in the U.K. in the 50s. Most of the crew wore coveralls, and the older guys wore ties, which really looked odd. The Gaffer had marked off the dimensions of the trench that I was to dig. I made up my mind that the best way for them to accept me as a crewmember was to pick up the shovel and get to work.

The work-site crew consisted of two other lads and a couple of older men plus the gaffer. We started at 9:00 a.m. and by 10:00 a.m. I had pretty much excavated most of my trench. The gaffer left the work site to run an errand. While digging I noticed some of the crew just leaning on their shovels observing my progress. Their expressions gave me a feeling that they did not entirely approve of the manner that I was digging the trench. A quick glance and I could see their trenches were not near as deep as mine. I concluded that I was digging too fast as far as they were concerned. Sure enough, one of the older men came over and bluntly told me that I needed to slow down. When I asked him why he told me, "Canuck, over here we're not paid to work fast, so take your time." This was my first taste of the post-WW2 labour problems of the U.K..

That day during the tea breaks and lunch break, the crew was sociable and curious as to why I had returned to Scotland after growing up in Canada. However, by the end of the first week, it became apparent that I was not really fitting in as far as the crew was concerned. The crew wanted me to slow down to their "drag-it-out" pace and I just wanted to get the dumb trenches dug and move on to some more interesting tasks. The gaffer did not seem to give a damn, one way or the other, what pace we worked, so I quit. Because this was the first hard labour, I had dealt with in years, my hands were sore and blistered. Aunt Kate thought I was not up to that type of work. I told her that was not the reason I quit. Further, I questioned the stupid work ethic of the crew and what seemed to be standard labour methods. The hardest part came when I was not willing to take their advice, and the crew stopped talking to me. I learnt then what they meant by the expression "he's been sent to Coventry."[15]

Somewhat discouraged by the split with my father and my first venture with employment in the U.K., I considered heading back to Canada. Reflecting on how hard I had worked to be with my family, I quickly banished the thought of leaving. A week later, Robert told me a mate of his knew of an opening in the plant where he worked. It was a metal fabrication plant, and the opening was for an unskilled labour position. Robert also warned me that I could run into the same labour practices I had experienced on the first job. I now realized that it seemed to be a deeply entrenched custom with the labour unions of the U.K. If one wanted to earn a living in the U.K. with the limited skills I possessed, it is much simpler to "do as the Romans do." Forewarned and willing to accept that which I had no control over, I applied, and they hired me for the position.

---

15   To "send someone to Coventry" is a British idiom meaning to deliberately ostra-cize someone. Typically, this is done by not talking to them, avoiding their company.

Memories of the plant are a bit vague; I do remember that they made these large metal signposts that were common for Shell Oil road signs. The work was not strenuous, and as I no longer felt the need to prove that I was capable of a hard day's work, the lads accepted me as one of them.

While I had left school at grade ten, my education had continued with correspondence classes in the army. So compared to most of the lads working at the plant, the manager may have considered me a bit too bright to be working as a labourer. One day, the director of the plant called me in order to assist in setting up a display for a special sales demonstration. At the time, he questioned why I was working as a labourer. He told me I really could apply for an apprenticeship programme to qualify for a better position of the firm. Somehow, much as I was enjoying family life and the job, I knew that I would not settle into any permanent employment there; it seemed I was a man torn between two countries.

I received my pay parcel weekly on Fridays; there was always enough money for me to pay Aunt Kate for my room and board, and a few pounds extra for play time. I had prudently put money aside to cover my airfare back to Canada for such time, as that decision could arrive. Robert and I would hit the dance halls on Fridays and Saturdays, and I was still dating Margaret occasionally. Leaving the dance hall, we would buy a fish & crisps U.K.-style wrapped in a newspaper. Our transport to everywhere was the double-Decker buses and many a night after dancing late, the buses were no longer running for many routes, so we walked the girls' home. Following the standard necking sessions on their doorsteps, we headed home. It was quite a hike to Sauchton Mains Loan at 1:00 a.m., but we had a laugh or two. With little regard for the homeowners, we occasionally stole a bottle of milk off their front steps. We attempted to cover our guilt by the theory the homeowner would call the milk delivery for replacement of the milk.

I would spend some Sundays with my Granddad Sandy; he was quite a character loved by the children of our family. However, the adults (his children) within the family did not share our good impressions of Grandad. Apparently, he had not been a very responsible parent, as he enjoyed the company of his cronies in the Rutherford Arms too much. He was a well-read man, and I enjoyed many nightlong discussions with my granddad on the affairs of humanity in general. I did not remember him as a child but my older brother and cousins told me that he was always very generous to all the kids of the family. He used to give us money for movies and sweets on Saturday mornings.

I had met him briefly earlier on my first trip to Edinburgh, and I grew to love him in the short time we were together. Physically and in personality, he reminded me of the Irish actor Barry Fitzgerald, diminutive in stature only. With a twinkle to his eye, Sandy's barroom humour reminded me of the character Fitzgerald portrayed throughout the film *The Quiet Man*. In the Scot's idiom, Sandy was "a wee man," physically maybe but not in personality. He always dressed in a rumpled tweedy-looking suit, shirt and tie with the typical flat cap worn by most men of the working class in the U.K. in those days.

During my earlier visit on my first meeting with Sandy, he was in his local bar; my father took me there to meet him. Sandy ordered three nips and three wee heavies. I was soon to learn this was his favourite, a nip of Bells Scotch and a half-pint of dark ale. Back in those days, bars of Scotland did not serve mixed drinks, particularly scotch and water with ice, unless you were in a hotel lounge, where they recognized a North American accent. Men drank their whiskies neat, but they did have a small jug of water on the bar for the faint-hearted.

At the tender age of 21, I had not developed my taste for whisky, so I picked up a water jug that was sitting at the bar and poured some water in my whisky glass. I then turned to Granddad and offered him the water jug, asking him politely, "Granddad, would you care for some water?" His response I will never forget. With an impish grin on his face, he said, "Water? Roddy I'm no needing a bath."

I once asked my aunt Kate, what it meant when you asked someone where a certain person was and the answer was, "He is away on a message."

She replied, "Why do you ask that?"

I told her every time I went to visit Sandy at his workplace, they told me he was off on a message.

Kate replied "Roddy, for most people that would mean, he's away on an errand such as shopping. However, if your Grandfather is the one in question, it means he is off to a bloody bar."

One of my favourite stories about Sandy occurred during the war years. Sandy was too old to serve in WWII. However, he served in the army for WWI. Like many men his age, he signed up as an air-raid warden. His warden's responsibility consisted of making sure when the sirens sounded that everyone in the Drummond Street neighbourhood made their way to the bomb shelters. The story goes that one night when the sirens went off, Sandy was in the Rutherford Arms[16] (the Mackay men's drinking hole) enjoying a nip or two. On the first shrill sound of the siren, Sandy grabbed his warden's helmet, blew his whistle and cleared the place out, sending everyone to the shelter. He then followed up, making sure everyone on his beat had made his or her way to the shelters.

Prior to the all-clear siren, the wardens were supposed to check in with the head warden of that region. That night Sandy did not show up for the check- in, so they went looking for him. The chief warden checked the neighbourhood, but could not find him.

Upon the "all clear" sirens, all the men from our neighbourhood returned to the Rutherford Arms to resume their philosophical or 'fit ball' discussions and enjoy their nips. The first man there went to open the door to find it locked (barred from the inside). They banged at the door, as they could hear someone in the bar singing. Finally, the bar owner climbed up on a couple of old boxes and looked through the window. His first words were, "Look no more for Sandy Mackay, that old bugger is in there having one hell of a drink of my whisky." That was another episode to be added to the legend of Sandy Mackay whilst in the service of his King and country during WWII.

16   One of the oldest bars in Edinburgh once frequented by authors Robert Louis Stevenson and James Barrie when they were students at the Edinburgh University.

Sandy in his younger years was very musical; he played the piano and the organ and apparently had an excellent voice. Possibly my love for music and singing was passed on via his genes. His voice must have been quite strong, as he liked to sing opera arias at times.

He lived in a very tiny bed-sitting room flat just up the road from the famous Grey Friar Bobbie Bar. Somehow, they had managed to move in a small organ that took up half the room. He had to climb over the organ to get in his bed (or was it the other way around?). One night when I had taken him out for a drink, I walked him home. He asked me up, as he wanted to play the organ for me. His landlady let us in as he forgot his key. It was 10:00 p.m., and I was thinking the other tenants might not appreciate Sandy playing the organ at that time of the night. I asked the landlady, "Will this not disturb the other tenants?"

Her response made me realise that Sandy was still a bit of a ladies' man, as she said, "Roddy, if it does, they will just have to move out."

My cousin Cathie told me that not only was Sandy proficient at playing the organ, he had an excellent voice as a tenor. Unfortunately, in his old age, he did a serious injury to his throat. He had a bad cold and stupidly decided he could cure it by cutting into his larynx to relieve the pressure. Apparently, he thought he could simply excise the cold with this procedure. My aunt Kate had to rush him to the emergency room where they treated the injury; sadly, he could no longer sing, and it left him with a very hoarse voice for the remainder of his life. Sandy also dabbled in the world of spiritualism; this may well have prompted him to commit the procedure he took on his throat. He never spoke to me of that experience, and I had a sense that maybe that day his odd curiosity may have prevailed over his common sense.

He was interested in a broad range of life's affairs and had a great sense of humour. I loved him and I always enjoyed his company. Sunday afternoons he enjoyed taking me to the Mound on Princes Street where we listened to all kinds of soapbox speakers. The speakers were mostly men speaking on topics as diverse as women's rights, war and independence for Scotland, politics and all the major religions. It was fascinating not only to listen to the speakers, but even more so to hear the wit in the responses of some of the hecklers.

The Mound drew big crowds, and I observed several men who could be best termed as professional hecklers. Quite often, the heckler knew much more about the topic than the speaker did. Sandy and I both enjoyed listening to this one little Irish guy go after some of the far-out evangelical religious speakers. He knew the Bible inside out; and would trip many of them up when they falsely quoted the Bible in attempting to make their point.

Edinburgh, like most of the U.K. in those years, observed Sunday, and most drinking establishments closed on the Sabbath. One Sunday, Sandy asked me to meet him in the city. On meeting him at the designated spot he said, "Come on, lad, we are going up to the Highlands." He then indicated a local bus for us to board.

I thought this a bit strange, as I knew a city bus would not be going that far north to the Highlands. When I queried him further he chuckled, gave me one of those sheepish grins and said, "Dinn'a worry, Roddy, you'll see when we get there."

We were on the bus for about 15 minutes, and I could see that we had left the city and were now out in what definitely looked more like the countryside. Finally, he tugged my sleeve, indicating for us to get off at the next stop. Stepping off the bus, I looked around the neighbourhood; it was mostly residential with few shops and a small hotel. Sandy led the way, heading straight for a hotel.

Upon entering the hotel, a man greeted Sandy and asked him to sign the book. Sandy said, "Roddy, sign it," then whispered for me to write the following: "We are travelers on the way to Inverness."

Upon signing the book, the man who had greeted us opened a door, and we entered a bar. Once I could see through the haze of cigarette smoke, I could tell the room was chock-a-block with men. The air was thick with smoke; men were drinking their pints and wee nips of whisky like it was payday on a Saturday night. Sandy, with a gleam in his eyes, was rubbing his hands and licking his lips as he headed straight for that bar. Practically every man at the bar greeted Sandy as we passed him by and found a place to sit. The barkeeper did not have to ask; he poured a wee nip and a half-pint of beer, and then set them in front of Sandy. For me, that day was a revelation on how the men of Scotland manage to enjoy their pints and whisky on the Sabbath. You get on a bus, head out of the city to the outskirts, find a hotel and sign the guest book as a traveller with a destination of one's making. Even though we never made our supposed destination, the Highlands, it was a memorable Sunday afternoon. As a think back on that day, I wish I signed the book with the fabled destination Brigadoon.

A Wedding in Scotland

My cousin Cathy and Carl made the big decision to get married, and it was fortunate for me this happened while I was with the family. Aunt Kate was soon busy supervising all the arrangements, including the guest list. When I inquired if Sandy had been invited, Aunt Kate gave me a very stern look, saying, "If he is, Roddy, you will have to be responsible for him." This was another hint of the shaky esteem held by the offspring generation of Sandy Mackay.

Anyhow, with little regard to any dire consequences, I accepted that responsibility. One day when Sandy was out, I called in to see his landlady, informed her of the wedding, inquired if she were kind enough to check his wardrobe, and told her I would pay to have a suit dry-cleaned. I had met her on a previous occasion when I walked Sandy home to his flat. Moreover, I knew that she had quite a soft spot for the old man.

He did have a decent suit that needed to be cleaned; I took care of that, his landlady laundered and ironed a shirt, and I polished a pair of shoes for him, so we were all set. Wedding day came and we all gathered in the church courtyard, greeting family and friends, and I noticed Sandy seemed slightly agitated. It struck my mind that maybe Aunt Kate might have given him a cautionary glare.

Following one of the Boy Scout golden rules, I came for the wedding prepared. I had wisely invested in a wee silver flask that I had topped with a dram or two of Sandy's favourite Bell's whisky. I took Sandy to a small concealment of hedges away from the milling guests. One wee nip and Sandy would be fine, ready to enjoy the ceremony. He gave me a big hug, whispering into my ear, "Ye are a fine lad, Roddy, a 'real Mackay."

Carl looked quite smart in his air force uniform and Cathy the beautiful bride in her white wedding gown. They made for a very handsome couple. I must have met all my relatives on that day but strangely did not remember my father or his new family attending the wedding. Much later Cathy told me her mum remembered all who attended, and he never came nor paid the courtesy of sending a card of congratulations.

I cannot recall where the wedding reception party was held, but it was not far from our Palaise dance hall. As I had not brought a date along, I did glance down the reception hall to see if there were any single girls. As there were none, I sneaked out and dropped into the Palaise dance hall. There I spotted a girl I had danced with and invited her to the party. Following the reception party the family retired to my aunt Kate's house. I walked the girl to her bus stop. Cousin Robert was feeling no pain when I arrived at the house, but he was kind of glaring at me. I could see he was angry, so I approached him, asking what was wrong. He responded with a bit of a snarl, "What the hell were you doing leaving my sister's reception and taking off to the Palaise?"

I was trying to explain and calm him down. I really did not think he would get that upset over the girl, as he also knew her from past dances at the "Palaise." My efforts were in vain, and then suddenly he took a swing at me. He missed and gratefully Uncle Robert jumped in between us.

Now I really felt bad so thought it best I leave the house at once. Outside and in stocking feet, I found myself in pouring rain. Confused as hell, I began to walk down the street. I finally stopped and sat down on a low brick wall. At this point, I took a swig of the little whisky that was left in my flask. I felt absolutely terrible and guilty that I had not only upset Robert but also possibly the whole family. My head was reeling now. I had lost a home with my father and was no longer welcome to the home of my Aunt Kate and cousins. As I sat there totally dejected, looking and feeling like a drowned duck, I heard voices calling my name. It was Uncle Robert and my cousin Robert down the street but heading towards where I was sitting. My first reaction was confusion. I did not know if I should run or wait and face them. Standing soaked in the pouring rain I decided best I face the music. The concerned looks on both their faces told me my decision had been right.

Uncle Robert looking at me and simply said, "Come on home, laddy, yee'l catch your death of a cold in this weather."

Cousin Robert grabbed and hugged me, mumbling, "Roddy; pay nae mind tae me, it was the whisky."

Then we walked back the short distance to home, laughing in the rain, and rejoined the party as if nothing had happened. I went to bed and thought about the irony of my situation. At the great expense, I had traveled back to my place of birth to find a family and a home. Yet, in the short period I had been in Scotland, I was more or less alienated from my father and had been very close to losing a home with my aunt Kate and my cousins. That night, I fell asleep with comforting and grateful thoughts, knowing I still had a family.

A couple of months after the wedding I began to have thoughts of returning to Canada. Much as I loved Scotland, I had a feeling that the opportunities for my future[17] were not available in the U.K.. Early on, I had been wise enough to set aside money for my return airfare to Vancouver so as one chapter of life ended, and another began. As I was leaving Edinburgh, somehow in the back of my mind was a strong feeling that I would return. It struck me; I was a man with some unfinished business that would have to be dealt with eventually.

My granddad Sandy came to the Waverly train station to see me off, as I would take a train south to the London airport. Neither of us knew at the time that it was to be our last parting. The image of Granddad Sandy standing upon the platform, waving good-bye as the train slowly pulled away, has never left me. The memory of that wee frail man, older than his actual years, a scarf wrapped tight around his neck for the cold winter day, saddened me terribly. I remember fighting the tears as I gazed at him; the train picked up speed, and then he was gone. As so many do in life when we are young, we think family and friends will be with us forever. However, that day there was something telling me that I would never see Sandy again. All I have left now is my memories and a photo of my granddad (when he was young master printer) standing in front of a printing press, likely taken in the mid-1930s.

It was sometime in the mid-seventies that I heard Sandy

---

17   Had I known how bad the unemployment situation was in Canada at that time I may have well considered staying in Scotland.

had died; apparently, he was walking through the streets of his neighbourhood when he collapsed and died. I hope he was returning to the Old Soldiers Home[18] following a good afternoon sipping a wee nip or two of Bell's whisky. He would have been [19] spinning tales with his elderly cronies, enjoying what he loved best. I will always regret that I did not have more time with him. I would have loved to hear about his life as a young man during WWI and his years as a professional printer.

My uncle Robert told me that the Old Soldiers Home gave him quite a sendoff with a full pipe band at his funeral service. Sandy was an army veteran of WWI; he never shared his war experiences with me. I also heard that my father was a wee bit chuffed that they had given his father, Sandy, such an honour.

On several visits to Edinburgh in the 80s and 90s, I made it a point to stop in at the Rutherford Arms. It was my way of paying some kind of homage to Sandy. On one visit I sat next to an elderly lady. She was chatting to the barkeep, her voice low and gravelly, and the thick Scottish dialect reminded me a bit of Sandy. When I ordered my next drink, I ordered one for her; sure enough, she asked for a nip of Bell's. She thanked me, asked my name, and I told her. Lifting her glass to me, she said, "Roddy, its nice tae be nice and I ken you are a nice laddy." That definitely brought a tear to my eye as I felt the mystical sense of Sandy's presence in the Rutherford Arms that day.

---

18   As Sandy was a soldier in WW1, veterans like him could spend their final years in the Old Soldiers Home.
19   Fittingly enough, Bell's famous logo reads, "Bell's whisky afore you go!"

VANCOUVER 1956–1960.

I returned to Vancouver broke, and was to remain pretty much in that state for the next two-and-a-half years. Never having heard the word recession, after few years of living in that economic state I did not understand the why, but I certainly felt the impact. The skills I had acquired as an Army Surgical Technician had no value as far as hiring on for a similar position with a civilian hospital.

During interviews when I presented my qualifications, interviewers told me … well, you're certainly well qualified to work here; however, the best we can offer is the position as a hospital orderly. My first basic medical corpsman classes had taught me skills that surpassed those required in this position. I was broke and hungry so decided best to swallow my pride and accept an offer from the Vancouver General Hospital. I was very disappointed knowing that the skills I had acquired in the army would be of little value as a civilian hospital orderly. If that were not bad enough, the only opening available during that time was for a position (ward orderly) on a male geriatric ward. Despondent as hell, I made the decision I would have to 'tough it out,' until something more interesting and challenging came up.

As is the nature with a job caring for elderly patients suffering physically and mentally, it was as depressing as hell yet at times could be unusually amusing. The patients were all long- stay and suffered various levels of arrested insanity. Many were not completely bed-ridden and liked to wander from bed to bed talking either to some absent friend, or sometimes to an inanimate object like a door. One we called "the collector" was constantly picking up dental works from others' bedside tables. He would gather the false teeth and store them in his bedpan. Fortunately for the owners of the teeth sets, the bedpan was clean when "the collector" was making his calls.

One old Scot who reminded me of my granddad Sandy would come to the ward office enquiring on train times for Glasgow. No matter what response you gave he would reply, "The bloody trains canna everr run on time, it's the fucking English bastards runnin' these trains I tell ye." If you attempted to walk him back to his bed, he would make threatening moves to hit you with his walking stick. I would use the Scot's dialect when I spoke to him, and this seemed to calm him down enough. There were moments when he could be somewhat rational, and I spent time chatting with him about Scotland.

An English gent, Mr. Rose, had a scholarly demeanor and possessed a very cultivated Oxford or Cambridge accent. He was constantly asking for a telephone. So I inquired of him, "Mr. Rose, who is it you wish to call?" His response was, "Mr. Stalin, of course; I have a message for him from Mr. Churchill."

The temptation of this opportunity overwhelmed me, so I found myself leading Mr. Rose to a nearby fire hydrant attached to the wall. On a prior occasion, we observed him talking to the hydrant. Then I gently eased the hose end out of the clip and handed it to him, instructing him to speak into the brass knob-end, loud and clear for Mr. Stalin, who is on the line. I left him to his serious task of conveying whatever international negotiations Mr. Churchill wished to share with Stalin. Of course, this was definitely a one-way conversation. He spent a good half hour speaking on our imaginary phone to his imaginary Mr. Stalin and when he finally hung up he called me over (I think at this stage in his fantasy. I became his secretary). Shaking his head, he said to me, "The Prime Minister may not appreciate hearing this, but I personally think Mr. Stalin is absolutely MAD and dangerous to boot!" Mr. Rose obviously suffered some form of dementia, but history proved he was spot on the mark with his opinion of Stalin.

I realise that many will think it was terrible for me to play a trick like that on my patient Mr. Rose, but I really meant him no harm, nor do I think it ever did. Quite the contrary, this provided Mr. Rose with hours of interesting conversations with his imaginary world leaders. It also provided a smile for us, the so-called sane ones.

I stuck it out at the Vancouver Hospital with my elderly friends for about seven months, but I was in a rut with no hope for a better position. Daily I checked newspaper employment columns. I could not resign, as I needed the job in order to pay for my rent, food, etc. The depressing nature of this occupation and the geriatric ward environment was affecting my mental health. It is extremely difficult to care for patients who are in this hopeless state, particularly if you are sensitive as I was and frankly, still am.

On one of my scheduled night shifts, there was another orderly whom I found difficult to work with. I had threatened to turn him in because of the abusive way he treated some of the patients. Yes, we at times played silly tricks on some of our patients but never in any way that would be harmful. At times a patient would have to be restrained, but we did all possible to avoid hurting them physically. This orderly was abusive and callous in the way he treated them, strong-arming them when they refused to move. That particular night he was attempting to give the Scot a bath. While the old chap could be stubborn and difficult to move around, with a little patience, we could move patients without harming them. I offered to help the orderly with the situation, which he declined, grunting to me, "I can handle this old bastard myself."

He then commenced to pull the old man's arm behind his back, much like a police officer would in a physical restraint situation, and shoved him into the shower stall. Seeing this I thought, what if this man was my Granddad? I came "unglued." I grabbed the orderly, swearing at him to take his fucking hands off the man. While the orderly was a bit stockier than me, possibly the rage in my face did it, as he backed off. He snarled at me, "Fine; you take care of the old bastard." With the assistance of another orderly, we calmed the old Scot, and then we gave him a sponge bath and put him to bed. I also warned the orderly who had been abusing the patients that he needed to find another occupation.

Riding the bus home in the morning, I found it impossible to get the episode out of my mind. I needed the job; however, the episode of the prior evening had me very disturbed. It also left me more depressed than ever. The following day I made an appointment with the head nurse and told her my intentions to resign. I did not go into details, but I did warn her that she had one employee who was not fit to be working with elderly patients. Leaving the hospital was the finale of my five-year medical career. My army buddy, Doug, had moved in with his mum who had leased a nice two-bedroom apartment. Doug asked me if I wanted to move in with them as he had a large room with two beds. It cut my rent expense in half, and this was as good an offer as one could expect.

Employment openings were practically nonexistent for people as ill-qualified as Doug and me. Both of us left high school to join the army, and we both had no other civilian trade other than our medical training. In those days, there were no unemployment benefits for army vets, no government programs for job training, etc. So, we took whatever came along, mostly part-time jobs washing dishes in restaurants, or hiring on with a company distributing free soap door-to-door. It was not a pleasant period of my life and had it not been for the good camaraderie of my ex-army pals I could have ended up on skid row. I retract that statement, as I have far too much pride to allow that to happen with my life.

Right about this time Doug and I located some of my other army buddies. This was not too difficult; all it took was a short trip to the old Cecil Hotel beer parlour, and there they were, Pete Topolnisky, Jack Adams and Joe Wilkes. All three had been unemployed but Joe was leaving town for a job up northern BC and Jack, lucky SOB, was hiring on with the BC Liquor Stores. I was happy to see them and willingly bought the first round of beer. We passed the evening with me filling them in on my recent activities and the six months in Scotland. As for them, they also experienced hard times. While we had goofed off a bit in our last days in the army, we were not lazy types or lacking the desire to do a good day's work.

In reflection, I am not sure how we survived that winter, but we did. I attempted to enter the merchandising trade as a clothing sales clerk. Each morning I would get up, shower, get dressed in my one and only decent suit, and head for downtown Vancouver. I tried every major department store and privately owned men's clothing shop. It was usually the same response: sorry, but we are not hiring. A few times the receptionist would invite me to fill in a form, and politely tell me in words like, "We will give you a call if any openings become available." That is a call that never materializes. About this time, I moved in with Pete, who had a bigger place.

We lived quite a distance from the Vancouver downtown area; I had no money for bus fare, so I walked the distance daily, rain or shine. Those of you, who know the northwest realise we get an awful lot of rain, thus BC is well known for its giant evergreen trees.

I had to cut pieces of cardboard to fill the holes of my one and only pair of dress shoes. Many a day I entered the employment office of a department store looking like a drowned rat. The constant, "Do you have any experience?" Their response always the, "No, sorry, at the moment we have nothing available." Answers like that finally got to me, so I packed it in for a week or so. My next venture was checking out restaurants; best I could get there were temporary jobs washing dishes. Usually, it could be for an evening or two at some of the larger food establishments.

One night I found myself feeling very low and depressed with what was happening in my life. Pete was out of town working on a temporary job. I had stayed in most of the day as the weather was foul, and I was broke, couldn't afford the price of a ticket to a movie. I went to bed at nine. After two hours, I was still wide-awake. I turned the bedside lamp on, and I felt like the four dismal walls of the room were closing in on me. I tried to read a book in an effort to take my mind off the misery I was feeling. Nothing seemed to work, and this led to thoughts of the purpose of my existence.

Next thing I knew I was contemplating ending my life. This led to thoughts of what method of suicide to use. Hanging or cutting my wrists seemed awfully gory. I got up and walked into the kitchen and there sat the kitchen gas stove. I sat there gazing at that old stove for some time. Sitting on top of the stove was a half-pint of whisky that Pete had left behind in his hasty packing for his trip. I got out of bed, picked up the bottle and sat down on the couch. It was a Canadian whisky that I really did not care for, but I managed to choke the entire contents down in two gulps. Then I walked over to the stove and turned the gas on and picked up a pack of cigarettes. Smoking my last cigarette was very likely the dumbest decision of my life. However, it did open my mind to a small seed of logic. To light a cigarette, I would not only be taking my own life but those of the couple who lived upstairs. Yes, while in my depression, I was entertaining the thought of suicide, but harming or killing others, that I could not bear the thought of committing. That moment of logic found me dashing over to the oven, quickly turning off the gas and opening doors to air the room out.

I quickly threw on some clothes and walked out in the dark, even though it was still raining hard. With rain pouring over my head and soaking me to the skin, it felt like it was washing away the turbulences of the madness I had just experienced. When Pete returned from his job, other than to tell him, I owed him a bottle of whiskey, I never divulged what had happened that night to him or anyone else. Over the years, I have experienced various stages of depression, but none ever brought me to that crucial stage. Thank God. I also learnt to be more open with my feelings and discuss times like that with close friends whom I trust.

Somehow, we managed to survive through the winter and spring. One day, my pal Pete and I went shopping for groceries as usual; we had no money in our pockets. Being a cold day we were wearing our old army great coats[20] with deep pockets. Here was the scheme: for every article, we put in the shopping basket; one would find its way to our pocket. One of us kept an eye out for sales clerks on the floor. We were smart enough to confine our takings to small items. Pete had an item in his hand that I could see; it was a can of Canadian brand sardines. I reached over, rapped his knuckle and said to him in a low voice, "Hell, Pete, not that brand, get the expensive Norwegian sardines!" I thought just because we were poor that was no reason to lower our standards. Yes, we had sardines on toast for our evening meal that day.

---

20   *These were heavy coats typically worn by soldiers for winter weather.*

Someone in our group discovered a free recreation club on Robson Street. Technically, the club was for merchant seamen, but they were a bit lax in their admission policies. On days when we needed a break from pounding the pavement, we started hanging out there. Next thing we knew the ex-army group was becoming friends with ex-seamen. The seamen mostly were from Liverpool, "Scousers."[21] These guys worked on the Cunard liner the *Queen Mary*. In that group, I met Phil Peers, who was later to become one of my best friends. Phil, his brother Eddy, Peter Hope and John Scott quit their jobs with the *Queen Mary* to settle in Canada. However, just like us, they also were experiencing hard times finding work of any kind.

That summer, Phil, John and I lucked out and hired on as temporary cabin/dining room stewards on the CPR Princess ships. It was a seasonal job for Phil and me over a two-year period. In my desperation to hire on I lied about my prior experience. I told them (the CPR employment office) my experience had consisted of working as a steward in army officer's mess lounges. During my first session in the dining room, Phil noticed my complete lack of the skills required for a first class dining room. For whatever reason, pity or what, Phil kind of took me under his wing and taught me the basics of dining room service. Had he not helped me, the Chief Steward would have fired my butt on our first return to port Vancouver.

---

21 Scouser is a nickname for people from Liverpool.

A LESSON ON HOW TO IMPROVE YOUR TIPS

Our first duty was to greet the passengers at dockside and assist them by carrying their luggage on board and up to their cabins. At the end of our first week on board the ship, I had noticed that a few stewards were receiving larger amounts of tip money than I was, and Phil was one of those. I had been working on the theory that the quicker I assisted passengers to their cabin and returned to the dockside; I could service more passengers. More passengers, I reckoned, would mean more tips. Realizing that my "tip theory" was not working I finally asked Phil what was going on.

He laughed and said, "Yes, I was wondering how long it would take before you would ask that." He also added that he, and some of the others were amazed that I hadn't broken a leg during my mad dashes up and down the decks' stairwells.

I told him about my "more passengers more tips" theory.

He replied, "Yeah that was obvious, but apparently it's not working" He then asked me exactly what I did for the passenger when we arrived at his or her cabin. I told him my routine consisted of entering the cabin, placing the luggage on the portable racks, and turning over the cabin key, exiting with a "thank you and good night."

Phil laughed again, and I said, "Come on, Phil, what am I doing different than you guys?"

He replied, "It is not what you are doing as much as what you are NOT doing!"

I asked, "What is it that I'm missing here?"

Phil answered, "It's all about service. People, no matter who they are, enjoy being waited on, pampered, or whatever you want to call it." His cabin service consisted of the basic service I provided, plus the following:, once he set the luggage down; he turned the bed covers back, puffed the pillows up, showed the passenger the bathroom facilities, tested the hot and cold taps, inquired if his passenger wanted a wakeup call, etc., etc. "By indulging the passenger with all those extra steps, most of them have reached into their pockets before I am ready to make my exit." He concluded his remarks saying. *"Don't be in such a mad rush; give them service and add a bit of personality and the tips will come."* Years later as a restaurant vocational teacher, I was to give my students that lesson using those exact words.

The end of summer found Phil, myself and other mates laid off and back to the unemployment status. The tough times drew us together, Phil's Liverpool mates, me, and a few of my former army pals. Sharing dark basement flats with rodents, we were really the original "Rat Pack." Unlike Sinatra's group, we lacked the money, talent and fame. Occasionally after we had a made a few quick dollars, we enjoyed a night out at the nightclubs. The booze, the dames[22], it was good fun with a lot of laughs. In the rough times of no jobs or money, when necessary we nicked food from the grocery stores as per earlier. We became highly skilled in cooking a shepherd's pie; breakfast most days we had beans on toast. We also were

22   We actually referred to the girls as "broads." I personally preferred the informal title "dames" just like dames in the song from *South Pacific,* "There is Nothin' Like a Dame."

quite adept at avoiding landlords on rent day. At one rental, the wife of the proprietor took a shine to our "Casanova," Pete. She was able to manipulate her husband, so we often could stall him on rent day. Most of us have stayed connected through the years, but Pete has mysteriously disappeared. Here it is 2017, and none of the lads have seen hide or hair of him. Pete being such a "Lothario," I sometimes wonder if an irate, jealous husband took a shotgun to my pal Pete.

Work was still sporadic and in our desperation, we latched onto anything that would provide us money to pay the rent, and buy food and a few beers at our local.

Meanwhile, I came home one night and Doug, who was working at a construction camp in the northern part of the province, had left a message with his mother. The message was great news; Doug's boss in the construction camp needed a couple more men, so I shared the good news of this opportunity with Phil. Next day, we hired on at their Vancouver office and caught a train to their camp that afternoon. We worked several months as labourers on the construction site of a power plant in a very remote area in northern BC, Shalath. Work was hard, and it was an extremely isolated area, but we had great, comfortable, clean lodging, good food, T-bone steaks, etc., and more importantly; we were making decent wages, finally.

The company had a holiday season policy that the married men would take a week off at Christmas to be home with their families. The single "bucks" were given the week off at New Year's; of course, this arrangement suited us fine, particularly for me, as the world knows the Scots love to celebrate New

Year's Eve. The New Year break came, and we caught the train into Vancouver, cash burning holes in our pockets, and we were anxious to let the good times roll.

First on our agenda was to make a few phone calls and check out the New Year's Eve parties. Lost track of where Doug got to, but Phil and I were sitting and having a beer in the hotel. We had decided we would hit a couple of parties with one of them taking place at the home of my army buddy, Jack Adams. Next on the agenda was girls; Phil had called an English girl, Ann, that he had met earlier, and I could tell at that time he was beginning to show signs of a man in love. I called a girl who said fine, but asked if she could bring along another girl. Fine by me, I said. OK, now we have the party site and the girls; now, what would the "Rat Pack" wear for a New Year's Eve party? Coming into the hotel we had passed a gents' clothing shop, which had featured men's tuxedos for hire. I said to Phil, "Hey, Phil, I have never worn a tux. Why don't we show these girls some class and rent a tuxedo?"

Phil laughed, telling me I was crazy, but said, "Let's do it."

I still have an old photo album with photos of that evening, and we were definitely enjoying ourselves. There is one of Phil and me posing in our tuxedos with cigs in our hands; as they once said, "Looking real cool, my man." You would have thought we were attempting a Frank Sinatra and Dean Martin look-alike photo shot. We had a great New Year eve and we celebrated New Years day in Seattle.

QUADRA PUB AND
THE IRISH CREW ASHORE

On our last night before heading back to the construction camp in Shalath, we decided to go to the upscale nightclub, the Quadra Club. The club had a membership-only policy, but we heard that they also allowed visiting seamen from foreign ships. So four of us decided to be Irish and approached the club, each of us mimicking an Irish accent. We signed the book as crewmembers of an Irish ship that was in the harbour. As we were signing in as crewmembers of an Irish merchant ship, it really behooved us to speak and act like Irish sailors. Here I was a Scot, who ad almost lost the brogue, and then we had the Liverpool accents of Phil, his brother Eddie and John Scott.

Regardless of funny accents and all, it worked, for the man behind the desk allowed us into the club. We ordered our drinks and were doing our best to top each other with who could do the best Irish brogue. Finally, this big guy, who had to be well over six feet, sitting next to Phil said in a very authentic Irish brogue, "Pardon me, but what part of Ireland are you "Scousers," from?"

Quick-witted Phil, with absolutely no hesitation, pointed at me and said, "It was that Scotch bastard at the end of the bar put us up to the Irish." Gratefully, considering the size of the Irish bloke, he laughed, and we bought our new friend an Irish whisky. The rest of the night went fine with all of us enjoying our libations and exchanging humorous stories, some real and some made up.

The next day it was back to the wilderness of Camp Shalath; we worked there for another couple of months. Phil was writing love letters to Ann, and I could see he was getting restless to return to Vancouver. Phil's brother, Eddie wrote and told us the job situation was improving so we both decided to head back to civilization. Doug stayed on.

I decided that now I had enough money to buy myself a new wardrobe, a couple of suits, blazer, slacks, and dress shoes, that I would venture another try at the men's-clothing sales business. It is amazing how a new wardrobe and some money in the bank can restore a man's confidence. I had also made up my mind on how best to meet the one requisite that I had failed to meet in my early job interviews. I thought it through and made up my mind, if they wanted a man with experience, then that is what I must become during the interview.

In checking the daily paper, *The Vancouver Sun*, I came across an advert for a part-time clothing salesman in a department store Woodward's, Park Royal, in West Vancouver.[23] I was up early next morning and got dressed in my new suit, white shirt and a conservative striped tie. I caught an early bus over to West Van and arrived at the store as they were opening up for business. I made my way up to their personnel office, and the secretary asked me to fill out the job application. The application was the first important hurdle to clear and if my strategy failed me, I was not going

---

23   Park Royal was the first shopping centre in Canada.

to see the other side of the store manager's office door.

I finally thought of a way that would involve my father; for once in his life, he might be of assistance to my future livelihood. It took very little imagination to set up a scenario whereby he became the proprietor of a business that never existed. On the application, I wrote for experience, "A gents' wear shop assistant in the family owned 'Mackay's Gents' Haberdashery Shop,' Edinburgh, Scotland." After I completed the application, the secretary checked it over and invited me to take a seat, alongside two other applicants.

Now came the difficult part. The secretary said, "Mr. Mackay, the manager would like to see you now."

Eureka! I would now cross the next threshold to my future. Now stage two arrived, applying for the position. Taking a deep breath, I entered his office; fortunately for me, in his greeting, the manager appeared to be a pleasant sort, as he extended his hand. Of course for me, this required a firm handshake, and one must politely wait until you are invited to take a seat. An application of an experienced salesman from Edinburgh, Scotland, must have caught his attention.

As he questioned me, I looked at him straight in the eye, and quietly but with confidence, told him of my experience in working for my father. Thankfully, my one major fear eased as he said, "Edinburgh, Scotland … someday I look forward to taking my family there for a visit." It had crossed my mind, what if the manager had once lived in Edinburgh and asked me to be specific as to the location of the shop. The very thought of that had my hands perspiring, so I simply slammed the door on that section of my brain and took a deep breath. The interview from that point became quite pleasant, as he was more curious about Edinburgh than my actual sales experience. He closed the interview and asked me if I could report for work the coming weekend; no need to tell you my response was affirmative, finally I was in like Flynn! It took great restraint for me to refrain from dancing out of that employment office.

They scheduled me for the weekend shift, beginning Friday morning. I arrived at the Woodward's store full of confidence that was quickly shattered when I viewed the store window display. In the menswear, window was a male store dummy looking very handsome in a new suit. There was also a very large sign that jarred my over-confident attitude. The sign read: "THIS WEEK'S SALE, MEN'S TAILOR MADE SUITS!"

When I first decided to sell men's clothing for an occupation, I made it my business to learn by observation. Every time I ventured into a menswear store, I would listen and watch closely to observe the technique of the salesmen. Helping customers try on suits, jackets, etc., while chatting up the quality, the fit and looks of the apparel did not strike me as being too difficult for a task. I also felt I had the right kind of personality for the job. However, measuring and fitting a man for a tailor-made suit, now that was a major oversight on my part.

Nervous as all hell I made my way to the menswear department, and introduced myself to the department manager. He showed me around the department, and then instructed me to restock a glass case with men's dress shirts.

It did not take much to figure out the system, and I began to relax. Around ten a.m., the manager, Bob, (he had put me on a first-name basis) told me he was going on break. That had me freaking out a bit as that meant I was the only sales clerk on the floor. With much haste, I made my way over to the table they used for measuring up suits.

I had barely opened up the book used to record body measurements when I heard a man say, "Can you help me? I would like to purchase a made to measure suit."

My initial thought as I panicked was, "Why the hell aren't you asking me where the hell the men's toilet is?" Breathe deep, I said to myself, and find some way to stall the man until Bob returns to the floor. By then I will have come up with some plausible excuse as to why I did not take care of the customer.

My stalling routine began with; "Sir, allow me to show you the various fabrics and colours we have available."

I barely got the last word out when he said, "I already know what I want," pointing to a sample. "That fabric in dark brown, and please don't waste my time"

Now, all I wanted to say was, "Listen, you impatient bastard, let me do my sales pitch first." However, I managed to keep the rude remarks from leaving my lips, and picked up the measurement tape.

The recording book did have the typical diagram of a man's body, and it outlined the various sections to be measured, i.e. the neck, chest, waist, arm length, etc. Thus this complete incompetent novice began measuring a suit. I was convinced this would be my first and last made to measure suit and quite likely lead to my instant dismissal. I was not satisfied with one round of measurement. I took two more measurements. Bearing in mind his last remark, "please don't waste my time," I decided it best not to chance any more friendly sales patter with this "bugger." Bob reappeared just as the customer was exiting the front door, and I was standing there somewhat shell-shocked. Doing my best to stay calm and appear (I hoped) professional, I said to Bob, "This measurement book is slightly different than the one I used in Scotland. Would you mind checking it to see if I have filled in all the required measurements?"

He barely glanced at it and said, "It looks fine."

In a very nervous state, I rode home on the bus, realizing I would have a whole week of anxiety. They did not schedule me to work until the following Friday. I was facing a week of sleepless nights, coupled with nightmares of that suit. I had visions of putting the jacket on the customer to discover one sleeve barely covered his elbow, or pant legs two to three inches too short or two long. My self-confidence was so low I considered calling in and tell them a big fat lie that I had to return to Scotland, as my father needed me, his health was failing.

Phil, of course, was busting his gut as I spilt my guts over this ridiculous saga. Friday arrived and with very mixed emotions, I had decided best to "step up to the plate," return to the scene of the buggered-up tailor made suit. Bob greeted me, asking if I had a good week.

Quite literally lying through my teeth, I said yes, I had a

swell[24] week. He did tell me my customer's suit had arrived back from the tailoring department, and I mumbled to myself "Well, that's just swell; I will be looking for a new job before the day is done!"

My customer showed up in late morning, and with much apprehension, I greeted him.

Taking his suit off the rack, I handed it to him and showed him to the customer changing room. As I paced back and forth, it seemed to take forever before he came out. I was convinced there would be one irate customer and one unemployed salesman. Forcing myself to look at the man as he approached, my day changed to wonderful sunshine and happiness; the suit was a near-perfect fit. What am I saying, near perfect? As far as I was concerned it was perfect. I walked him over to a full-length mirror, and with restored confidence, I pointed out all the finer points of the fitting. He did give me a somewhat curious look that seemed to say, "What the hell, did you expect it not to fit?"

Before the day was done I had laid claim to a new tape measure that I draped over my shoulders, and I proudly walked the floor looking every bit as if I knew what I was doing. I approached every male customer in the near vicinity with a greeting of, "Good morning, sir, may I assist you; we have a terrific sale on made to measure suits today."

By the end of the month, I was working a five-day week in a reputable store and enjoying my new vocation. I stayed with them for four months of so and then a new adventure

---

24   *For you youngsters, "swell" meant good in the 50s, or what you call bad when you mean good!!!!*

for some of the "Rat Pack" was on the table for discussion.

One night when we were home watching the "telly," Phil decided to share his feelings about Ann. In Ann, he felt he had found the love of his life. Those may not be his exact words, but it amounted to much the same. He was definitely in love, saying what a beautiful woman she was, and telling me she looked very much like some former English actress (I can't recall the name). Next thing I knew he was talking serious arrangement, long-term, with Ann (marriage).

Me in my typical selfish bachelor mode did not see this in any other light than the pack was about to lose our key man. It did not take long before we realized that Phil was serious, and the top man with the "Rat Pack" was actually ready to give up his freedom as a bachelor for the chains of matrimony.

Ann and I had not hit it off in our early social gatherings. I think she thought I was a shallow type of person with absolutely no interest in life other than pretty girls and partying. Far be it for me to argue her assessment of me during that period. However, at times I also did regard life as something more than the superficial fun-seeking way we lived. Reading had always been my great resource, and exposure to matters such as world affairs, history, etc. It was at this stage that I began to recognise the difference between well-written books and the lesser types. If I read and enjoyed books by certain authors, i.e. John Steinbeck, Earnest Hemingway, Charles Dickens, Bertrand Russell, etc., I would seek out other books they had written. Yes, I even tackled Tolstoy's *War and Peace*. I loved to engage her in small debates of politics and other social topics, such as the differences between those who live well and those who barely get by in life. This I did partially with the intent of trying to impress on her that I was not the shallow person she perceived I was. That, yes, I knew there was more to life than "wine women and song." I doubt very much this changed her mind then, but she seemed to enjoy our conversations. Over the years, we learned to not only accept each other; we became good friends.

In 1960, Phil's brother Eddie travelled down to San Francisco for a short holiday. He was enjoying it so much he decided to find a job, which he told us was easy, and he settled in. Unfortunately, he did not have the necessary visa or work permit when the immigration department caught up with him. Therefore, it was back to Vancouver for Eddie, where he began to tell us how great life was in San Francisco. Jobs were easy to find, there were decent apartments with reasonable rent, and the nightlife was fantastic.

It did not take long before several of us were having serious thoughts of moving down to the U.S. Here I was finally with full-time work, but financially just barely meeting monthly expenses. At that time, Phil and I were sharing one of those dark and gloomy basement apartments that were all we could afford. Someone in the group did some serious research on what it would take to enter the U.S. legally. At that time in the late 1950s, the basic requirements seemed to be to either have a sponsor or be able to show some financial security. None of us had a sponsor, and as for financial security that was very questionable. On further inquiry, we discovered that for an individual who met all their other requirements, a savings account of $1,000 would meet their criteria. Not one of us had that amount in the bank, but it did not take long for us to figure out how to come up with an agreement on how to meet that requirement.

PART IV

1960-2010

California Here I Come

By late 1960, we somehow managed to collect enough money to meet the financial means qualification for immigration to the U.S. Phil, Eddie and Peter, with his wife Lilly, were the first to file. Phil and Eddie received their visas, and in no time they packed up and headed south to San Francisco. Following them was Peter, Lilly, and their two children, and then bringing up the rear was yours truly. Phil was the one who encouraged me to make the decision to immigrate. By the time I arrived, Phil and Eddie had full-time work at one of the top hotels in San Francisco, the Fairmont. Peter was working in a high-class restaurant, Rolf's, close to Fisherman's Wharf.

Once the U.S. granted my papers, I made my farewells to my army buddies, Doug, Pete, Jack and Joe. The 'bon- voyage,' party, I'm sure, must have been a good night in one of our regular pubs. For me, the next step was to book a ticket at the Greyhound bus station and head south to that bustling city by the bay, San Francisco. Phil had an apartment, and I slept on a couch until I found my own place. On my first night, the lads took me down to Fisherman's Wharf, and we had dinner and a few beers. I feel fortunate to have experienced that early period of the 60s living in San Francisco. The wharf, where we spent a lot of our leisure time during those years, was not the overblown extravaganza it has become today! You could drive your car and park (no parking meters in those years) within a few steps of the restaurants, cocktail lounges and boats.

The next day I arose early, put on my best suit, caught a cable car to the City Of Paris, a very fashionable department store owned by a French family. They interviewed me, and I was hired on the spot; that kid full of self-doubts, with an inferiority complex a mile long, had changed.

A month later, I found lodging out in the suburbs, a room with shared kitchen and bathroom facilities. Commuting back and forth to work and home on the bus and cable cars was relaxing. It gave me plenty of time to read books or the morning paper; meanwhile, Phil and the others all had jobs in either hotels or high-class restaurants. Their British accents helped them get hired in these first-class food establishments, as Americans generally enjoy foreign accents, particularly if they speak recognizable English.

Somewhere along the line, Phil slipped back up to Vancouver, married Ann and brought her and her sister Barbara down to San Francisco. Phil worked most of his years in the hospitality trade at the Fairmont Hotel. He became the maître d' of the Venetian Room, where all the top stars of the day like Frank Sinatra, Ella Fitzgerald, Dean Martin, and Sammy Davis Jr. performed. Occasionally Phil could slip my date and me into the Venetian Room. With great professional decorum of a first-class maître d', Phil would greet ne with a, "Good evening, Mr. Mackay, your usual table?" Then he would lead us to an excellent table, close to the entertainment being featured that night.

I saw such stars as Ella Fitzgerald, Jerry Lewis and Tony Bennet. Believe me that really impressed my various dates. I did miss one night when the real Rat Pack was in town. Phil told me Sinatra, Sammy Davis Jr. and Peter Lawford were feeling no pain when they arrived at the Venetian Room. During the evening, "Chairman of the Board" Sinatra offered the busboy $100 to drop a waiter's tray loaded with glasses behind Sammy's chair. According to Phil, Lawford, being the gentleman that he was, tipped the kid $50 and told him to disappear.

Yes, that was a fun, crazy time of my life. I remember having to inform one date, "No; we cannot dine at the Venetian Room every weekend." I did not tell her that I could not impose on my friend Phil, nor could I afford to dine at the Venetian Room regularly. She did not seem to accept that so I promptly removed her from the proverbial little black book. For the first time in my life, I was not exactly short on girls to date.

I worked at the City of Paris for a little over a year, and then changed jobs to work with a chain outlet, Bond's clothing stores. Their merchandise was not as fashionable or expensive as the merchandise I had sold at the City of Paris; however, my paycheck was considerably higher. I was selling more clothing because the prices were far more reasonable. Within a year, they promoted to me to the position of floor manager.

With the promotion, I bought my first car, a flaming red Austin Healy Sprite sports car. Here I was buying a new car and had never been behind the wheel. I had to take one of my sales people with me to drive the car out of the car lot.

The same guy, Malcolm, taught me how to drive my new toy. My boss's secretary, a cute redhead, asked me to take her for a ride, so we began to date occasionally. In no time at all, I was blazing around the streets of San Fran and over the Golden Gate Bridge to Sausalito in that hot, zippy little sports car. Yes, I picked up a ticket or two, but life was great and I was having a ball. Some of my married pals possibly worried that I was having too much fun and began to mention that maybe it was time for me to settle down. I felt I was not ready for that stage of my life.

My good mate Pete Topo came down to San Francisco for a visit. I took a few days off from work, and we drove to Los Vegas, the fun city. We hit several casinos. Pete wanted to gamble, but me, the non-gambler; I was more interested in checking out the girls. So, there was Pete at one of the card tables with me standing alongside enjoying a cocktail and girl watching. "Whammo"! Straight across the room I spotted two very attractive women standing close to one of the coin machines. One was a blonde and the other a brunette. My intense view centered in on the beautifully tanned brunette wearing a dazzling white dress. As I gazed at her, the song "Some Enchanted Evening" came to my mind. I just stood there enjoying the view when suddenly the brunette's beautiful eyes glanced at me, and we exchanged a smile. Doing my very best to stay cool, while my heart was racing, I tapped Pete's shoulder and said, "Don't look now, but I have spotted two beauties across the room and behind us. I said, "Eyes to the rear, soldier."

Taking a moment, Pete casually turned around and with

smile, lighting up his face said, "Sir Roderick, I do believe we should rescue those two fair damsels from the dangers lurking in this house of ill repute!" With that, he turned in his cards and scooped up his chips as we prepared to make our approach.

Before we took one step on this venture, knowing my buddy's Casanova reputation, I warned him the brunette was mine.

His response was, "Hey, you should know that gentlemen prefer blondes."

That remark cracked me up, and we were both chuckling as we approached the women. With years of training in the dance halls on how to meet a woman for the first time, I felt reasonably confident. I said to the woman of my choice in the semi-deep tone of Italian actor Rossano Brazzi, "Some enchanted evening you will meet a stranger ... and I do believe he has just arrived, Good evening, ladies."

It worked. They laughed as we exchanged names. Smiling at me, the brunette told me her name was Joan and said, "I loved that movie *South Pacific*." Her smile reassured me that I did not need to worry about my pal Pete. He, in turn, was quite happy and chatting up Joan's friend.

Let me summarize here by saying the four of us had a wonderful two days doing Los Vegas: seeing different shows, dining out and dancing. She was an excellent dancer and with my love of dancing, we very seldom came off the floor. I hate to say it, but Vegas being what it is, Pete and I initially had wondered if the girls might be professionals working for the casino. I was delighted to learn that this was not the case. I was definitely intensely attracted to Joan. When I said good-bye the next day, I had a new phone number in my book. Joan told me she lived in Tracy, California, and said she would love to see me again. That was a given; if I had to move mountains that was going to happen.

I visited her a few times in Tracy, meeting her at restaurants but never at a home address. This did concern me but not wishing to lose her, I did not dare venture to question further. She came down to San Francisco a few times, and I took her out to dinner and the nightclubs. Yes, it was not long before I had Joan on my mind night and day. One weekend I called her to tell her I had a couple of days off and could drive over to Tracy to see her. Her voice was a bit choked, and I sensed she was crying as she began to explain to me that she was married and had two kids. She and her husband had been having problems. He had moved out but now they decided to save their marriage for the sake of their children. She told me how she really cared for me and was so sorry. I felt like the floor was collapsing under me as the phone dropped out of my hand. I sat down and, yes, wept like baby. The phone rang later that night, and as there was no caller ID back then, I had no idea who was calling. I did know if it were Joan, that just the sound of her voice would only tear me apart.

Yes, it was a whirlwind and stupid affair, but I had fallen deeply in love with her. I spent countless miserable nights walking the beaches of the Sunset District and all I could think of was Joan. Every love song I heard on the radio could tear me apart.

As the wise pundits tell us, time does eventually mend a

broken heart. Close friends like Peter Hope and Phil Peers knew what I was going through and did their best to bring me out of my emotional mess. I found myself returning to the depression stage that I had suffered in Korea. Thoughts of suicide finally drove me to seek the help from a doctor. During the third session, he said, "You know you have had a lot of turmoil in your life; maybe you might try following your friend's advice."

I likely told him, "Doc, that is easier said than done" as I exited his office. Finally, I began to think that possibly my married friends were right. At thirty years of age, maybe I needed to be thinking in terms of marriage and a family. As I began to heal that is exactly what I felt was missing in my life: a family and home.

As I was recovering from my emotional problems, I began to have serious problems with my ear condition. I decided to make an appointment with an ear specialist, a Dr. Neil Mulcahy. This turned out to be an excellent choice. Through surgery, Neil eliminated the mastoid problem in both ears. That condition began when I was still in the army. Surgery and treatment actually prevented further loss of my hearing. Neil also had a nurse assistant, Carol, who had a close friend, Orris. They had been friends since nursing school. That is how I met and began the relationship with my first wife. She was beautiful, intelligent and personable. Orris was also a nurse for another top ear specialist in the city. We dated for several months, and then I proposed and she accepted. We had a small wedding with close friends, and Orris's father and mother drove up for Los Angeles.

Within a year, on December 19, 1964, we had a baby girl, and we named her Christine. Without a doubt, she was the nicest Christmas present a new father could receive. I quickly began to call Christine my Little Princess, and I think that rather stayed with her, as in her adult years she has a slight touch of royalty in her personality. I really began to think that finally my life was taking a turn in the right direction. Orris stayed home with the baby, and that worked out fine, as in exchange for free rent we managed an apartment complex.

My job at Bonds was going along fine. Then, one day, the boss's secretary called to say the boss wanted to see me in his office. With some trepidation, I went upstairs to his office, wondering what was going on. Chris, the boss, was a former WWII Marine, and he was strictly a no-nonsense kind of man. My being a Canadian Army vet cut some slack in our work relationship. As I sat down, he came straight to the point and told me that Bonds was going to build a new branch store over in Walnut Creek. He said he was happy and impressed with my management of the menswear department. To that end, he was going to recommend me to the New York office for consideration in their selection of a manager of the new store. I was more than excited at the prospects of managing my own store, yet aware that this would entail a much heavier load of responsibilities and longer hours. Regardless, I thanked Chris for putting my name up and told him I was definitely interested. This new store was really still in the planning process, so I had plenty of time to decide.

Oddly enough, shortly after that offer my brother in law, A.G., called me asking if I would be interested in managing a bowling centre. His family owned this business, and it was located in a small country town, King City, about 150 miles south of San Francisco. It was a newly built bowling lane with billiard tables, restaurant and cocktail lounge. We had driven down to King City on weekends, so I was familiar with the business. However, as I told A.G. on his first call, I knew absolutely zilch about managing a bowling centre. He explained to me he knew that, but placed value on my previous experience in the food and beverage business. He also told me the restaurant and cocktail lounge was their major sources of profit. It was difficult evaluating these two offers received in the same proximity of time. I asked A.G. to give me time to think this over and discuss it with Orris.

From the day I had arrived in San Francisco I loved the city, but now as a new family man with a baby girl, my perspective of life was changing. It was about that time major changes began to happen in the city, one being the invasion of the hippie culture. In those days, most people would have considered me a "straight or square kind of guy." So there was our choice, did we want to raise a family in the big bustling city surrounded by hippies, or move to a small town in the quiet countryside.

It was not that many years ago that I had been trudging the streets of Vancouver unemployed, seeking any type of work. Now I had to make a choice between two management-level job offers. Store manager for Bonds was likely a year or more from materializing, whereas the King City offer was immediate. I decided on the King City offer, so I called my brother-in-law to accept his offer. Before I left the city,

I picked up a business manual on restaurant management. I realized there were gaps in my past food and beverage experience that I need to work on immediately.

Learning to operate a bowling centre and my life in King City was new and challenging. However, first, I need to introduce the Andrus family that hired me to manage the business. A.G. was my brother-in-law, and he owned and managed a pharmacy in town. His brother Hugh was the head physician of the Mee Memorial Hospital of King City. Their sister Nancy was their business secretary of their properties and businesses. Their father, a retired physician, was the driving force to build the King City hospital. The town folk referred to the elder patriarch of the family quite simply as, "Old Doc," and Hugh, the head physician of the hospital, as "Young Doc."

Doc was retired for several years prior to my arrival. Over the five years, I knew Doc; he remains lodged in my memory as a most unforgettable character. Besides his tall physical stature, Doc was a big man in many ways: great sense of humour, intelligent, outgoing personality, yet quite blunt-spoken in expressing his opinions. If he sensed someone was talking sheer nonsense, he was not shy about telling whomever, "That is pure bullshit." In his younger days in university, he was an all-round athlete who excelled on the gridiron, basketball and track.

Most of the town liked and respected Doc; envy accounted for his few detractors. He played golf every day the weather allowed and late afternoon was his happy visiting hours. Friends, particularly a man known as Pappy, would come over to Doc's house. The house reminded me a bit of the Ponderosa home of the TV Cartwright family. Doc, an atheist, was married to a lovely woman, Leora, who as a Christian attended church every Sunday. Their relationship was as loving and caring as any married couple I have known. Doc was a well-read man and could carry on intelligent conversation on a wide scope of subjects. Most days he and Pappy would play chess and converse on various topics.

Doc had little use for politicians or the entire political system. The only system he did believe in was Technocracy. I had never heard of it. He shared several gazettes from the organization with me, and at the time I felt there was much merit to their system. However, as I said to Doc, to implement Technocracy would surely result in a blood bath. Quite often, he and Pappy, who was a Christian, would have some lively debates on these two topics, religion and politics. Of course, Doc's relaxation hours were mandatory in his house. This is how I entered into Doc's small, intimate special gatherings. I normally took a break from the business at 5:00 p.m. and stopped by his home. Doc enjoyed scotch on the rocks, and JB was his favourite drink. When his JB was running low, I would order a case for him from our spirits distributor.

I considered it a privilege when Doc invited me to stop in and visit during these late-afternoon sessions. I found the conversations in Doc's home both stimulating and always interesting. I count them as some of the most fascinating and enjoyable hours of my life.

Doc had a special family tradition that I feel would benefit many families in this fast-paced electronic world.

Each Saturday morning Doc would have all the grandkids over for breakfast and a special program. Leora would cook up bacon and eggs, and all the rest. Following the breakfast, all the dishes were cleared from the table. Then Doc would open up the main purpose of this special gathering. There were six grand kids at that time and all in their teens. Each Saturday, one boy or girl was pre-assigned to pick and speak about a topic of their choice. The one mandatory rule was that nobody was allowed to interrupt the speaker until he or she had finished speaking.

I appreciated Doc inviting me to attend and observe a couple of the breakfast club meetings and was so impressed with the mature way these youngsters spoke and listened on their chosen topics. Nobody interrupted the speaker and the youngsters actually listened to each other. I recall making a resolution to implement that programme with my kids. In sad retrospect, like so many excellent ideas, I never followed through. A simple concept like this would work well in a home of harmony with both parents involved. Unfortunately, at the time our house was lacking in that respect. Orris was prone to migraines that had her bedridden quite often. She could not tolerate any noise from the children, so at times like that I took them with me out or to the bowling centre.

Quite often on a nice sunny afternoon, Doc would ask me if I had time to take him out for a drive in his big, old Cadillac. The drives were mostly just touring around the farm sites and fields surrounding King City. He enjoyed talking with the farmers, and they would always have a box of vegetables for him to take home to Leora. I recall one farm where the farmer, and his wife were outside the house. Following a typical conversation of crop yield, weather, etc., the wife asked Doc what she could take for a headache. Doc, with a wink to the farmer and little grin, said, "I think what you need, Myrtle, is a nice, quiet, romantic night and early to bed with Don (the husband). That's as good a prescription as I can give, and it's a hell of a lot more fun than an aspirin." As we drove off they were both standing there shaking their heads, but smiling happily. I rather think that just maybe they followed Doc's prescription that day.

In recent years as I drive past King City and the farmlands, it saddens me as the inevitable demise of the small farms has taken place. What was once a myriad of crop farms—tomatoes, lettuce, and cabbage, corn—is now one vast vineyard.

In 1969, our daughter Tara was born, and I can best describe her as a lovable and a very active, high-octane little girl. Our home was close to the school with a huge playing field in our backyard, so she and Christine had plenty space to play. One year when Tara was four or five years old, my wife called me at work, frantically telling me that Tara was missing, and she could not find here anywhere. I told her to calm down, and I would be straight home; the bowling centre was about a half-mile from our home. Prior to the call, I had been counting the cash registers for the day. One of my waitresses came in and said that a truck driver told her there was a kid trying to climb up onto one of the big semis parked in our lot. I told her to ask Roberto, my assistant manager, to go check it out.

So now, as I rushed to my car, my brain was racing. "Wham, a kid is in our parking lot. What size kid and is it mine?" Out the door I went running, looking for Roberto; I finally spotted him, and couple of other staff members, gathered at the front right side of a big semi-truck. They are all standing there with benign smiles, gazing at a curly-headed little girl who has managed to haul herself up to the lower step of that mega-sized truck. Yes, that little girl was my daughter Tara. Guess what, that little girl grew up with a wanderlust that never left her. We lost Tara in 2012; she died in a tragic road accident in her pickup. Just writing that sentence chokes me up, I miss her so much.

My Brother Rob ...
and Two New Brothers!

A very important and memorable turn in my life took place during my King City years. I finally located my older brother Rob. In one of life's peculiar circumstances, this came about with the help from a stranger in King City.

One morning I was setting up the cash register in the cocktail lounge. The TV had been left on, and I was about to turn it off when I heard the newscaster mention Edinburgh, Scotland. It was our local station giving the local news, so I decided to stop and hear the rest of this news item. Coincidentally, the item regarded a King City man doing research for U.S. Department of Agriculture. In the broadcast, they said he would be travelling to Edinburgh in a couple of weeks to attend a conference. My new involvement with the Scottish Society and pipe bands awakened feelings of family and the land of my birth. I obtained the phone number of the chap and explained part of my family history. I told him that unfortunately over the period from 1955 to the present date, I had lost track of my Aunt Kate's address. Recently, I had written her but the letter returned with caption, "No forwarding address." I asked him if he could be kind enough to go to the last address I had for Kate and inquire of the neighbours as to where she might have moved. The name of the chap I was talking to was Marion. He said he would be happy to follow through with my request. In less than a month, I received a letter from both Marion and my aunt Kate with her new address.

Aunt Kate's first letter explained that my brother Rob had been searching for me for years. He had come up from London a few months after I left Edinburgh and returned to Canada in the 1950s. He was amazed that I had come back to Scotland, as somehow he thought; a Canadian family had adopted me and changed my name.

Within a matter of days, the first letter from Rob arrived. The handwriting and spelling of the letter was excellent. I was amazed as I thought possibly due to difficulties he faced growing up he may not have attended school on a regular basis. He enclosed several photos, of him and his wife Sylvia. One photo was a formal portrait of them posed in front of a large painting, Sylvia dressed in a lovely evening gown, and Rob dressed very smartly in a blue blazer, regimental tie, and gray slacks. It was the image of a couple who might well have belonged to the upper class society of England. My first reaction was pure amazement by their surroundings and the way they were dressed in that photo. I immediately sensed that he had done quite well in life. If he had spent his early years on the streets, it appeared that he had ended up very successful and had prospered. Possibly Rob was one of those rags to riches stories. My first letter to him included my phone number, and I told him I would immediately make plans to come visit him in London.

Several days later, he phoned. Orris answered the phone and, on hearing his English (not a Scottish) accent, assumed it was my mate Phil playing a joke on me. Rob, very confused, answered emphatically, "No, no, it's me, Roddy's older brother Robert Mackay in London!" As soon as I was home, I called him back to tell him I had booked a flight to London, and we would be over there in a couple of months. He responded by telling me he did not think he could wait for my visit. Sure enough, within two weeks I received a call from him, informing me he was in Las Vegas. I was beginning to sense that my big brother was a fast and high wheeler-dealer kind of man. After I got over the initial shock and happiness, yet mixed with a bit of anger that he had seen fit to go to Las Vegas first, I began to scheme as to how I could do a 'number' on him.

Among many friends whom I had acquired while managing Ranch House Lanes Phil Vincenz was a regular customer. We had become good friends over the course of Phil doing daily business at the restaurant, and we both were members of the Lion's Club. Phil, like many of my friends, had heard the news of Rob and me finding each other after 35 years of separation.

That night Phil came in for dinner and invited me to sit at his table and have a drink. I told him what my brother had done, and while I was so happy, I was very frustrated that he stopped over in Las Vegas, whilst I was left here panting like a puppy. I told Phil that if there were some possibility I could get to Las Vegas, I would go to their hotel and somehow surprise the hell out of him. In my mind, I had a scheme that included making contact with the hotel manager, telling him of the situation and seeing if he would go along with a little joke on my brother Rob. Later, learning that my brother Rob was a "high roller," I'm sure the management would have been happy to assist in our surprise plot.

The plan included borrowing a bellhop's uniform and delivering flowers and a bucket of Champagne to his room. When he answered the room doorbell, I would announce, "Room service, sir, we have a special parcel to deliver from a Mr. Mackay of King City." I would also mispronounce our name as most Yanks do. As Rob had not seen me since I was five, I was betting he would not know me.

Phil, who owned a small two-seat plane, not only thought the plan was brilliant; he immediately volunteered to fly me there. I did not hesitate to take him up on his offer, telling him I would go home, talk to the wife, and call him right back. What happened next I consider one of the biggest regrets of my life? I told my wife what I had in mind and of Phil's fantastic offer to fly me to Vegas. I could tell from her expression that she did not think much of the idea. This was but one of many areas where we disagreed. However, I take the responsibility for making the decision to decline Phil's generous offer. This first meeting with my brother Rob after all those years of separation, I really wanted to make it special and memorable. Phil's offer … I should have accepted with no hesitation and that should have been the end of the discussion.

Following his Las Vegas visit, he rented a car to drive down to Los Angeles; you see; he was determined, regardless of his kid brother's impatience, to see as much big-city action as possible. I learnt much later in a bar conversation in London that by driving the rental at the highest speeds possible, he burnt the engine out. Finally, he called to tell me they would be flying up to San Francisco and asked if I could pick them up there. Naturally, there were the hugs, tears and all the emotions flowing as we met at the airport that day. While I can't recall much of what we said to each other, the first question my brother asked almost floored me on the spot. He said in his Cockney accent, "Roddy, did Alex and Billy go to Canada with you?"

I had absolutely no idea of whom he was asking, so naturally my response was with some trepidation. "Who the hell are Alex and Billy?"

A very strange look came over his face as he answered, "Our brothers."

Wondering if this was a stroke of his Cockney humour, I answered him with, "Rob, what in hell are you talking about? You are the only brother I have."

I was dumbfounded. I *had* no younger brothers, and yet here was Rob telling me otherwise. It didn't make sense. At the same time, his tone was so earnest that it could not have been a joke.

It was as though I had just instantly acquired two younger brothers from nowhere. The ground below my feet felt a little unsteady, and I wondered what other information had been kept hidden from me. What else had the U.K. welfare system taken from me besides my childhood when it shipped me off to that deplorable place in Canada, the Fairbridge Farm School?

Well, following a strange and lengthy conversation, at age 37 I was to discover for the first time in my life that I had two younger brothers. Complicating matters, nobody in the family seemed to know where they sent Alex and Billy [25]during the family split-up of 1939.

We decided to spend a few days showing Rob and Sylvia around San Francisco. At this point, I was beginning to feel the town of King City would not be of much interest to my high- flying brother. He could not stop raving about the sights of Las Vegas and L.A. Matter of fact about the second or third day in King City, shaking his head; he asked me why I had moved from a beautiful city the likes of San Francisco to a small, hick town like King City.

My response was quick and short as I told him, "For the sake of my kids," and then we dropped the conversation. He was impressed that I was managing a business and had a nice home. The local newspaper interviewed and took photos of us and printed the story of our reunion. I did all I could to entertain Rob and Sylvia, and a few of my friends put on a special Western-style barbecue.

One morning he came into the bowling centre with me to check it out. I also had to make a cash drop-off at the bank and a short 1:00 p.m. business meeting to attend. To keep Rob entertained, I dropped him off at a Western-style saloon on the main street. The owner, Steve, and I were good friends, so I introduced my brother and asked Steve to entertain Rob while I took care of business. My errands took the full hour, and as I entered the bar, I could hear men laughing. At the center of all this vocal humour was my

---

25   More on Alex and Billy in a later chapter.

brother Rob. There were about a dozen men, a mix of farmers and cowboys, in the saloon. One of the guys had loaned my brother his cowboy hat and Rob was doing an impression of John Wayne. Nobody, including myself, ever heard anyone doing John Wayne with a Cockney accent. It was hilarious. He entertained everyone, including Steve, the owner, telling them Cockney jokes. They all thought he was funny as hell and were very disappointed when I showed up to pick him up. On the way out, he turned and said, "All right boys, I'll see ya later at the OK Corral."

Once in the car, he said, "Roddy, five more minutes, and I'd have had a six shooter on my hip." I was happy he had enjoyed himself that day in a Western saloon. After he left for home, men who had met him that morning would stop me on the street and tell me, "That brother of yours is a hoot and funny as hell," and ask how he was doing. I've seen and heard a lot of guys doing impressions of John Wayne, but my brother Rob with his Cockney accent was the funniest and wildest.

Time went fast and when they left, in spite of our different ways, I felt we had bonded as brothers. I found Rob to be a bit of an enigma. It was apparent he was doing quite well financially, but his line of business remained a bit of a mystery. When I posed the question, he answered with a bit of a smirk, "Whose asking, the FBI?"

Later, he told me he was a bookie[26] and owned a betting parlour. This profession is legal in the U.K. Rob's wife Sylvia,

---

26   A bookmaker....somebody who takes bets and pays winners, this is a legal business in the U.K.

whom we often called Sylvie, was an absolute jewel and all my King City family and friends commented on what a nice woman my brother had married. As it happens in life when you are enjoying a special time, their visit was son over. It was time to drive them back up to the San Francisco for their flight home to London. With much sadness we parted; however, that was eased knowing that we would be visiting them in London in a few weeks.

We only had a month and half to wait out our trip to the U.K. I was as anxious as a little kid waiting to be returned to his home and family. The magic day arrived and Orris, Christine and I took off on a charter flight loaded with British ex-pats, like me, most of them from Scotland. Everyone was celebrating; the stewardesses earnt their money on that flight, keeping up with the beer and drink requests.

Next morning, our flight landed at Prestwick Airport. Once we had cleared immigration, I collected our luggage, and we settled down in the passengers' lounge to wait for Rob. He had told me he would drive up to Scotland and pick us up at the airport. We had agreed that we would spend a week in Edinburgh, and then he would drive us down to London. So we sat and watched all our fellow flight members being picked up by their families. After an hour wait, I decided to phone Rob's home and find out what was happening. Much to my surprise Rob answered the phone; he went straight into an apology, explaining that due to business, he was unable to make it up to Scotland. Of course this being years before cell phones became common; he had not been able to contact us. Yes, I was sorely disappointed, but decided we just had to make the best of it and arranged transportation into Edinburgh. I hired a cabbie to take us to the train or bus. In loading our luggage, I noticed we were short a suitcase (mine). Orris was sure that all the cases were there before I went to the phone booth, but had no idea what could have happened. I reported it to the airport security, gave them my two U.K. addresses, and they assured me they would contact me when it showed up. Frustrated but determined not to let the two incidents spoil my homecoming, we made our way into Edinburgh. Aunt Kate had invited us to stay with her. It was a small, cozy flat but somehow we managed the sleeping arrangement. First item on my agenda was to find a phone box and call Rob to tell him about my lost suitcase with all my clothes. He just laughed and told me not to go out and buy anything; if it was not located he would take me out shopping in London.

Quite honestly, this mix-up in our plans worked well as I wanted to visit longer with Aunt Kate and Uncle Robert first. I felt guilty and needed to apologize to her and Uncle Robert for my not staying in touch all those years. It was good telling her and Uncle Robert how grateful I felt for them taking me into their family back in the fifties. Uncle Robert said, "Dinna fesh yerself laddie you are family." They were the first to give me the wonderful warm feeling of being part of a FAMILY!

One of the most memorable days of our time in Scotland was taking my cousin Robert, his wife Joan and their son Gary to the Braemar Games. Queen Elizabeth and the royal family were in attendance and while we certainly did not have the privilege of meeting her, I did meet the lead Drum Major of the Massed Bands. On hearing my name was Mackay, he said, Well, that is a real Highlander's name." Christine and Gary, who were close in age, had a fun-day chasing my cousin's dog around the park.

We stayed in Edinburgh a week, just long enough to see the sights within the city and get reacquainted with all my cousins and their families. Then we took the train down to London. Rob picked us up at the Kings Cross station and took us to his home. He lived in Streatham, which at the time was a fashionable area in London. Typical of the area, his house was a large, older style home and quite comfortable, with spacious rooms. During his trip to the U.S., Rob had noticed how Americans loved their showers, so he had installed a shower in our assigned bedroom. He also laid out on the bed a wardrobe of new clothing for me: a blazer, two pairs of slacks, four shirts, and a pair of shoes. Laughing, he told me I would have to take care of buying my own underwear. Amazingly, all the clothing fit me well; of course, Rob and I are similar in size. When I asked how much I owed him, he replied, "Nothing, they fell off the back of a lorry." That is an expression used by the Cockneys basically there way of telling you " it's none of your business," He also had a classy motor, an Aston Martin in which he drove us to all the top tourist spots in London. Yes indeed, we took in the Changing of the Guard; the biggest thrill in that episode was my brother ignoring a police barrier and driving right behind the Regimental Band. I felt sure they were going to pull him over, but he got away with it by shouting out the window to the closest police officer that he had American press in the car. The security back then obviously was not near as tight as it is these days. This was one small incident of several, but it was indicative of how my brother would flaunt the law.

On our second night, Rob had arranged a family and friends welcoming party, and here I was to meet my sister Minnie, her husband Alec and their son Alec. We got quite emotional as Minnie told me how terribly sad she had been when they took me away and sent me to Canada. They never told her where they were sending me, and she cried for days. Other than that, it was one great happy celebration, which went on until the wee hours of the morning. I met Rob's family: daughter Suzy, sons Barry and young Robbie, his friends and business associates. We had music organized by a DJ who had me in stitches with his Cockney dialogue. I danced with my sister Minnie that night, and sadly it turned out to be the one and only time we would dance together. A few years later, she fell into a deep depression and never fully recovered.

During the evening, Rob introduced me to one of his neighbours, Harry, who was a professional musician. He was playing trombone with the London Symphony Orchestra, and he invited me to come with him to a rehearsal the next morning. I took a small recorder and began to imitate an American newscaster interviewing Londoners. I still have that tape and pull it out every now and then; it is hilarious. Cockneys are quick-witted and once you can understand their lingo their humour will have you rolling with laughter. The only person not enjoying the evening was my ex-wife. She felt upset with people drinking and could not stand the fact that we were all enjoying ourselves. Yes, we were having fun and laughing, with some of us a bit tipsy, so she retired to our bedroom. Of course, that upset my brother and his wife Sylvie, I went up to the bedroom and attempted to pacify her. As I expected from past experiences, this only exacerbated the problem, she yelled at me and said she wanted to go home. That just blew me away; I told her we were celebrating a thirty-year family reunion, followed with, "What the hell do you expect us to do, celebrate over a cup of tea?" Full of anger, I rejoined the party, determined to put the ill feelings aside and continue celebrating with my family.

The next morning, in spite of the "morning after" symptoms, I was up early. I apologized to Rob and Sylvie for my wife's ill feelings. They were more understanding than I was. Rob told me Harry had called to pick me up; he said it was best I go ahead with Harry, enjoy the day, and they would take care of Orris. I had a wonderful morning listening to the orchestra, followed by a couple of hours of recuperation in their local. There was a mix of musicians, actors, and the general conversation was witty and funny, and I had a delightful time just listening to them. I didn't dare attempt to match wits with them. By some miracle, Rob and Sylvie had calmed Orris down, so we spent the rest of the holiday with some semblance of peace.

Rob was anxious to find and give me a gift. I told him there was no need; he did enough already. Earlier, he gave me a gold sovereign ring during his visit to the states. Stubbornly, he insisted, saying, "Surely I can find an article for your kilt uniform that would be hard to find in the U.S."

I realized this was going to give him as much pleasure as to myself, so I told him that yes, I could use a Dirk.[27]

Rob asked me, "What exactly is a Dirk?"

As I was explaining, he interrupted, saying, "Oh, yeah, we call it something different over here."

Over the years, I came to realise that this is one of my brother's funny idiosyncrasies. He will never admit to being completely ignorant on any subject. The kicker of this little incident came later that day when he came home with the item I had requested. However, when I removed the item from the parcel, I discovered he or one of his men had bought or purloined an antique WW1 German bayonet. I laughed but not too hard, as I did not wish to rub Rob's ego the wrong way.

He responded by telling me, "Roddy the man (an expert) told me that it was a genuine Dirk. What the hell do you Yanks know about Dirks anyhow?"

Recently going through boxes in the attic, I came across my big brother's gift, the German bayonet, and noted the serial number. I decided to search the web to check it out. I found it is a genuine WW1 German bayonet, and it is currently valued at approximately $1,000. I must remember to tell Rob this on my next call; very likely he has forgotten.

One night he invited me out to his club; while he was visiting some mates at another table. A guy who looked like a character out of *a certain movie featuring Marlon Brando* sat down at our table. He introduced himself as one of Rob's

---

27   A dirk is a long thrusting dagger that is often worn ceremonially with the kilt in Scottish Regiments.

mates and told me, "Rob sent me over to look out for you."

Like most of Rob's associates, he had a thick Cockney accent. He knew whom I was and that I was visiting my brother for the first time in London. At this point in the short time that Rob and I had been together; I was beginning to sense that my Big Brother had done more in his line of work than being a "Bookie." As mentioned earlier, he owned a very nice house in a posh area of London. He was driving very expensive cars so it was apparent whatever he had done in life; it had resulted in some handsome financial success. As I was sitting and talking to this mate of Rob's, I quite innocently asked him where my brother's business was located. He gave me a bit of a funny look and replied, "Roddy; your brother's place of business is wherever there is a pound note to be made, and this section of London is Rob's place of business." I decided it might be prudent at this point to change the topic and commented on how good the band sounded.

As it happens in life when you are enjoying yourself, all too soon it was time to say good-bye, pack up and head back to the good old USA. There was also a natural feeling of guilt of having left our youngest daughter Tara with family friends at home. With mixed feelings of leaving my brother Rob, Sylvie family to rejoin my American family, we flew home.

The Andrus family welcomed me back, and I told them within a week we could schedule a business meeting. During my vacation, I gave a considerable thought to both our marriage and our future in King City. I had worked hard and long hours in that business, building the restaurant and bar trade up, so we were finally showing a profit. However, the bowling section was a major financial drawback that was next to impossible to resolve. The complex had far too many lanes for the size of the community. With our cash flow, the cost of leasing the sixteen pin-setters was insurmountable. I reviewed this with A.G. and family. My advice was that I negotiate with AMF, the owners of the machines, to remove six of the pinsetters. We would use that floor space for a banquet community room. Once we completed the renovations, we put the business up for sale. In a matter of weeks, it was sold and, of course; with that reality, I had now sold myself out of a job. The five or so years in King City had kept me busy. My one regret was it had cut down on time spent with my daughters. However, the experience of managing a business on my own was of value both in business and managing Scottish Festivals. A.G. and Doc took us into their family and included us in all the family celebrations. I will never forget them. Sadly, A.G. and I both encountered serious problems in our relationship with our wives, the sisters. I think in both cases, they were extremely unhappy living in a small town. Of course, there were other differences within the two marriages.

Unfortunately, as happens too often for so many, our marriage fell apart, the major cause being we were definitely not compatible. The split left me feeling terrible about disrupting the lives of my young daughters.

I never knew much about my mother, as she had disappeared when I was a very young child. I always assumed she had died. In the early 1970s, however, I learnt she was very much alive, moving to London and remarrying. My father, of course, had remarried as well, and both had children in their second marriages. What was more; they actually kept and raised those kids, unlike us? My father even went on to have a very successful career with the U.K. Defense Department. When he was posted in Burma as a civil-service officer, his new family had a good home and the money to hire housemaids and other help.

By all accounts, both of my parents simply absolved themselves of any responsibilities as our caregivers. Though it may seem harsh, I can only conclude that our parents effectively abandoned the five of us. I, like my older brother and sister had, remain quite bitter about it. I don't hold any grudges against my half-sisters, though. None of it was their fault, and we've become very close over the years.

When our parents absolved themselves of all care-giving responsibilities, they left us to a heartless child-welfare system. It was a system that shipped well over hundred thousand children overseas to Canada, Australia, New Zealand, and South Africa. Frequently, the social workers didn't even wait for children to be abandoned; they snatched penniless children right off the streets. They would never see their families again.

It had nothing to do with the war; this scheme had been in motion since well before the First World War ever began.

Many feel, as I do, that the main goal of the U.K. welfare system was to get rid of poor children who presented a financial burden to the country and relieve overcrowding in cities. By the same stroke, they could populate colonies with homegrown British stock.

I can just imagine one of the aristocrats mingling with other bigwigs like Ebenezer Scrooge at his club when he proposed, "Let us be rid of these filthy little guttersnipes— ship them to the colonies, I say!"

A New Life in Monterey, California

During the process of our divorce, I applied for a new position, managing a private club in Monterey.

One might wonder how or why I had the confidence to raise my goals in seeking a management position of a private club in a plush resort area, following my experience of running a bowling centre. Experience taught me there is a far greater learning curve in operating a struggling business than a successful one. When the available labour market is weak, as it is in small towns, a manager learns patience in his dealings with his employees. I learnt very quickly how to control both labour and food/ beverage costs. When forced to lay off employees, as happened with my office manager, I was prepared to personally handle the payroll and take on other office responsibilities. I had learnt how to deal with the vendors, many of whom naturally would do their 'damndest' to oversell their products. For example, when I first took control over the business, in checking my inventories, I discovered we had a storage room with enough paper supplies to last six months. I told the sales rep to remove and credit us for five months of his supplies, or I would be doing business with one of his competitors. Those were but a few examples that I feel honed my management skills to go after the position I was seeking in the Monterey area.

A good friend lined me up to have lunch with the director of food/beverage of the Pebble Beach Lodge. The director was a former Brit. That turned into a plus for me as we hit it off pretty well, particularly when I gave him a bit of my Scots and Cockney dialects. He informed me that presently, they were remodeling a casual dining/ barroom to be called the Tap Room. They would be hiring a manager for that room, and he told me to make an appointment with the personnel office to go through the formalities. I could not believe my luck and thanked my friend for setting up the appointment. The one hitch was that I would be waiting at least two months for the remodel of the Tap Room to be completed. In order to keep my family finances in order, I needed work ASAP. Right about then I heard that a private men's club was interviewing candidates for the position as a manager. I checked it out, interviewed and was hired on a trial basis.

At this time during my life, along came a new friend, Jim Anderson, who was to make a great impact on my future. I first met Jim shortly after I hired on for the position of managing this club; one of my friends had warned me that the club had a reputation for hiring and firing their managers. Between the impending divorce, separation from my family and selling a house in King City, I was going through severe emotional and financial pressure. In spite of the warning of a reliable friend, I decided I had to take the job.

The club was a well laid-out, modern facility with a spectacular view of the Monterey Bay. The original developers built it as a resort hotel, and then they ran into serious financial problems. At that stage, a local group of Monterey executives took it over and converted it into private men's fraternal club. I was very naïve, knew nothing about the fraternal club, but I was impressed with the facility and enthusiastic over the challenge of managing the club's food and beverage entities. The committee that interviewed me informed me that my first tasks as a manager would be to resolve a few of their operational issues, i.e., high food and labour costs and security of their liquor stock room. With my experience, I felt confident I could meet that challenge and agreed to a period of three months to prove I was capable of managing the club and dealing with the problems.

In order to accomplish the goals I had set, I undertook long hours, working six or seven days a week. My working hours varied, many days with opening the facility at 7:00 a.m. and many nights closing at 2:00 a.m. Driving 100 miles round-trip from my house in King City to Monterey was killing me, especially on days when I worked from 7 a.m. until 1:00 a.m. In an attempt to cut the long drive, I posted a bulletin to see if possibly one of the members had a spare room that they might consider renting. Oddly enough, Jim was the one who responded. He was facing similar problems, a divorce, and his primary home was miles away near Fresno. Like me, he did not want to uproot his children, so he had rented a small house with two bedrooms in Pacific Grove. We discussed and agreed on the rent and terms; I moved within a week later. We found we were quite compatible in our ways and personality to share a home the size of a small cabin. In reminiscing, I have often described our experience as being similar to the TV show back in the 70s, *The Odd Couple*. Jim was Oscar and I definitely matched the role of Mr. Neat, Felix. We were both beginning to enjoy our new status of independence. I sensed that his marriage, like mine, had ended due to incompatibility. Both of us also felt that other than staying connected with our children, the parting with our wives was to be a final decision. We both worked hard and met the heavy responsibilities that came with our jobs.

After a month of reorganizing my workload at the club, I eased up on the long hours. Naturally, as young men who enjoy the company of women, we would go out on a weekend night to local nightclubs and hotel lounges that had a band for dancing. Yes, we both had been faithful to our wives, and now we were quite simply enjoying our new freedom and meeting new women. Another plus to our friendship was that Jim, and I have a good sense of humour and enjoy a laugh. It still amazes me that the simple act of renting a room from a man who knew nothing more about me than I did of him led to our lifelong friendship.

Just prior to the end of my three-month trial, I developed a list of solid recommendations to propose to the club's house committee, which consisted of approximately eight members who more or less made the final decisions about the running of the club facilities. At a special meeting, I presented a written list of how I proposed to resolve the club's problems. They had cited this task when they hired me. Nothing I proposed was disruptive, such as laying off employees or cutting off food or liquor distributors. From the day, I was hired, I compiled notes of what I observed. I also made it a point to discuss and listen to staff members, from the chef to the dishwashers to the head bartender. To each, I politely asked general questions about their individual duties, hours, etc. I informed each employee if he or she had any suggestions or problems that were job-related to let me know, and I would be happy to meet with them.

I also prioritized meeting with the various food and beverage distributors who were our suppliers. One company representative appeared to be tight-lipped and told me he did business only with the chef! This was his crude way of telling me, "Mr. New Manager, butt out of our business." I recognized this as a red flag warning for me. Though angry with his snotty reply, I kept my cool, thanked him and walked away. However, I immediately researched that problem quietly on my own. I did this quite simply by tracking how much of their product was used, reviewing their invoices and talking to the chef. From all my notes over the three months, I prepared an outline of my recommendations that I would present to the club's house committee as agreed on at the end of my first three months. Prior to this meeting, I also talked to Jim. As an active member, I felt his input would help in presenting my ideas to the committee. Jim did forewarn me about the possibility of opposition from two of the members on the committee.

Now came the meeting night. While I was slightly nervous, I felt confident in presenting my list of recommendations to the committee. Without going into great detail here, I listed the problems they had given me. To each problem, I gave the causes as I had observed, then explained how together we could resolve the issues. It was apparent that most of the committee agreed with my recommendations. That is, other than the two whom Jim had warned me could present problems. There were questions from individuals that I was prepared for and answered each one as intelligently and succinctly as possible. Then one of the two Jim cautioned me to be careful with began his harangue. He sarcastically implied that my recommendations were a waste of time and unnecessary. The chairman, wishing to save me further embarrassment, thanked me for my report and said they would review it in a closed session later in the week. I left the room feeling less confident, and also somewhat pissed off.

A few nights later, Jim came home and said he had overheard a conversation that took place in the club exercise rooms. Apparently one of the committee members, in a conversation with another member, said, "Well, sure as hell, we made a mistake hiring that new guy as manager."

I asked Jim if it was Dick C., and he responded, "How did you know?"

I told him how he had been the one man at the meeting who was completely negative and sarcastic. I also knew exactly why he was opposed to me as a manager. Besides being a house committee member, he owned the meat company that controlled all our meat purchases. I went into that meeting knowing who he was, so I had purposely not made any mention of cutting his company off. My recommendation was that we needed to pull in the chef and go over the problem with him. What I did not know then was that he was plying the chef with booze, etc.

Two other issues I had raised were how the cash was handled through the office and why there were at least three sets of keys floating around for the liquor storage room. Word

of that got back to the office manager, who confided with one
of the officers at the club. Yes, the initial warning I received
came crashing down on me like an avalanche. I stayed on
a few more months as the head barman while I waited for
another management position to open at Pebble Beach.
Fortunately for me, the manager of food and beverage at the
Lodge was still interested in hiring me. I did take one last
shot of revenge as I was leaving, by tipping off a committee
member that I knew who the member was who had a key
for the liquor storage room. I also witnessed him loading
liquor in his car. He asked me who it was, and I told him that
was for them (the house committee) to figure out as I was
no longer their manager. I love that old idiom, "What goes
around comes around."

Shortly after, out of the blue one day, Jim asked me if I
were interested in a teaching position with the school district.
My first reaction was, as the Brits would say, "Jim are you
taking the Mickey out of me?" I told him I left Fairbridge at
high school level I never attended college, and questioned
how could he offer me a position as a teacher? Actually, with
hopes of qualifying for the Officers Corps Training, I had
taken several academic classes during my military service.

He explained to me that California had a special
programme of vocational training for high school students
and adults called the Regional Occupation Programme. The
qualifications listed to teach for that programme were that
the individual had to have five to seven years of experience
at a management level in a specific trade. I actually qualified
in two occupational fields, retail and restaurant management.

Jim also said that he had been able to observe me working with young high-school students. I had hired and trained several teen-age students to work in the dining room at the club. He cited that as the reason he felt I would be a good fit for this occupational programme.

With Jim's assistance, I gathered all the necessary documents, and then applied to the personnel office of the Monterey Peninsula Unified School District. In short order, they call me in for an interview with the director of the ROP. Quite honestly, I was somewhat amazed when he hired me. In spite of proving that I had management skills, that old feeling of self-doubt and inferiority complex from my childhood days was still with me.

As required, I took and passed classes at San Jose State University to earn my teaching credentials. A few years later, I passed a certification license process to teach at the community college level. I put that credential to good use, teaching restaurant management at Monterey Peninsula College. Thanks to Jim, I enjoyed a rewarding 25-year career teaching young people entry-level skills for employment in the food and beverage industry. I also met a beautiful woman on the teaching staff, my wife of 34 years, Betty. Ironically, within weeks of my taking the teaching position, a new chairperson of the club called and asked if I would reconsider hiring on for the manager's position. He apologized for the way the club had treated me. He also thanked me for the recommendations that I had given that caused my dismissal. They had finally realized my advice had been right "on the mark." Subsequently, they fired the chef, ceased doing business with the meat company, fired the office manager and removed the two members who had caused the problem. Of course, I refused the offer but thanked him for his consideration. I also told him as a food and beverage manager, I found it very difficult taking directions from a group of tradesmen like plumbers, electricians and carpenters who served upon the house committee. I added it would be just as ridiculous for me to be giving them directions on their specialized trades.

My first assignment with the school district was to teach a summer school class. This being a smaller class and short summer session gave me time to prepare my course outline and objectives and that worked out fine. Of course, one of the real benefits of my new employment of a teacher was taking the summer vacations if I wished. This enabled me to go over to the U.K. and visit family in both Scotland and England.

During one short holiday in Bournemouth, brother Rob dropped me off at his "local."[28] Every night, my hosts, as assigned by my 'big bro,' were my nephew Barry's young mates, two "Scousers," the brothers Paddy and John. These two were fun-loving guys. Paddy's biggest joy in life was to sing and play the guitar. His all-time favourite singers were not the Beatles, but John Denver. I also met another fellow Scot, Alex Davidson, who was working for a big oil company in the Saudi desert. Alex owned a home in Bournemouth and Sterling, Scotland. When he retired, he sold the Bournemouth house and settled in Sterling. Betty and I have exchanged visits with him and his wife Pat over the years. On the last night of my Bournemouth visit, following a few farewell nips

---

28   A "local' is one's pub most frequented by him and his mates.

of whisky, Paddy repeated several times how he longed to move to the U.S. Following a whisky or two, feeling quite magnanimous, I offered him my card and said, "Paddy, if and when you get over there you just give me a call. I'll be happy to put you up."

So it came to pass just as sure as God made little green apples, the Dalton brothers showed up one day on the doorstep of my home in California. Most of my U.K. trips over the past 40 years have been split between visiting my family in Edinburgh and family in England. Two families, cousin Robert[29] wife Joan in Edinburgh and my cousin Alec and wife Karen have always generously taken us into their homes during our visits. Betty and I are always happy and delighted when they come visit us in California.

---

29   Following a stroke Rob was confined to wheelchair in his later years and died several years ago.

A SECOND CHANCE AT MARRIAGE AND FATHERHOOD

During my third or fourth school year, I noticed a very attractive teacher by the name of Betty Griffin. I noticed her quite often on her way to class; she was holding the hand of a little blonde-haired girl. My too-quick assumption that this lady was married proved much to my delight to be in error.

Since my divorce, I had been enjoying the dating game, so I was not too anxious to plunge into a long-term commitment of marriage. Strangely enough, my mate Jim was doing exactly that. There came a day when Jim announced that his bride-to-be would be moving in and his dog, Watash, and the renter (me) would have to find new digs. Maybe Jim's decision had some influence on my rethinking my single status. Because suddenly Betty was the only woman, I enjoyed being with, and I began to date on a steady basis.

Meanwhile, the divorce left my daughters unsettled, particularly Tara, the youngest. Tara's mother felt she could no longer handle her, so she turned custody over to me.

One day, Betty, Brianna, Tara and I were out driving in Betty's car. Then out of the blue, my Tara posed the question, "Dad, why don't you marry Betty?"

For a minute, I thought we were on the Art Linkletter TV show, *Kids Say the Darndest Things*. Besides not wishing to disappoint her and for more solid reasons, that was exactly what I did.

With not too big, a budget, Betty and I planned and

organized our entire wedding. Besides being a beautiful, intelligent woman, she is talented in so many areas and very resourceful. The wedding took place at Betty's church. It happened to be in the early stages of construction on the new church building. Our vows took place with a bulldozer as a background. Daughters Christine, Tara and Brianna were bridesmaids. Betty looked stunning in her white wedding dress. I did my best for the role of a handsome groom in my formal kilt attire. At my side, my best man Bill Merriman was also kilted. Not being one who always follows tradition, I invited two other good pals to participate in the best man role, Michel d'Avenas and Harvey Hillbun. Michel piped for the wedding, and escorting us to the wedding site was Harvey, six feet plus and all decked out in his Sherlock Holmes cap and cape. Harvey belonged to a select group of Sherlock Holmes admirers called the Diogenes Club. My ushers were the Liverpool lads, John and Paddy, wearing formal tails. Prior to our wedding, I doubt they had never worn a tux dress shirt or tie. Paddy volunteered to sing one of his favourite songs, "Annie's Song," a big hit by John Denver.

Like many a groom with nerves gone awry, I stupidly charged John and Paddy the task of transporting the Champagne to the reception hall in Carmel. When I arrived at the church site, one look at the lads and I knew my Champagne inventory would be minus several magnums. I grabbed Paddy not too gently, snarling, "How the hell are you going to sing the wedding song in your drunken state?" Besides cursing, I threatened him with great bodily damage if he screwed up our wedding song. Well, that day Paddy sang our wedding song as beautifully as his hero John Denver once did. Unfortunately, one of my friends, who shall remain anonymous, forgot to hit the button to record the song.

Following the wedding, we wended our way to the reception in Carmel. I hired a band called Cheeky Spanks; they were brilliant. A strong contingent of my pipe band mates was invited (I think). We had a mini-pipe band from the Prince Charles Pipe Band led by Bill. Flying up from Los Angeles, we had the Farrar brothers, both professional Highland dancers. Of course, Betty's Mum and Dad drove in from Tucson, Arizona. Her parents, being a teetotal couple, had me somewhat concerned with us serving alcohol. This situation did present me with an intricate and challenging problem. I was sensitive to their feelings; however, a Scot, particularly a kilted one, going dry on his wedding, that was not on in my books! Before the guests arrived, I surreptitiously tucked a whisky bottle under our table, the tablecloth concealing it nicely. Now that Paddy had sobered up somewhat, I gave him instructions occasionally top my teacup up with a dram of scotch when nobody was looking. While I was up dancing, they decided to move that table for the purpose of cutting the wedding cake. Yes, there I was, quietly dancing with Betty's mum when this huge whisky bottle came rolling across the floor. Horror upon horror, the bloody bottle rolled towards Mum and me. Making like Fred Astaire, I quickly and gracefully glided into a turn, taking my mother-in-law in the opposite direction of the rolling whisky bottle.

The band took requests and, yes, soon enough a bunch

of my British mates, including yours truly, were on the stage singing "Flower of Scotland" and Paddy singing more John Denver songs. Then the mini-pipe marched in, piping for the Highland dancers. As mentioned earlier, two young lads, the Farrar brothers, who were champion dancers, danced for us that day. To me, it was one of the happiest days of my life; so many good friends surrounded us. Sadly, as I am reflecting on that wonderful day of 33 years past, so many of those dear friends are no longer with us.

In 1983, Betty became pregnant and gave birth to a baby boy; I selected the name Angus. However, the womenfolk outvoted me, so we had to go with my second choice, Iain, and all approved this. At an early age, with a little encouragement from Dad, Iain learnt to play bagpipes and this opened the door for his father. The poor lad his destiny as a piper established whilst he was still inside his mother's body. I would hold a music recorder loaded with pipe band music on top of Betty's abdomen. Naturally, the tape held only music played by world champion bands. Those were wonderful years for me as a father; my son and I shared a common interest. Iain's first instructor, a very talented musician, was another of my best friends, Michel d'Avenas. Michel and I organized the Monterey Scots Pipe Band, so I was doubling up as a drummer, drum major and manager of the band.

The San Francisco-based pipe band had a youth band, the Prince Charles Jr. Pipe Band. This band included kids Iain's age, so I talked to Bill about Iain joining the junior band. Soon we were travelling and participating in games all over California, Oregon and Washington. We also travelled overseas to Scotland to compete. This was a wonderful opportunity for any youngster. The pipe major of the Grade 2 bands promoted Iain up to the senior band. That band won the Grade 2 World Championship held in Glasgow, Scotland, in 2000. Together we enjoyed travelling to various Scottish Games in the U.S., Canada and Scotland. Our trips to Scotland also gave me the opportunity to introduce Iain and my daughters Tara and Christine to all their U.K. family members.

Due to my connection and activities throughout the world of bagpipes, I count myself fully blessed with the many friends I have made worldwide. We often use the expression, "It's a small world," which brings to mind my reconnecting with a former Canadian Army Cadet, Bill Merriman, in the early 70s. Bill and I met as teenagers at Camp Vernon in the early 50s; from there we both travelled our separate ways in the world. Fast-forward to 1971, when Bill and I met during the Pacific Coast Pipe Band Association annual meeting in Morro Bay, California. Following the meeting, we lifted a few drams and spun memories of Camp Vernon. Bill and another couple of chaps formed the Prince Charles Pipe Band. Bill has taught hundreds of kids to play pipes. I doubt if there is any other person in California who can come close to matching his record in teaching youngsters in our musical field. Of course, all pipe bands include drummers, so with his organizing the complete band; many kids also developed their skill in drumming. Over close to forty-plus years, I have observed at least two generations of Bill's kids become highly skilled musicians. Several now playing in the top-grade pipe bands. Megan Canning (nee Harington),[30] a piper, competed in two of the best Grade 1 bands around the world, both winning the World Championship. Megan is the first U.S. woman to achieve that honour.

Bill and I both put a lot of effort into our involvement with pipe bands and organizing Scottish Games. Many will testify that Bill and I always enjoyed meeting our mates after the games in the beer tent. Pipe bands celebrate when they win the big silver trophy and also need to drown their sorrow when they lose. We participated in the Scottish Games in Pleasanton, Santa Rosa, Monterey, Los Angeles, Seattle, San Diego, Vale, Victoria, Canada and the World Championships in Glasgow, Scotland. Yes, in spite of a few with one major skirmish, our friendship has endured for well over forty years.

My passion and return to the world of bagpipes began in the late 60s, drumming and drum majoring with the local pipe band. Both my daughters became Highland dancers. With one of my best friends, we put together a competition pipe band, The Monterey Scots Pipe Band. In addition to all this side activity, in 1969 I became involved in organizing and managing The Monterey Scottish Games and Celtic Festival. This was an event I managed for close to forty years, with the help of a few dedicated committee members. When I took it over, we had a budget of less than two thousand dollars; when I finally retired in 2010, it was $100,000. Over those years, we contributed thousands of dollars to worthy charitable causes.

---

30   Megan's dad, Jim Harrington, a fellow drum major, is also one of my special buddies.

Since retiring as the manager of the Monterey Games, I stay involved as a drum-major adjudicator. Judging the drum- major contest alongside my mates Jim Harrington, John Nichols and Dave Cubberly annually at the Pleasanton Scottish Games. It has become the highlight of my year. At 82, I am the elder of the group, so these young pups love to "take the mickey out of the old man." It's all good fun.

After Fairbridge, I didn't play football in an organized team for decades. But then life brought me back to my favourite sport. At age 65, I was hired to coach the varsity football team of a public high school[31] in Monterey, California.

My varsity team was a mixed group of Hispanic, black, and white kids. There were six other public high schools and two private schools in our league.

I saw the pattern of rivalries from my Fairbridge years repeating itself when our rag-tag team faced off against the wealthier kids. My boys were equally determined to prove their mettle in the field as we were against Qualicum.

The match brought a psychological element in addition to the physical. I cautioned them to behave well out there and not forget the values of sportsmanship, just like Doc, our coach at Fairbridge, did.

One day when they were out in the field against a private school, I saw the boys playing much tougher than they usually did. It was a good game, and they played tough, and in the end, we were victorious.

---

31   Here I use the American convention. The public schools of America are not the provinces of rich as I knew them.

Just as we were preparing to leave afterward, the coach of the opposing team pulled me aside for a talk.

He was very polite, but he had an exasperated look on his face as he told me that someone stole a team jumper from one of his boys.

My heart sank a little as I heard it. I promptly unloaded the bus and searched all of them and their bags.

There was no team jumper from their school to be found.

I smiled to myself as I got through the last bag. My boys hadn't let me down. I was proud.

With a touch of smugness, I said to the coach, "Well, you can see it was certainly not one of my lads; guess you better line your own team up for a search."

My football coaches' experience had yet another twist in store for me. Following a year-and-a-half bout with treatment for prostate cancer, I returned to coaching soccer, this time would be a different school. It was a school for the sons of the rich folks, a private school.

I can now say that, thanks to soccer, I have experienced coaching both sides of society's class divide and found it quite interesting.

The private- school kids did best in academics, either because they were brighter or because the well-funded schools had the resources to serve them best and give them more individual attention. As a result, I found it easier to coach them in positioning and strategy. They picked up the principles quickly.

In contrast, several of the kids on my public school team had difficulty maintaining the grade-point averages required to participate in athletic programmes. I could lose some of my top players in the middle of our season due to poor grades. I would have to change strategies and assign players to different positions to compensate.

However, when I had a full team, those kids played a tough and hard game. And while the private school kids tried hard, they simply lacked the raw physical determination and the grit of the kids from the other side of the tracks.

Return to Fairbridge

In 1982, one of my closest school friends, John H., called to let me know a group of Fairbridgians had decided to organise a school reunion.

I was unable to come to the first reunion in 1983 as my son Iain was born that week. However, because attendance had been so great, the organizing committee decided to make it a biannual gathering. I made up my mind to come to the next one in 1985.

When I went, the experience was strange, almost surreal. I found out that many former students had vastly different perceptions of what took place at the school. At times, I wondered if we had all lived in the same school. As I listened to the banquet speeches and private conversations, I left under the impression that Fairbridge according to the speaker had been a wonderful experience for many. This didn't match up with my recollections at all.

I came home and began to wonder if my memories were screwed up, and it hadn't actually been as bad as I remembered, or if I had simply been extremely unlucky.

I needed to understand better. I needed to make sense of these contradictions.

At my second reunion, I vocally expressed some of my grievances against the school to several of the "old boys"— the migrants who arrived in the early years, around 1935 to 1940. Most of them, but not all, enjoyed living in the school and remembered it fondly. They did not like how I challenged their pleasant memories.

Much like the old boys, the migrants who had arrived in Fairbridge after World War II also thought life at the school was fairly decent and didn't want to believe it could've have been as bad as I and others described. At the same reunion, an older guy interrupted a private chat with one of my former cottage-mates as we traded grievances about our old school. In a snarling tone he said, "You have something bad to say about Fairbridge, take it elsewhere!"

I recognized him as one of my former boxing teammates. I said, "OK, Rab, where's the ring and what time do you want the fight to begin?"

He wasn't quite sure whether I was serious or not, but I laughed and that defused the situation.

During the reunion banquet, the guest speaker and former patron of Fairbridge, Lady Dodds-Parker, harped on and on about "the joys and happiness of our wonderful childhood years at Fairbridge." It seemed like my memories were being cast even more in doubt than before.

Later that night, ten or twelve of us gathered at a large in the hotel bar for a beer. That was when one of the chaps said, "Where the hell was I when all this bollock's happiness was dished out?"

His statement broke the floodgates.

People agreed in unison, and suddenly they were eager to share their stories of terrible childhoods at Fairbridge. Some spoke about being abused in the hands of certain staff members and the bullies. One woman's memories were so painful that she could not hold back tears while she spoke.

A young professor, who was doing research for a thesis

about Fairbridge and the U.K. Child Emigration Act, was also in the room. At one point, I turned and told him, "You should really be taking notes. This is the other side to the story."

He didn't take my advice. And his paper certainly didn't tell the stories that unfolded around that table.

At the time, it did not occur to me to write a memoir so that the other side of the Fairbridge experience could be told. The concept took hold shortly after I was reunited with my missing younger brothers after a separation that had lasted over sixty years.

When I was searching for my brothers, I dug deep into the history of not only our Fairbridge School, but also the whole United Kingdom child migrant experience. What I found was far bigger than I could have imagined. A piece of British history that had remained swept under the rug for decades, and quietly claimed thousands of children. Their stories are equally mixed; ranging from decent to terrible.

Many years later at one of our school reunions, I heard that both the S Cottage bullies had turned into hard-core criminals. Upon leaving the school in their teens they turned to crime and were working the streets of Vancouver. Both spent much of their adult lives in and out of prison, and I also heard one of them died in prison. Frankly, I was not really surprised.

Another time Hughie and I—both in our late fifties by then—were reminiscing about our Fairbridge years when he said, "You know, Roddy, I never understood why, when you and I were pals at the school, you would often pick fights with me."

I shook my head and chuckled wryly. "Hughie do you remember the two bullies in S Cottage that terrorized us day and night?"

"Yes."

"Those two would pull me aside and order me to pick a fight with you, or they would beat the shit out of me."

After that, we shared a good laugh about how his big sister Agnes would pull me aside and slap me for picking on him when she heard about the fights.

In spite of the mean and strict teachers at Fairbridge, some of the day school teachers treated us well. One of them was Mrs. Williamson, one of my first teachers at Fairbridge. I met one her again during one of our reunions in the early nineties. During the banquet, she came over to my table. She seemed very shy and tentative when she asked if I remembered her.

I didn't recognise her at first glance. I was a bit flustered and about to apologize when she told me her name, and that she'd was one of my early primary teachers.

The recognition hit but vaguely. It had been a very long time, she had been amiable and good with us younger kids back then.

I invited her to join us at our table so we could catch up. She said she had a little surprise for me,

then took out a piece of paper that had turned dark yellow-brown with age. Sentences in a child's handwriting were penciled on it. Turned out it was an essay I had written as an assignment in her class.

She pointed out the title at the top: "The Navy Boy Rody."

I was laughing already. At that age, I still hadn't mastered spelling my own name. But, 'Boy,' could I come up with a hilarious story to go along with it. She read the whole essay aloud and it had all of us laughing. We spent a wonderful evening reminiscing.

Nowadays, the chapel still looks almost exactly the same it did when I was a boy. It is one of the very few buildings at Fairbridge that has survived intact and in its original state. Most of the other buildings have been torn down or remodeled long ago.

The chapel, built in 1939, has survived in its original form over 75 years as of the writing of this memoir—the only building of its size in the area to make it so long. Many of us hold the chapel in high regard for that reason. The British Columbian government designated the building as a Heritage Site.

Keeping it in good repair is the Alumni Heritage Committee and the Chapel Society. Ron Smith, who now resides in are modeled after what was once the Fairbridge office. Ron is the president of the "The Fairbridge Chapel Heritage Society." Without Ron and his volunteers, this wonderful old building would be close to ruins today. He not only keeps up maintenance, but he also regularly cleans and winds the old clock. Its gears are still turning.

Some things about the chapel have changed. The glorious pipe organ is no longer there; it is currently housed in Christ Church Cathedral in Victoria. The chapel is not used as a church anymore. It is rented out for weddings, special events, and sometimes even social functions.

But during our annual reunions, we hold a short service

in the chapel to honor our Fairbridge brothers and sisters whom we have lost over the past year.

During one of the more recent reunions, we held a short service for the dedication of a newly installed chapel window, complementing the beautiful original glass stained glass panels overlooking the altar. The window was dedicated in the memory of Hughie's older brother John, who had died of brain cancer at Fairbridge shortly after he arrived in the school. Hughie dutifully came and sat in the front row, stoic throughout the whole service.

When I attend these services, I walk in and seek out the same spot on the pew where I used to sit each week in my school days. The wood has been worn smooth over the decades. As I sit, my mind wanders back to the Sunday services of my younger years. I can almost hear the pipe organ sounding and the choir warming up with the first hymn. Mrs. Green and the bullies are gone now. If I concentrate real hard, I can imagine my young schoolmates in their Sunday best sitting in those pews, exchanging glances with each other before the sermon begins.

THE PHONE CALL

During the initial reconnection with my older brother Rob in 1971 It was then that I first learnt I also had two younger brothers, Alex (Sandy) and Billy.[32] It was then that I made the decision some day in the future we would find Billy and Alex.

Rob and I exchanged visits where we both met all our U.K. and U.S. family members and close friends. Rob following his first visit fell in love with the U.S. and in the late, 90s came over with his wife Sylvia and bought a house. While Rob and Sylvia lived here, their son Barry and his wife also moved to Monterey.

For a few short years, I was able to enjoy part of my U.K. family as my neighbours. It seemed so good to be talking to my family on the phone or jumping in my car to drive crosstown to visit, celebrating birthdays and getting together for barbecues on all those special occasions that many families often take for granted.

Due to their age and future ailments inherent within the aging process, Rob decided that he and Sylvie best return to the U.K. There they have the benefit of what this country sorely needs, a National Health System.

In addition to Barry, several of his mates already moved here; all this through one visit I made to London and Bournemouth. Back in the early 80s my brother owned and managed a hotel in Bournemouth. Over the years, I heard so many funny stories of how my brother, and his family ran that

---

32   As per my earlier footnote, the full story of the Mackay Family Reunited is the makings of a new book that I am working on.

hotel. To my mind, it could have well been an inspiration in the making of a British Telly comedy.

During a visit to Birmingham in 1998, a friend drove me to the site of the old Middlemore Homes. I expected to find a scene from a WWII documentary, the structures looking worn-down and dismal.

Much to my pleasant surprise, I found a bright, cheerful setting—the exact opposite of my childhood recollections. It was a warm and sunny day, and the well-tended gardens surrounding the buildings were blooming. The buildings themselves were not gray; they were red brick in a traditional style. The main structure was converted to an educational facility. The smaller building still housed homeless kids, although they were probably experiencing better childhoods than we did.

Following a long and fruitless search of thirty years for my missing brothers, I was at the point of giving up the venture. Attempts consisted of inquiries to the Fairbridge Society, U.K. government, British Navy, City of Victoria, Canada, and Liverpool, U.K., archives, searches for my childhood records; all were in vain. Even my own family, those who had known them as babies, had no idea where they had been sent.

On one occasion while hosting a dinner in Monterey, California, for the leader (at that time) of the Scottish National Party, I requested his assistance. I explained my situation and gave him a paper that contained the limited information I had on my brothers. He looked at me straight in the eye and with great sincerity told me that as soon as he returned to Scotland, he would do what he could, and I would definitely hear from him. I was desperate and naïve enough to believe he was different from far too many politicians. To this day, I have not had one word from the man, and very likely if asked he would claim he had never heard of me.

Finally, one of my Fairbridge mates advised me to try the Child Migrant Trust in the U.K.; I contacted them and shared what scarce information I had gathered.

The search ended with a phone call.

A quick glance at the caller ID showed an international call originating from the U.K.. It was four o'clock in the afternoon in November 2000 here at my home in California. I quickly did the math: midnight in London. My pulse began to quicken. No one would place a call at such a late hour— unless it was very important.

With shaking hands, I picked up the receiver. The caller identified himself as Steve Kuti from the Child Migrant Trust. My heart pounded, and my breath grew short. Three months earlier, I contacted this organization asking them to help find my two younger brothers.

"You might want to have a seat," Mr. Kuti said. "I have something very important to share with you."

I did as he instructed and focused all my attention on his next words. "Roddy, we have reason to think we have finally located one of your missing brothers, Alexander Mackay."

Waves of emotions swept over me in a cascade of confusion: shock, laughter, tears, and indescribable, immense joy.

At long last, I would be reunited with my two youngest siblings.

My journey to that long-anticipated reunion began on a bright, sunny autumn day in October 2001 on Highway 101 heading north to San Francisco International Airport. I had made this drive many times over the years. However, on this particular day, I was as excited as that proverbial kid on Christmas Eve, brimming with anticipation. Today, I would be boarding a flight for the U.K. to meet my brothers! With me was my wife Betty and son Iain; my daughters Christine and Tara would take a later flight and join us at our destination.

At age 67, after over sixty years of separation, I was finally going to meet my long-lost brothers Alex and Billy. It also was going to be the first reunion where all of us—Rob, Minnie, me, and Alex and Billy—would be all together in one place. The only sad thought I had about this wonderful family reunion was that our Aunt Kate and Uncle Robert would not be with us, but even that could not put a damper on my mood for long. I was overwhelmed with sheer happiness as I made that drive on the busy freeway to San Francisco. By the time we arrived at the airport, parked the car in long-term and made our way to the main check-in desk, I was so thrilled, I felt as if the jet couldn't fly fast enough.

The entire main concourse of the airport was strangely empty. Missing was the usual hustle and bustle of thousands of people on the go, rushing, pushing their way through to check-in desks or departure gates. One could practically have driven a car through the main doors straight up to the check-in counter without hitting a soul. While it was a great relief to stroll through the empty airport, it felt eerie and quite spooky.

The reason why it was like that was because barely a

month had passed since the terrible tragedy of 9/11. All major airlines had cancelled or rescheduled many flights, and people in general did not feel safe about air travel. For the first and likely last time of my life's experience in airports, there was absolutely no one lined up at the check-in counter. We still had an hour or so to wait prior to boarding. I noticed Betty glancing nervously at a gentleman wearing a Muslim head scarf. It was a reaction that many people had in the aftermath of that terrible day.

To relax and kill some time, we headed to one of the airport cafés for a cup of coffee and a snack. Again, no one was waiting in line, so we had instant service from the one and only server on duty.

I said to him, "It looks like they have really cut back on the airport staff."

"Yes, sir, and likely will be that way for quite a while. We're afraid," he replied.

Our flight was booked well in advance of that tragic date. Before we left, a Monterey TV news reporter asked me if I was nervous about flying.

I simply told him, "This trip for my family is far too important for any further delay."

I was not trying to brag or show false courage. I figured that in this unsettled world, there would always be some type of threat or danger. My family and I had over sixty years to catch up on. I was determined not to waste one more day.

Our flight was called. We boarded the plane, took off without incident, and soon reached cruising altitude. I relaxed in my seat, lulled by the whirring of the engines and gentle rumbling of the plane, and thought how appropriate it was that, to mend this family that had been broken; I was going back to the place where this incredible story about my life all began and the last place we had all been together: Edinburgh, Scotland.

The first celebration took place at my nephew Alec and his wife Karen's home. Alec is my sister Minnie's son. Attending was our long-lost brothers: Alex with his wife Gillian and daughter Ruth, and Billy with his wife Edna and son Kevin, who flew over from their home in South Africa. Sandy lived in a small village, Chinnor, which was only about a two-hour drive from our older brother Rob's home.[33] Senior brother Rob, his wife Sylvia, and family were there also.

Our new niece Ruth organized the main reunion celebration in the village of Chinnor, where we met many of their village friends. Sandy was very active as a deacon with the local church. The party was in the church hall and well organized by Ruth. However, for some of the Mackay clan, tea and non-alcoholic punch were not exactly our style for a sixty-year family reunion.

My U.S. family and I proceeded by train to Edinburgh; Sandy, Billy and their families drove up to Edinburgh. It was important to me that they meet the Gray families. It was the Grays, Aunt Kate and Uncle Robert, who had taken me into their home back in the early 50s. As per my expectations, the reunion in Scotland took place at my cousin Robert's golf club with an open bar. Those present at this reunion included cousins Robert and wife Joan, their son Gary, his

---

33   *Both brothers were very unaware that they lived in such close proximity.*

wife Heather and their young boys, cousins Jean and her husband Bill, Dorothy and her husband John, and Norman with his wife Margaret. We simply relaxed, all of us in good cheer, finally enjoying being together as a family that thus far over some sixty years had existed only in the name.

During this visit, I finally learnt what had happened to my two younger brothers after our family broke apart. Alex and Billy went to an Edinburgh infant's home, probably by my father's signature. From there, they were eventually sent north to the village of Huntley, Aberdeenshire, Scotland. They were fostered out to an elderly couple who were expecting to foster care a pair of older, able-bodied boys that would help them with work on the farm. Alex and Billy were practically still toddlers.

It seemed fitting that on our reunion, my brothers and I would visit the house where we began our lives and one of the last places we were still together.

A secretary at Scottish Births and Deaths Registry Office had given me the exact address. I had expected to hear the name of a hospital when I called to inquire into the details of my birth. Instead, she told me, "You weren't born at a hospital; you were born on Drummond Street."

Jokingly I responded, "Wow, dropped naked at birth on a cobblestone street? No wonder I have had this attitude problem."

She didn't seem to get it. "Oh no, sir, not the street, you would have been born at the listed home address on Drummond Street."

So I learnt that my mother had been one of the many

women living in tenement apartments of the day who delivered their babies at home. These women would be extremely lucky if they had a midwife to assist them. So I assume my entrance to this world was a difficult one.

After that, I was not a quiet baby. My aunt Kate once told me I was a "greeting bairn," which is a common Scots term for a bawling baby. I never asked what prompted that kind of "greeting" out of me.

The term still applies, although as an adult, I developed the uncouth habit of swearing to replace my crying, much to the annoyance of my dear wife. Not very polite, I admit, but it does give some relief.

The old tenement building was still standing. I didn't know what to expect from it, but I didn't expect much because I knew our family had been poor.

I stayed close with Alex and Billy as we walked toward the old structure. We each silently took it in, waiting to see if any latent memories would resurface. None came.

It was a dreary and forlorn stone structure, darkened with age and soot. The inside was hardly more pleasant than the outside. The chilly draught made me shiver. The walls were riddled with cracks. The common stairwell was filthy and reeked of urine, telling of countless drunken men staggering home and taking a piss in the hallway because they couldn't hold their bladders.

We found flat number 13, our childhood home, and peered inside. Standing in the threshold, I felt I was looking at the cell of an early 19th century debtor's prison.

The flat consisted of only two small rooms, and the sparse, run-down interior was terribly depressing. We turned the tap on to find it ran bone-chillingly cold water. Three families shared the bathroom in the hallway.

It was a scene right out of a Charles Dickens novel. Where was Fagin? I half expected him to round the corner at any moment.

I couldn't imagine how two adults and five children lived in those two tiny rooms. But this was the norm for thousands of poor families in the major cities of the U.K. in the 1930s.

The three of us were grateful we had no memory of living there.

On the other hand, I thought back to the time I had stayed at my Aunt Kate and Uncle Robert's place: a three-room tenement flat in Edinburgh not much larger than this. I remembered the small space being cozy, warm, and cheerful. You knew you were in a loving home.

I will be eternally grateful to the Child Migrant Trust. The reunion of my family following a sixty-year hiatus came about through their endeavours. The Child Migrant Trust, founded by Margaret Humphreys, has reunited hundreds of families, mostly in Australia where she first established the CMT. [34] They and they alone assisted me in locating my brothers, finally reuniting our whole family. From the day, I began the search for my brothers; there was no assistance forthcoming from the U.K. government,[35] the Fairbridge institution, nor the Canadian government.

---

34   *To understand the full story of the U.K. Child Migrant scheme I recommend Margaret Humphreys' book, "Oranges & Sunshine."*
35   *On the recommendation of Margaret Humphries, the founder of the Child Migrant Trust, the U.K. government did set up a special fund for reunification families for their former child migrants*

Last Visit with My Cousins

In 2006, I spent some time visiting with my cousins Cathy and Jean in Edinburgh. Jean was undergoing chemo treatments for cancer, and Cathy was there to give her sister all the support and love she could. Years earlier, Jean's husband Bill had also gone through a bout with cancer of the throat, and it had seriously affected his voice. Bill and Jean also lost their two children as young adults to Cystic Fibrosis. It was only during two prior visits that I really had had the opportunity to spend any time with Jean, Bill and their daughter Gail. Gail had been fighting the disease that had taken her brother some years earlier. I do not use the term "fighting the disease" lightly. I think too many times it is used when, in reality, it simply means the individual has or is suffering from the condition, as in my case with prostate cancer. With Gail, it was different. She knew she did not have that long to live. Gail, with her positive and cheerful attitude, kept her family and friends from dwelling on her fatal condition. She took time to help me look for some special artwork in Edinburgh and drove me to the airport when it was time to go.

She was a brave young woman, and I will always remember her for the cheerful, positive attitude, her thoughtfulness and her amazing courage. During Gail's last months of life, she once said to her mother, "Mum, be happy. I am grateful for the ten years more than the doctors had predicted."

Later on, Jean also had the same fighting spirit with her own fatal illness, cancer. The last night I was visiting with Cathy and Jean, we had supper in Bill's local pub. After supper, Jean was tiring so she and Cathy retired to Jean's flat. Bill and I had a couple more drinks, and then headed up to the flat. The sisters were sitting and having tea in the kitchen. Jean said, "Well, here we have Mutt and Jeff; one canna speak and the other one is 'deef.'" Bill and I had a good laugh over that; it was a sad yet hilarious scene. Jean had lost all of her hair and couldn't stand wearing a wig, so she had flung it off and was sitting there scratching her baldhead. Cathy was teasing Jean good-naturedly about the wig.

In the same lighthearted spirit, I facetiously said, "What the hell, why don't we do what we used to do in the old days? Let's all go to the Palaise and have a dance."

It was to be the last time for all four of us to be together, yet the tears I fought back that night were a mixture of sadness and laughter. Jean died in July of 2007; she told the doctors to take her off the chemo, as she was tired of constantly feeling sick and wanted to die with the dignity as a human. My next visit to Edinburgh will include a gravesite visit to the Gray's family plot. The Gray family took me in for a short period of my life and gave me an insight of what a caring, loving family is all about.

THE FORMER GUTTERSNIPE
MEETS THE PRIME MINISTER

In 2010, I was one of two former child migrants from Fairbridge invited via an email to London, England, where Prime Minister Gordon Brown made the well-publicized apology. The apology was to cover all the U.K. Child Migrants sent to Canada, Australia, New Zealand and South Africa, well over 150,000 children. The email invitation included the following information: Mr. Dave Lorente, Home Child Canada founder, called the editor of our School Association Gazette, Pat Skidmore, and asked if she and her mother Marge,[36] plus one male Fairbridgian, would be willing to be representatives of the U.K. Child Migrants of Canada[37] at the London apology ceremony.

There was a deadline of 24 hours to accept this invitation. The official invitations came later from the U.K. High Commissioner of Canada, Mr. Kevin Farrell. It stated that Prime Minister Gordon Brown would give a Formal Apology to the Child Migrants at The Palace of Westminster, scheduled for Feb. 24, 2010.

Our *small* delegation of seven Canadians would be representative of over 120,000 former U.K. Child Migrants sent to Canada from 1833 to 1948. It is my understanding

---

36   *Marge was one of the 87 girls sent to Fairbridge in 19XX. Due to her age, daughter Pat accompanied her*
37   *There is some confusion over the classification of a Child Migrant. Fairbridgians of Canada and Australia are indeed Child Migrants. The U.K. government classifies <u>all children</u> who were part of the mass child emigration from the U.K. to Canada, Australia, New Zealand, South Africa, etc., as Child Migrants.*

that there were approximately 30,000 sent to Australia.

We had barely two weeks to make our own travel arrangements; a special committee of the U.K. government arranged our lodging, etc., in London. On arrival, we learnt that a large group of forty former Australian Child Migrants was invited to the ceremony. There were also small groups from New Zealand (four) and South Africa (one). [38] With the extremely short notice and the significant difference to the number of Aussies invited, compared to our tiny Canadian group, some of us wondered if including Canada had been a last-minute decision. To this day, I personally feel there should have been more Canadians invited. The members of the Fairbridge Canada Association numbered approximately 100 at that time. We are the few surviving Child Migrants left in Canada.

Initially, one of the U.K. government coordinators invited me to respond on behalf of the Canadian Child Migrants to the Prime Minister's Apology. Later, that invitation was rescinded, possible due to a political or the time in the schedule. An Australian responded to the Prime Minister's speech.

I received instructions to book my flight tickets ASAP; due to my health problems at that time, they included my wife Betty to accompany me on this trip. Later, I received compensation for all my out-of-pocket expenses. We landed in Heathrow, London, and a committee member met us and

---

38   *The child migration to Australia continued well after ours in Canada, ending somewhere into the 1970s. This would explain why today's surviving Child Migrant numbers in Australia exceeds that of Canada.*

drove us to the hotel. There we met up with Marge, Pat and a few others who would be representing Canada.

We were invited to a reception the next night prior to the Westminster Apology. The committee taxied us over to the hotel where the Aussies had been booked. The reception was in a large banquet-style room. Our small group was on one side across the room with our cousin Aussies on the other side across the room. As we glanced across the room at the large numbers of Aussies (40), our tiny contingent of six from Canada seemed even smaller. With one of the Aussies as cheerleader, we gave Margaret Humphreys a robust, old-fashioned British "Hip, Hip Hurrah."

Of course, she was the person that I was determined to meet. I walked across the room and introduced myself to her. Then I thanked her personally for the major role her organization, the Child Migrant Trust, had played in reuniting my family in 2000. They assisted me in locating my two youngest brothers following a separation of 61 years. The story about my family was likely not too different from that of many former Child Migrants standing across the room that night. Most, if not all, had received no assistance in reuniting with their families, from the either the governments or the institutions where they had been sent.

The reasons the Australian Child Migrants later become the focus of all the speeches during the Commons session of The Formal Apology were due to the tireless efforts Margaret Humphreys and her Child Migrant Trust. It was in Australia that Margaret as a social worker began investigating why these thousands of children had been taken from their families in the U.K., then shipped to Australia. Her workload was so great the C.M.T. opened up two offices in Australia. Because of her tireless efforts in their behalf, it is not difficult to understand why our Aussie cousins became the focus of attention during the Apology ceremony that was to follow.

The next morning, with what I think was some of that childhood excitement flowing through our minds, we were all up early for breakfast. After all, it was a very rare occasion, likely the only time I would be invited to the Palace of Westminster.

From our hotel, they transported us over to Westminster; on arrival special, nametags were issued. I jokingly said to someone in our group, "These name badges are a lot classier than the name labels they tied around our necks when they put us kids on the ship to Canada."

As we passed through security police and metal detectors to enter Westminster, I created a slight stir with security. I was wearing my kilt uniform, and I had gone through the metal detector when one of the guards stopped me and asked very politely, "Sir, are you wearing one of those small Scottish daggers in your sock?"

I said, "No with the security levels being what they are today I decided to leave it at home. By the way, the correct name of the wee dagger in my sock is 'Sghian Dhu.'"

We both laughed and he said to his mate, "Well, Charlie, we know now how to question the next 'kiltie,' that comes through."

The idea of packing my kilt uniform for this trip germinated during a phone conversation with one of the U.K.

reps. He said to me, "I hear you are Scottish."

I answered, "Yes, born in Edinburgh."

He then said, "Do you know that the Prime Minister is also a Scot?"

I responded, "Indeed; I do and to honour this occasion; I have already packed my kilt!"

He chuckled and said, "I'm sure the Prime Minister will enjoy meeting a fellow Scot."

There were actually two official ceremonies of the Apology, the first by the Prime Minister during a regular Parliament session. In addition, several members of Parliament stood and added their sentiments. Prime Minister Gordon Brown apologized for the U.K.'s role in sending more than 130,000 children[39] to former colonies where many suffered abuses. He expressed regret for the "misguided" Child Migrant Programme, telling the Commons he was "truly sorry."[40]

Following the Prime Minister's speech in the Commons, the minister coordinating the event invited all the former Child Migrants to a private gathering to meet the P.M. Here the Prime Minister repeated the Apology, but spoke to us in a sincere, meaningful manner. My own feelings were that both the formal and informal apology by Prime Minister Gordon Brown was genuine and straight from his heart. He recounted the terrible mistakes committed by government-sponsored agencies, which resulted in far too much abuse and suffering of Child Migrants and their families.

I had the honour of meeting and shaking hands with the

---

39   Canada alone had taken in 100,000, by far the largest number of children.
40   His full speech is available on the web.........

P.M. As I anticipated, as he walked about the room shaking hands, he had noted the kilted man among the crowd. He came over to our group, and I shook his outstretched hand. As I was shaking his hand, I said to him, "Prime Minister, I think it would help if I could round up several thousand of us in kilted Scots to vote for you in the upcoming elections." It was a moment of levity, and the Prime Minister could relax and have a laugh.

Unfortunately, a few short months later in the general election, Gordon Brown was voted out of office. However, as far as all the former Child Migrants are concerned, he goes down in history, as the first Prime Minister of Britain who cared enough to recognise and apologize for the terrible cruel system of the Child Migrant Scheme. That's when I thought of the appropriate title for the photo of this significant occasion: "The Guttersnipe' meets a Prime Minister."

THE END

EPILOGUE

This memoir began with all my focus specifically centered on my early life as a child migrant. I've spent the last seven decades doing my best to keep those gloomy childhood memories dormant, in a state of permanent hibernation. I felt as though dwelling on those hellish years would have eventually earned me a one-way ticket into the state hospital. Turns out, a little dwelling on those years helped me permanently close the book on that chapter of my life.

Now in my 80s, I've finally figured out the key to separating myself from my dismal childhood that I've spent so much energy to keep suppressed. All I had to do was get it down on the pages you hopefully just read. Now, my tragedy is no longer a burden I must carry alone. Since it's all down on paper for anyone to read, I feel like I've taken the power of the pain away that I've been carrying on my back for all these years.

Truth is, my story is just one of 329 different perspectives of the 329 individual children sent to Fairbridge. Some still hold the school in high esteem, while others experienced abuse at the hands of staff members and bullies. And Fairbridge was a hotbed for abuse, although many, including some of my former schoolmates, deny it to this day.

For the past 20 years, I've spoken and worked with various people and organizations that have expressed a desire to assist me in my efforts to bring the child abuse that took place at Fairbridge to the attention of the Canadian Government. As of December 2017, we haven't had any success…yet. However, there are two organizations, The Child Migrant Trust and the Scottish Government Inquiry of Child Abuse, who are both still actively looking into this endeavour.

My optimism is waning that we will ever receive an apology or any resolution from the Canadian government for the abuse we endured at Fairbridge. The Canadian and U.K. governments take some responsibility for allowing children to be shipped during WWII over the Atlantic, which was teeming with Nazi submarines.

All said and done, my life has been happy and productive despite a tough beginning. The successful search for my siblings and family was one of the most wonderful events of my life. And marrying my wife, Betty was one of the best decisions of my life. But there's been tragedy in my adult life as well.

Since Christine had to work on her birthday in 2011, we took her down the coast to Big Sur for a birthday lunch the following day. We dined outside on the patio, taking full advantage of the sunny December day and the natural majesty of Big Sur. It was a perfect spot to celebrate our daughter's birthday.

After lunch, I dropped Christine off at her condo. Just as I walked inside the front door of our house, the phone rang. It was Christine. She could barely catch her breath as she cried into the phone to the point of near-hyperventilation. She was finally able to calm herself down momentarily, just enough to relay something about her sister Tara. Through the sobbing and crying, Christine said that her sister just died in a terrible car accident.

The immediate adrenaline-soaked devastation that filled my body was almost unbearable. I felt like I needed to crawl out of my skin. I felt helpless. I didn't know what to do with myself. There's no agony comparable to losing a child.

Tara was spirited and energetic; she was always filled to the brim with life. Six years later, writing about her death still hurts tremendously. The universal adage, "A parent should never have to bury their child," is a perpetual nightmare for those unfortunates who go through it.

Tara had built a picturesque water pond in her backyard. I took some of the large flat rocks that she had collected and built a waterfall and pond in my front yard. I named it "Tara's Waterfall" in her memory. It continues to give me some solace when I see folks stop to admire it. In 2001 I was diagnosed with prostate cancer.

The news threw my life into a tailspin, especially since I was told the cancer had metastasised after I had already undergone surgery and radiation. However, thanks to several miracle drugs, the cancer has been contained, and 17 years later, I'm still alive and kicking. I just can't kick as hard as I used to. This year, my oncologist advised that the drug I had been on, no longer worked on me. The meds cost $8,600 for a month's supply, but through my school retirement health insurance, I only had to cover $50 a month. Unfortunately, the Monterey Peninsula Unified School District terminated all retiree health plans in 2016, which left my wife and I scrambling for a new health policy. That's a whole other story.

By spring of 2017, I was left with one treatment choice… chemotherapy. Like most cancer patients, chemo is the most dreaded treatment. All the years that I've lived with the disease and took the prescribed drugs, I didn't have any painful symptoms. There would be some side effects, but nothing I couldn't handle. But chemo is about as unpleasant as it could get. Many obits include the cliché: "he or she battled cancer for years."

I view the situation as, enduring an unwelcome guest who's moved into my body—if I could just show the little prick the front door. As a realist, I recognize that there is no cure for my condition, and I do my best to make every day count. I've had unconditional love and support from my wife Betty, my daughter Christine and many other wonderful family members and close friends.

I lost my brother Sandy (Alec) to Parkinson's a couple years back. Presently, one of my closest friends Bill suffers from the same disease. He lives north of us in San Rafael; we visit when we can and I call him frequently. It's easy to see that it's more difficult to navigate through daily life with Parkinson's than it is with my ailment. However, Bill never complains. In spite of all the terrible symptoms he suffers regularly, he remains upbeat. At times, when I begin to feel sorry for myself, thinking about Bill's health struggles cures me of any self-pity. Fortunately, Bill's wife Jeannie is a strong and caring woman similar in that respect to my Betty. We are blessed to have these beautiful souls as our brides.

Acknowledgements

Several friends not only encouraged me, but a few also assisted me in writing my story. I owe many thanks to my longtime schoolmate, Roy Myhill, whose incredible long-term memory filled in when mine failed, and to my volunteer editor, Dr. Dan Murphy, who edited the first draft of the manuscript. I would also like to thank my editors, Joyce Krieg and Adam Joseph, for going through the material from beginning to end and polishing it to bring it to full potential, and my publisher, Patricia Hamilton of Park Place Publications.

Most of all, my eternal gratitude goes to my dear wife Betty who has patiently tolerated years of incessant ramblings about my past and that damned Fairbridge cottage mother.

Made in the USA
Las Vegas, NV
11 February 2021